Taking Up the Cross

New Testament Interpretations through Latina and Feminist Eyes

Barbara E. Reid, O.P.

Fortress Press
Minneapolis

TAKING UP THE CROSS
New Testament Interpretations through Latina and Feminist Eyes

Copyright © 2007 Augsburg Fortress. All rights reserved. Except for brief quotations in critical articles or reviews, no part of this book may be reproduced in any manner without prior written permission from the publisher. For more information visit: www.augsburgfortress.org/copyrights or write to: Permissions, Augsburg Fortress, Box 1209, Minneapolis, MN 55440-1209.

Proceeds from this book will benefit CODIMUJ and *Nuestra Casa*, The Diocesan Women's Office and their Center in San Cristóbal de las Casas, Chiapas, México.

Cover graphic: copyright © Segundo Huertas / ArtBox Images / Getty Images
Cover design by Danielle Carnito
Interior design by Douglas Schmitz

Library of Congress Cataloging-in-Publication Data
Taking up the cross : New Testament interpretations through Latina and feminist eyes / Barbara E. Reid, editor.
    p. cm.
Includes bibliographical references and index.
ISBN-13: 978-0-8006-6208-0 (alk. paper)
ISBN-10: 0-8006-6208-3 (alk. paper)
1. Jesus Christ--Crucifixion. 2. Women in the Bible. 3. Bible. N.T.--Criticism, interpretation, etc. 4. Bible. N.T.--Feminist criticism. 5. Liberation theology. I. Reid, Barbara E.
    BT450.T35 2007
    232'.4082—dc22   2007016302

The paper used in this publication meets the minimum requirements of American National Standard for Information Sciences—Permanence of Paper for Printed Library Materials. ANSI Z329.48-1984.

Manufactured in the U.S.A.

11   10   09   08   07   1   2   3   4   5   6   7   8   9   10

Contents

*For valiant women whose struggles for dignity
and life daily give birth to hope.*

Acknowledgments

I AM DEEPLY INDEBTED TO a multitude of persons for their help with this study. First, I want to thank my congregation of Dominican Sisters of Grand Rapids, Michigan, and my colleagues and the administration at Catholic Theological Union in Chicago for their unflagging support and for allowing me a sabbatical in the academic year of 2002-03 in which to travel, study, and write. I am most grateful to the Association of Theological Schools and to the Lilly Endowment, who granted me a Faculty Fellowship for that sabbatical, providing the initial funding to enable this project. Catholic Theological Union graciously granted me academic leave in 2005 in order to continue the writing. I wish to thank as well the Aquinas Center at Emory University, particularly Mary-beth Beres, O.P. and Jan Sebacher, as well as Dean Russell Ritchie, Professors Gail O'Day and Karen Scheib at the Candler School of Theology, whose hospitality to me as visiting Dominican scholar in the Fall of 2005 helped me move toward completion of the manuscript.

The extraordinary hospitality I received from communities in various parts of Latin America and the Hispanic community in Chicago made possible numerous round-table conversations with Latinas of various social locations and cultural backgrounds. In México, my profound gratitude goes to the Benedictine Sisters at the Centro de Desarrollo Integral de la Mujer, Santa Escolástica (CEDIMSE) in Torreón, particularly Patricia Henry-Ford, O.S.B. and Maricarmen Bracamontes, O.S.B. For introducing me to friends in Chiapas, I am grateful to my colleagues Michel Andraos and Gisela Gründges-Andraos. My thanks go especially to Sr. María del Carmen Martínez, O.P. and the women of Coordinación Diocesana de Mujeres (CODIMUJ); to the Dominican community in Ocosingo, particularly Gonzalo Ituarte, Pablo Romo, and Sisters Dorys and María; to Rev. Delle McCormick and the community at Melel Xojobal and the women in Amatenango to whom she introduced me;

and to Dominican Sisters Socorro, Josefina, and Begoñia, and the women of Altamirano.

On a return visit to México in 2005 with my colleague Richard Gaillardetz, we enjoyed the extraordinary hospitality of Miguel Alvarez, C.S. in Mexico City, who also arranged for us to meet at length with Don Samuel Ruiz, retired bishop of San Cristóbal de las Casas. Deep gratitude to those who shared their wisdom and hospitality with us in Chiapas: Sr. Josefina from the Chancery in San Cristóbal de las Casas, Fr. Joel Padrón, indigenous theologian Pedro Gutiérrez Jiménez (Petul), Miguel Pickard from Centro de Investigaciones Económicas y Políticas de Acción Comunitaria (CIEPAC), Jorge Santiago from Desarollo Económico Social de los Mexicanos Indígenas (DESMI), Conrado Zepeda, S.J. and the Tzotzil community at Takiu'kum, and the community of Las Abejas and their Mesa Directiva in Acteal.

I am most grateful to Fr. Michael Gilgallon, who introduced me to the people and realities of La Paz, Bolivia. I want to thank his coworkers and students at the Pastoral Universitaria Normalista Arquidiocesana (PUNA); my hosts in the Maryknoll community; members of INTER (working with religious in formation); professors and students in the social work department of La Universidad Mayor de San Andrés (UMSA); Cati Williams, Berta, and the Aymara women at Centro PachaMama in El Alto; Sr. Anita and the community in Rio Seco; Sr. Anitawa and the Aymara community at Salud Integral in El Alto.

In Cochabamba, Bolivia, my profound thanks to Steve Judd, M.M., Director of the Maryknoll Language Institute (IDEIM), whose repeated invitations to share biblical perspectives on mission continue to stretch and enrich me; to the Maryknoll sisters Shu-Chen Wu, Associate Director of IDEIM, Marilyn Belt, and Joyce, and to JoAn Leo, O.P., Director of Instituto Boliviano de Teología a Distancia, for their ever-gracious hospitality; to the team of Oficina Latinoamericana de Servicios para la Misión (OLASEM): Tom Henehan, M.M., Jhonny Montero, Líder Lijerón, Gabriela Zengarini, O.P., Samuel and Cecilia Stanton; to Tania Avila Meneses, and her mother Gregoria and the community from the parroquias de Colcapirhua, Quillacollo; Fr. Roberto Tamicho and the professors and students of missiology at the

Catholic University; and Vicenta Mamani Bernabé, who introduced me to a spirituality of Aymara women.

In Lima, Perú, my gratitude goes especially to Holy Cross Sisters Patricia Dieringer, Josefina, Carmen, and Noelí, for their generous hospitality; to long-time friend and brother, Kevin Kraft, O.P.; to Sr. Adriana and the women at Capilla San Martín in the area of Surco in Lima; to Sheila Curran, R.S.M., in Villa El Salvador. In Chimbote, Sisters Lillian Bockheim, O.P. and Margaret Mary Birchmeier, O.P., from my own congregation, provide ongoing inspiration in their work with women at Maternidad de María and Centro de Obras Sociales.

In Chicago, my thanks go to Alicia Gutiérrez, S.H., Rayo Cuaya de Castillo, S.H., and Manuel Villalobos, C.M.F., who facilitated conversations with Hispanic women from St. Pius V parish in Pilsen, and Immaculate Heart of Mary and Holy Cross Parishes and surrounding neighborhoods.

I am grateful those who have helped me test out the ideas for this book in classrooms, retreats, and continuing education sessions in various venues around the U.S., Canada, Australia, Aotearoa-New Zealand, and Ireland. In particular, thanks to Fr. Joseph Cameron, Clare O'Neill, C.N.D., and parishioners at St. Willibrord Parish in Verdun; to Mary Ann Beavis and Friends of Sophia in Saskatoon; and to Fr. Patrick Flanagan, Fr. Barry Sullivan, Veronica Lawson, R.S.M., and Margaret Mary Brown, O.P. in Ballarat, Australia. To my dear friend, Helen Bergin, O.P., warmest thanks, and to Elaine Wainwright, R.S.M., Fr. David Tonks, and Fr. John Dunn in Auckland, and to the Redemptorist community, especially Frs. Brendan O'Rourke and George Wadding, at Marianella in Dublin.

Special thanks to Donald Senior, C.P., Gary Riebe-Estrella, S.V.D., Dr. Amy-Jill Levine, and Dr. Warren Carter, whose endorsement of this project from the start helped secure grant monies. My heart-felt gratitude to Leslie Hoppe, O.F.M., for his constant encouragement and support. Warm thanks to my colleague Steve Bevans, S.V.D. and to Jude Sicilano, O.P., for ongoing support and encouragement and to my colleagues in the Department of Biblical Literature and Languages at CTU: Dianne Bergant, C.S.A., Barbara Bowe, R.S.C.J., James Chukwuma Okoye, C.S.Sp., Laurie Brink, O.P., Thanh VanNguyen, S.V.D.,

Barbara Blesse, O.P., and Rabbi David Sandmel, who have taken on an extra load at times to free me to research and write. To my local community members: Justine Kane, O.P., Megan McElroy, O.P., and Joan Thomas, O.P., great thanks for their daily support, and to Mary Ellen McDonald, O.P., Carmelita Switzer, O.P., Marjorie Vangsness, O.P., Donald Christensen, James Heller, Bert Gohm, Sue and Denny Williams, Jan and Carl Krave, whose lifelong friendship sustains and nurtures me. To Margaret Leddy, Sr. Anna Santiago, O.P., and Carmen Nanko-Fernández, profound thanks for their helpful feedback on the manuscript. To my mother, Christine Reid, my aunt Marguerite Ewald, my brother Ronald Reid, and my sisters and brothers-in-law, Jeanne and Terrence Hissong, and Rosemary and Gregory Fournier, and to Peggy and Frank Meegan, my deep gratitude for sharing my interest in the women of CODIMUJ and for financial support that has contributed to the building of Nuestra Casa in San Cristóbal de las Casas. To the women of Sarah's/Sophia's Circle, Peggy Leddy, Mary Ellen Knuth, Peggy Meegan, Mary Neven, R.S.M., Maricarmen Bracamontes, Anne Bond, R.S.J., Mary Yan Mei Jiao, S.S.J., Reba D'Costa, RNDM, Lois Prebil, O.S.F., Jane Nienaber, O.S.F., Judith McGinley, O.P., who have fed my feminist spirituality, deepest thanks. Special thanks to Neil Elliott and Tim Larson at Fortress Press for their wisdom and guidance in bringing this project to completion.

My profound gratitude to all who have shared with me the meaning of living in hope while taking up the cross.

A final word regarding the bibliography: The bibliography found in this book is select. A full bibliography for this book is available on the Fortress Press Web page (http://www.augsburg fortress.org/store/item.jsp?clsid=187305&productgroupid=0&isbn =0800662083).

Introduction

ABOUT TEN YEARS AGO, WHEN I was teaching a graduate course on the Gospel of Mark, a student first alerted me to the dangers inherent in how we speak about the cross. We had come to chapter 8 and we were discussing Jesus' dictum to his disciples and to the crowd: "If any want to become my followers, let them deny themselves and take up their cross and follow me" (Mark 8:34).[1] In the midst of the discussion, a student raised her hand and spoke passionately about how deadly that verse can be. She worked in a shelter for battered women and she recounted to us that time after time, when women finally break the ugly silence about the abuse they are suffering, they usually do so by seeking help from their priest or minister. More often than not, she told us, women are advised to go home and to endure this suffering as their way of carrying the cross. Our discussion that day in class took a very different turn. It sparked my own ardent interest in looking at the ways in which Christians understand and speak about the cross and what effect that has on the way we live.

The cross is the symbol that stands at the center of Christian faith. This symbol and the narratives we tell about it bind Christians together, give meaning to our world, and guide the way we live.[2] When we remember the death of Jesus on the cross, we do so both in ritual and in narrative. Remembering and retelling the story of the cross, however, is not a static thing. In this dynamic process, we constantly retrieve images of the past to serve our needs to make meaning in the present.[3] When we speak about the crucifixion of Jesus, we necessarily move into the realm of mystery and paradox, which can only be expressed in metaphor, images, and symbols. At the same time, we bring those into dialogue with concrete, real lives in which suffering and death cry out for meaning.

When we turn to the biblical legacy, we find the New Testament replete with a vast array of diverse metaphors, as the authors struggled to express what it meant for Jesus to be crucified and what "taking up the cross" implied for their communities. No one theological explanation dominates. No single metaphor or image captures the essence of the cross and resurrection. Each metaphor contributes a brilliant tessera to the mosaic of meaning, yet even when all the New Testament tesserae are arrayed before us, the mosaic is still incomplete.[4]

It matters which metaphors we adopt to make meaning of the cross, for each carries not only theological but also social, political, cultural, and ethical implications. As Renita Weems observes, "Philosophers and critics of language . . . have shown repeatedly that the impact of language—and metaphors in particular—on a culture is no small thing. Metaphors remind us what is imaginable. Language influences our thinking about what is true, real, or possible."[5] Visual images, including depictions of the cross, also play an important role in shaping spiritual tradition. In the late medieval and early modern eras, for example, the habit of gazing upon religious images for the purpose of imitation and transformation became prominent. Undergirding this spiritual practice is the maxim: "one becomes what one imagines, one becomes what one sees."[6] As we examine in this study some of the images and metaphors of the cross, we will attend not only to their biblical provenance, but also to the ways in which they shape the imagination, both individually and communally, and the kinds of actions and attitudes they foster in us. Some of our traditional images need to be laid to rest, and other images need to be retrieved and reborn.

In this book, I explore five different clusters of metaphorical interpretations of the cross found in the New Testament. In each chapter, I analyze the biblical roots and the ways in which the metaphor can function, both in deadly directions and in liberative ones. I do this in conversation with women from a number of venues, in both Latin and North America. I offer in each chapter an exploration of stories of biblical women who emulate the crucified Christ and who may provide models for contemporary women. In chapter 1, I focus on various meanings of "a life given for others," including metaphors of sacrifice, ransom, scapegoat, justification, martyr, and friend. In chapter two, I turn to the image of Jesus as obedient son who goes to his death in accord with the will of God. In the third chapter, I examine Jesus' execution as a prophetic martyr who speaks truth to power. The fourth chapter examines a cluster of images including Jesus as healer, reconciler, and forgiving victim. The final chapter centers on Jesus' death as birthing new life. These metaphors do not exhaust the rich array found in the New Testament, nor is it possible in one book to fully explore the significance of each image. My aim is to bring into dialogue stories of real women who carry the cross today with New Testament ways of making meaning of Jesus' crucifixion. By bringing together theological reflection on the cross by Christian women of diverse social and cultural perspectives, I hope to broaden horizons of understanding and solidarity. By also looking to stories of New Testament women who exemplify "taking up the cross," I hope to offer female images of the Crucified One that validate women's experiences of suffering and discipleship. In this way, I hope to open a space for making meaning of Jesus' crucifixion and resurrection that can lead to liberation and transformation.

Stories of women are central to this book, but it is by no means intended for women only. While I hope to aid women in their efforts toward meaning-making and transformative praxis, I also hope that men will find this book a helpful tool in developing further understanding and solidarity in action with their sisters in Christ. As well, I hope this study will further both scholarly theological investigation and pastoral practice in ways that engage the biblical texts as powerful allies in the work of peace-building, reconciliation, and justice by Christians across lines of gender, race, culture, and socioeconomic position.

> "God doesn't want us to suffer."
> —Dominga, El Alto, Bolivia
> 27 March, 2003

THROUGH LATINA[7] AND FEMINIST EYES

Being conscious of my own privileged position as a white, middle-class, well-educated North American woman, I have attempted to listen to the voices of women whose experiences with poverty, oppression, and violence give them a different perspective on making meaning of the cross and the resurrection. I have entered into conversations with women from a number of communities in Latin America—Mexico, Bolivia, and Peru—as well as with U.S. Latinas in Chicago. These communities are part of a predominantly Roman Catholic culture that has traditionally made the cross central to their interpretations of suffering and death. In addition, many of the women speak from the richness of indigenous spiritualities of Tzeltal, Tzotzil, Quechua, and Aymara cultures. From their vision of the cosmos, they taught me other ways of understanding harmonious relations with God, the earth, and one another. I do not attempt to analyze the social, political, or cultural realities of my dialogue partners, but I will describe them where appropriate.

Our conversations with one another have caused me to ask different questions and to see other perspectives as I interpret the biblical accounts of the crucifixion and resurrection. I have met women who are part of the "crucified peoples" of Latin America[8] whose daily lives are marked by the threat of death from poverty generated by unjust social and political structures or from violence within their homes and on their streets. I have found that my initial puzzlement and revulsion toward the bloody, tortured images of the crucified Jesus that are so abundant in Latin America changed to humble reverence when I could see that, for those who live in situations of utter degradation, the only consolation is that Jesus knows and shares the depths of their suffering. Their hope in God, who raised Jesus from the dead, is tenacious and is deeply grounded in the conviction that the cross is the only route to new life. It is a lively hope that manifests itself in struggles for justice and liberation. I have found, too, that, as Jon Sobrino describes, crucified peoples are not simply victims; they, like the Suffering Servant in Isaiah, play a saving role in history.[9] They expose the lies about systems that claim to work for the betterment of all, while in actuality these systems exploit poor peoples and make the rich even richer. Crucified peoples witness to the gospel in extraordinary ways through their solidarity and cooperation with one another in community, their openness to receive and give love, and their determination to find God at the center of everything.

In turn, I hope this book will be of service to the women and men in Latin America who have befriended me, as they continue to reflect on and live their way of the cross. I hope not to falsely appropriate other women's stories. As my colleague Cármen Nanko-Fernandez asserts, "The process of accompaniment employs a metaphor of 'walking with' another, not stealing their shoes."[10] I do not claim to speak for other women whose reality is vastly different from my own. Rather, I hope to continue to learn from them how together we may open new pathways of theological conversation and solidarity toward mutual liberation. The path is not the same for all. The way "carrying the cross" can be liberating differs according to particular cultural and historical circumstances. It is not the same for those in positions of privilege as it is for those in the midst of struggle for survival. Liberation for the former requires relinquishment while learning to accompany the latter in their struggle for life and empowerment.[11] This is not an easy path of simply making connections with one another, but one that requires a person of privilege to confront the terror of difference[12] and her own complicity in systems that sustain injustices.

My approach to the biblical texts is through Latina and feminist liberationist perspectives. As a feminist,[13] I envision the interpretive enterprise in the same way as Elisabeth Schüssler Fiorenza:[14] it is a dance of Wisdom that consists of diverse hermeneutical[15] moves and turns. There are seven basic steps of biblical interpretation that interweave in spiral movements toward liberation.[16] The first is a *hermeneutics of experience*, in particular the experience of women, both contemporary and biblical. The starting point for reflection is the reality that a majority of women struggle daily against multiple structures of oppression, including gender, race, culture, class, age, and ethnicity. Next is a *hermeneutics of domination and social location*, which reflects on how social, cultural, and religious location shapes our experience with a particular biblical text. It then analyzes the potential of the biblical text for either legitimating kyriarchy[17] or fostering justice. The third step is a *hermeneutics of suspicion*. With this move, the interpreter recognizes the androcentric[18] bias of the biblical texts, most biblical commentaries, and many common-sense assumptions. Thus, the interpreter approaches the text, not with immediate acceptance, consent, and obedience, but with caution—recognizing that it could be dangerous to one's health and survival.[19] Fourth is a *hermeneutics of critical evaluation*, by which one weighs the oppressive tendencies and the liberating possibilities of the text. Recognizing the performative power of the text, one questions, "What does the text *do* to those of us who submit to its world of vision and values?"[20] This is not a question that can be answered once and for all for an individual text but must be done again and again in a variety of social locations.

A fifth step is a *hermeneutics of creative imagination*. With this step, interpreters dream of a world of justice and well-being for all, in which imagination is unleashed with drama, music, dance, poetry, storytelling, and ritual that brings to life new possibilities. As Schüssler Fiorenza asserts, "What we cannot imagine will not take place."[21] Sixth is a *hermeneutics of remembering and reconstruction*, which aims to retrieve the traditions of women that have been forgotten or covered over, placing women's history and struggle at the center. Strategies for this step include (1) assuming that women were present and active in history; (2) distinguishing between texts that are prescriptive, that is, forbidding women from a certain activity that they are, in fact, doing rather than being descriptive of reality; and (3) contextualizing and reconstructing texts and information in their variegated cultural and religious environments, not only in terms of the dominant ethos, but also in terms of alternative movements for change.[22] Remembrance involves, not only the retrieval of the triumphs of women, but also a *memoria pasionis*—a "remembering of texts of terror,"[23] of horrendous abuse of women, with the objective that such things never occur again. Finally, there is a *hermeneutics of transformative action for change*, which undergirds the entire dance. This move articulates a vision for a new humanity, a new global ecology, and a new religious community, in which relations of domination

> "It's not enough to just cry out to God—you have to take action!"
>
> —Robertina, Chicago
> 26 October, 2002

inscribed in texts, traditions, and everyday life are transformed by God's power at work in communities of believers into relations of equality, dignity, and mutuality.

Within these seven steps, I engage historical-critical methods of biblical interpretation with the goal of understanding the theological intent of each evangelist in the original context. I also employ insights from social science criticism to help sketch the social and cultural world of first-century Jews and Christians. I use literary approaches to unfold meanings conveyed in particular words and in the narratives as cohesive stories. I examine the rhetoric of the texts, looking for what attitudes and actions they seek to provoke in the hearer. Each of these methods is a key that opens up a portion of the meaning.

Latina feminists and *mujeristas*[24] share much in common with other feminists in aims and methods of biblical interpretation.[25] Our goal is the same: personal and social transformation that entails the elimination of suffering born of violence and injustice.[26] Like other feminists who begin with a hermeneutics of experience, Latina feminists emphasize *lo cotidiano*, "daily life," not only as the starting point, but also as the primary locus of theological reflection. *Lo cotidiano* refers to both the ordinary "stuff" of life and the processes of speaking about and reflecting on it.[27] An important distinction in the methods of Latina feminists is the recognition that the experience of the majority of women is one of poverty, oppression, and misery.[28] Commitment to analyzing the scriptures from the perspective of the poor is constituent of a Latina feminist hermeneutic.[29] Another key component of Latina methodology is reflection from *mestizaje* and *mulatez*,[30] that is, being a racially and culturally mixed people and living with peoples of other cultures. Theologizing from such a place contributes to a new understanding of pluralism and values diversity and difference.[31]

Another indispensable aspect is the communal dimension. Theologizing is not a task done in solitary isolation, but from a shared experience in community. Creating relationship in community is essential. A growing emphasis on ecofeminism—that is, attending to right relationships among all the elements of the cosmos—is shared by Latina and other feminists.[32] Akin to feminists who use a hermeneutics of suspicion, Elsa Támez speaks of a hermeneutics of distance and approach. Hers is a dual movement of distancing oneself

> "We women carry the whole history of suffering for our families, our people, we take up the suffering of all our brothers and sisters."
>
> —Sofía, La Paz, Bolivia
> 24 March, 2003

from traditional interpretations and approaching the text with questions that arise from the sorrows and joys of daily life.[33] Another important aspect in Latina experience is popular religiosity. Practices, signs, and symbols from medieval Spanish Christianity mingled with religious beliefs and rituals of African and Amerindian cultures are not regarded as primitive expressions that need to be evangelized, but as a positive reservoir of values for self-determination.[34]

Repeatedly, it is stressed that women be subjects of their own history, not objects of study.[35] Latinas, like other feminists, emphasize that such theologizing does not remain a purely intellectual endeavor but is intimately tied to praxis. While some feminists may envision the process as one that moves from reflection on reality to critical analysis, which then results in transformative action, Latinas never separate thinking from acting. Isasi-Díaz insists, "*Mujerista* theology is not reflection upon action but a liberative action in and of itself."[36] Characteristic of the majority of Latina feminist academics is that they straddle two worlds: the scholarly world of universities and seminaries and the grassroots communities of believers. Some live in poor barrios, choosing to share in the struggles of the majority while guiding local communities in liberative ways of theologizing and reading the scriptures. The ability of Christians who are illiterate or who have little formal education to do profound theological reflection and to be powerful agents for change cannot be underestimated.[37]

Biblical study is a most important entrée into theological reflection and liberative praxis.[38] In each of the groups of women with whom I dialogued, scripture is held in highest esteem.[39] If something is in the Bible, it is regarded as true. There is a thirst among Latina Catholics for better knowledge of scripture, not only for making meaning in their own lives, but also to be able to dialogue better with evangelical Christians who are adept at quoting chapter and verse.[40] There is also a hunger to become more skilled in interpreting the biblical word, to move beyond literalism and to find freedom and empowerment. Examples abound of how grassroots Bible study has led to transformative change for women and for their communities. The next section discusses a few of these with whom I have been privileged to walk.

CENTERS FOR WOMEN

In the Diocese of San Cristóbal de las Casas in the state of Chiapas, Mexico, a vibrant network of women's bible study groups, coordinated by CODIMUJ (Coordinación Diocesana de Mujeres, "Diocesan Council for Women"), is now more than thirty years old. Its initial roots came from the leadership of Don Samuel Ruiz, bishop of the Diocese of San Cristóbal de las Casas from 1960 to 2000. Having participated in all the sessions of Vatican II, Don Samuel was greatly influenced by the emerging vision of church as the people of God. In addition, by his own account, he was "converted" by the indigenous people of the diocese[41] and became increasingly committed to theology and praxis from the perspective of "option for poor." It is within this context that he became more and more attentive to the women of the diocese. He was pained at their silence and their servile behavior. When he would try to greet them, they would keep their heads down and cover their faces. If they did speak, it was in the tiniest voice, barely audible. It troubled him when he visited their homes that they did all the serving but never sat to drink the coffee with him or to join in the conversation with the men. He saw how men traded them like animals, bartering for their bride price. He noted that, in mixed groups, the women remained completely silent. It was from these experiences that he resolved to try to work directly with the women, apart from the men. To do so, he engaged the help of the religious women working in the diocese.

After trying several different tactics, they finally began to form grassroots groups of women for Bible study and reflection, a model that began to blossom.[42] The first of these groups were formed in 1968 under the leadership of women who went door-to-door, inviting other women to participate. Little by little, women learned to read the scriptures through the "mind, eyes, and heart of a woman," finding allies for transformative change among the biblical women. They have learned to ask critical questions about interpretations of biblical stories that have been handed down to them from patriarchal perspectives. They have gained self-esteem and have learned to claim their human rights. They have also worked with men to help them come to value women's dignity and wisdom. They have grown in their understanding that they have choices. They have gained ability to confront problems in the family and in the community and to look for the root of the problems. They analyze reality at the local, zonal, national, and global levels. They are working for changes toward a more just and equal society for women and men, as women's participation has increased in all spheres: social, cultural, political, economic, and ecclesial. They teach their children differently from the way they were educated. For many, "taking up the cross" no longer means passive acceptance of suffering that comes from abuse or injustice but rather signifies the struggles and hardships they choose to endure in order to learn and proclaim the gospel. In 2004, CODIMUJ acquired a donation of land and monies that allowed them to begin building Nuestra Casa, "Our Home," a center where the women now have their own space to meet, pray, and study together.

A similar center is in Torreón, a city in the state of Cuahila in north-central Mexico. There, the Benedictine Sisters of Monasterio Pan de Vida have made a fundamental option to work for the advancement of women, particularly those who are poor. They have founded CEDIMSE (Centro de Desarrollo Integral de la Mujer, Santa Escolástica, "Women's Center for Wholistic Development, Saint Scholastica"), where they have made biblical study and reflection a key component of their ministry. Like the women in Chiapas, praying with and breaking open the Word goes hand in hand with working for women's rights and human dignity. Daily prayer with gender-inclusive language and female images of God nourishes the new understandings learned in seminar settings. Weekly meetings, summer courses, and occasional workshops aim to help transform the realities, not only of the women, but of the whole family.[43]

> "Before I became part of this group of women who learn from the Bible about God's love, I was like the woman bent over for eighteen years. I had no sense of my dignity and worth. With the help of the others, now I am standing up straight and I am learning how to walk again. I know now that Jesus did not come to make us carry a cross—he came to free us from suffering."
>
> —Gloria, Torreón
> 9 November, 2002

Similarly, Holy Cross Sister Patricia Dieringer, Director of Caritas International in Lima, Peru, has found biblical study the key to the program she has developed to end domestic violence. In the courses she has created to train couples, she uses games, role play, discussion, and, at each stage, reflection on biblical texts. This is aided by instruction about historical and cultural contexts, both of the contemporary and the biblical worlds. The aim is to deconstruct false myths about women's value and roles and to build homes without violence, grounded in biblical spirituality.[44] Sister Patricia notes that oftentimes, men quote scripture to defend their rule of women and the household (Col 3:18; Eph 5:21-33). When women find something liberative in the text, it is important for them to be able to show it in the Bible to their husbands.[45] Another effort visible in Lima, which has spread throughout Latin America and the Caribbean, is the *Curso Intensivo de Biblia* ("Intensive Course on the Bible," CIB). This began in 1988 in Brazil in response to a need that arose from the popular reading of the Bible in *comunidades de base*, "base Christian communities." The courses include components in feminist hermeneutics and gender perspectives and have as one of their aims the empowerment of women.

In El Alto, Bolivia, Aymara women gather at *Centro Pachamama*,[46] under the direction of Berta Blanco, accompanied daily by Maryknoll lay missioner Catherine Williams. Approximately 1,200 women participate in the workshops provided at this diocesan center. The seminars focus on leadership, human rights, politics, gender issues, mental health, and scripture. The center also trains women in handicrafts. Affirmation of Aymara identity and their traditional vision of the cosmos interweaves with study of scripture and women's rights. Through these efforts, "more and more women are speaking out for themselves with confidence against injustice, oppression and discrimination."[47]

STORYTELLING

Telling One's Own Story

In each of the communities with whom I interacted, telling one's story is of vital importance. As women have claimed their power to tell their story and to interpret it through the lenses of scripture in life-giving ways, they are eager to speak their word. They recognize that each one needs to *echar su grano*, "plant her seed," not only for her own well-being but for that of the whole community. In groups such as those just described, women recognize that sharing their stories is not idle talk or gossip. Rather, as women speak their truth with the expectation that their story will be heard and held in reverence, storytelling becomes a means of empowerment, of claiming that the events in women's lives and they themselves as persons are important. Moreover, they affirm the revelation of the divine within their daily lives and recognize themselves as agents of Holy Wisdom. In finding her own voice, a woman gains confidence in her ability to interpret her story authoritatively and claim self-determination. Sharing in community, the similarities among the stories become clear so that women see they are not alone. Moreover, the systemic causes for their suffering become more obvious, which helps them begin to strategize together to confront unjust structures.[48]

Telling the Communal Story

Social analysis plays a key role in strategizing for change. In communal gatherings, women become adept at identifying systemic causes for suffering at the personal, local, zonal, national, and global levels. As they move from resignation, "*Así es; Dios lo hizo así*" ("That's the way it is; God made it so"), to the realization that "God never wanted us to suffer; God wants us to be happy," a retelling of the biblical story is crucial.

Telling the Biblical Story

Methods such as those described help women relate the biblical story to their own lives in ways that encourage them not only to say "we need to pray more," but also to strategize for transformative action. As one leader commented to me, "Women need to know that their suffering has meaning. But we need new images of God, and

> "Women need to know that their suffering has meaning."
>
> —Amparo, Centro Bartolomé de las Casas, Lima, Peru 10 April, 2003

of human beings. We need to see the God of life who defends life and the value of life for all."[49] It is such images of God and of Jesus that I hope to elaborate in the chapters that follow. How we understand the image of God presented to us in the crucified Christ is of utmost importance. As Elizabeth Johnson asserts, "The symbol of God functions."[50] How one speaks about God is the crucial theological question in the face of women's struggles for human dignity and equality. "What is at stake is the truth about God, inseparable from the situation of human beings, and the identity and mission of the faith community itself."[51]

There are strong obstacles to overcome in order to do this kind of theologizing. As María José F. Rosado Nuñes describes, liberation theology, the very movement in Latin America that helped empower women to theologize from their experience, is also the same movement that has relegated women's struggles to the background.[52] This has happened as hierarchies have been established in overcoming inequities. "Overthrowing capitalism, as the existing political and economic system, is made the 'priority' task. Women are generally told that the process of social change requires priorities and strategies. And they then have to wait at the end of the line for their liberation . . . they have to disappear, serving other struggles than those specifically their own."[53] The notion that the liberation of all is dependent upon and intimately intertwined with the liberation of women is still not widely understood. Moreover, in formal theological discourse, the only kind of theologizing by women that is welcomed is that which does not "rock the already-established theological foundation."[54] Investigations that keep women as a "topic" and that delegate to women only theology "about women," as if women were a kind of special interest group, serve to keep in place the existing ways of looking at the world. Raising critical questions about the exclusion of women from positions of power and decision-making in the church or lifting up women's preoccupations about sexuality, reproduction, or violence directed at them is seen as disloyal to the more general struggle for survival.[55] In local Christian communities, it is rare to find women's groups such as those described previously that have as their purpose the empowerment of women. Mothers' clubs more often serve a system that uses women's gifts without having their own liberation at heart. Despite these obstacles, biblical and contemporary foremothers can help blaze the trail.

FOREMOTHERS

In the past three decades, other scholars have made significant contributions toward a theology of the cross from a feminist liberationist perspective. Mary Daly is among the first to observe how "the qualities that Christianity idealizes, especially for women, are also those of the victim: sacrificial love, passive acceptance of suffering, humility, meekness, etc. Since these are the qualities idealized in Jesus 'who died for our sins,' his functioning as model reinforces the scapegoat syndrome for women."[56] The insight that the abuse of women and of other victimized persons is intimately related to Christian theologies of the cross has been further developed by theologians such as Rita Nakashima Brock, Jacqueline Grant, Mary Grey, Carter Heyward, Elizabeth A. Johnson, Chung Hyun Kyung, Kwok Pui-Lan, Elisabeth Moltmann-Wendel, Luise Schottroff, Elisabeth Schüssler Fiorenza, Dorothee Sölle, Regula Strobel, Delores Williams, and others.[57]

Some, like Joanne Carlson Brown and Rebecca Parker, have concluded that Christianity is an abusive theology that glorifies suffering and perpetuates victimization by convincing persons who are oppressed to suffer violence willingly. They see that the promise of resurrection persuades women to endure pain, humiliation, and violation of their sacred rights to self-determination, wholeness, and freedom.[58] Rita Nakashima Brock has called attention to how such formulations as "God sent his Son to die" lead to justification of child abuse.[59] Further, Anna María Santiago,[60] chronicles how the imitation of the silent, suffering servant keeps abused women from taking the necessary first step of breaking the silence about their abuse to begin to take action toward healing. Other scholars, such as Delores Williams,[61] reject the idea of the cross

"Seventy percent of married women experience domestic abuse. Eighty percent of the population is Catholic, but religion doesn't help women deal with the abuse. Priests don't know what to do. Women hear from their own mothers, 'You just have to carry this cross. You have to simply endure it.'"

—Paz, Director of Centro ¡Sí Mujer!, Torreón 7 November, 2002 or Christ's suffering as redemptive. They believe it is his life as a praxis of protest against injustice and solidarity in defense of life that is redemptive. Elisabeth Schüssler Fiorenza points out that the notions of innocent victimhood and of redemption as freely chosen suffering enable militarist and capitalist societies to persuade people to accept suffering, war, and death as important ideals for which people have died and for which it is still worthy to die. For women, a theology of the cross as self-giving love is even more detrimental than that of obedience because it colludes with the cultural "feminine" calling to self-sacrificing love for the sake of their families. Thus, it renders the exploitation of all women in the name of love and self-sacrifice psychologically acceptable and religiously warranted.[62]

Some feminists, such as Elisabeth Moltmann-Wendel and Mary Grey, insist that while paradoxical, the cross can yet be a symbol of life.[63] It is this last position that I would also like to adopt as I bring the fruits of foremothers and sisters working in the disciplines of Christology, systematic theology, and pastoral studies into conversation with my present work in biblical studies. I do not aim to give definitive interpretations or final solutions to the complex questions raised in this study. My hope is to provide a tool with which a conversation between contemporary women, the Christ of the gospels, and biblical women can open new life-giving avenues of theological reflection for present day believers. While the focus of this book is on the cross, we do this reflection from the stance of those who already know Christ resurrected and the new life that signifies. Each image of the cross carries a corresponding set of meanings concerning the resurrection. That investigation will need to be taken up in another study. The words of the Nobel Prize-winning poet Julia Esquivel capture the paradox that underlies talk of cross and resurrection. In her poem "Nos Han Amenazado de Resurrección" ("They Have Threatened Us with Resurrection"), she speaks about the "endless inventory of killings since 1954" in her native Guatemala.

"and yet," she says,

"We continue to love life

and do not accept their death!

They have threatened us with Resurrection
because we have felt their inert bodies
and their souls penetrated ours
doubly fortified.
Because in this marathon of Hope,
there are always others to relieve us
in bearing the courage necessary
to arrive at the goal
which lies beyond death. . . .

They have threatened us with Resurrection
because they are more alive than ever before,
because they transform our agonies,
and fertilize our struggle. . . .

They have threatened us with Resurrection
because they do not know life (poor things!)

. . . Accompany us then on this vigil
and you will know what it is to dream!
You will then know
how marvelous it is to live
threatened with Resurrection!
To dream awake,
to keep watch asleep,
to live while dying
and to already know oneself
resurrected![64]

CHAPTER ONE

A Life for Others

JESUS' DEATH AS ATONEMENT FOR SIN

As I HAVE EXPLORED THE meaning of the cross with many different groups in the past five years, all agree that the first answer that comes to mind for most Christians when asked, "Why did Jesus die?" is, "He died for my sins." This Pauline formulation (1 Cor 15:3) and the further elaborations of atonement theologies, most notably that of Anselm of Canterbury (1033–1109), have taken hold as the foremost explanation for the death of Jesus. When asked to elaborate on what "He died for my sins" means to them, many women speak of their unworthiness of this gift from Jesus and how they suffer with him, "taking up their cross" and following him (Mark 8:34). For many women, Jesus' sacrifice on the cross is translated into their own lives:

> He taught us how to sacrifice, how to give our lives for others, how to be humble and not self-centered. We sacrifice especially for our children, for our husbands, for our families. When there is not enough food, we give the best portions to our children and husbands. We sacrifice so our children can go to school, selling whatever we can in the market. We do not follow our own desires, but offer up our lives for theirs.[1]

A woman from Chiapas describes her daily sacrifices:

> I cannot read or write; I have to be content with knowing how to cook and sew. I get up at four o'clock every morning to get water and gather wood and start the fire for breakfast. I do all the housework and I work in the fields alongside my husband as well, with my youngest baby strapped to my back. I get no pay for any of my work. Men can spend money as they wish, and many waste it on drink; we women are completely dependent on what our husbands give us. At the end of the

17

day, my husband relaxes while I keep tending the children and fix dinner. Afterward, there is more work to prepare for the next day. I don't ever rest or have a day off. Who would carry out my responsibilities? God has made it this way, we have to be humble and sacrifice for others.

Having developed awareness through a women's Bible study group in San Cristóbal de las Casas, another woman remarks,

The worst thing was that we women regarded this situation as natural. We believed that this is just the way things are; there is nothing that can be done about it. We felt trapped; we never thought of ourselves as having value in ourselves, or of being capable and free to make choices and decisions about our own lives. Sorrowful, solitary, silent, and enclosed: this was our reality inside our homes in our daily lives—lives that we did not choose and that we thought we had no way to change. In our prayer, we would cry to God asking why he had determined this life for us. Our faith did not help us change anything; we believed that God had decided that it should be so. All the suffering we endured we accepted as our way of carrying the cross.

> "When men have free time, they like to watch soccer. When women have free time they use it to visit their mothers, clean house, take the children where they want to go. They are always using their time to serve others, never taking any time for themselves."
>
> —Fiorenza, Centro Bartolomé de las Casas, Lima, Peru
> 10 April, 2003

For many women, being Jesus' disciple means carrying the cross with him, enduring every type of suffering, including that which comes from abuse or injustice. Within the framework of atonement theologies, many women have internalized the message that they are sinful and unworthy of anything good in this life.[2] In some

> "In my Hispanic culture, women are the ones who consciously carry the cross."
>
> —Rayo, Chicago
> 26 October, 2002

cultures, as with indigenous women in rural Chiapas,[3] Aymara women in Bolivia, and Quechua women in Peru,[4] they have been taught since their earliest days that their whole purpose in life is to serve others, especially their husbands and children. Some parents lament, "It's only a girl," when female children are born. From their first moments of life, many women are schooled in self-deprecation and subservience. Any desire they might have for an education or to develop their gifts in ways that would make a contribution beyond the family is squelched. Self-sacrifice for the sake of others is the highest value. Linked with this is an acceptance of all manner of suffering—even physical, verbal, and emotional abuse, especially at the hands of their husbands. This is thought to be a woman's way of carrying the cross with Jesus. Lacking awareness of their rights, they internalize a sense of guilt for sin and regard any suffering as deserved punishment. Preachers reinforce the notion by elaborating on stories of biblical women as sinners, beginning with Eve, whom they present as the source of all evil.[5] In many areas of Latin America, there is an added factor—"a collective sense of guilt that is rooted in [the] culture. A sense of suffering with Jesus frees one a little bit from this guilt."[6]

The notion that Jesus' life was given for others[7] is a multi-faceted one that fuses together several interrelated images and interpretations, among which are sacrifice for sin, ransom, justification, scapegoat, martyr, suffering just one, sacrificial lamb, and friend who lays down his life for his friends out of love. We will examine the biblical roots of these images, analyzing their pitfalls as well as their potential for liberation. The Johannine image of Jesus as friend who lays down his life for his friends out of love is one that is particularly promising. We will see how this self-gift of a friend is replicated in a number of images of biblical and modern-day women who pour out their lives in love for others.

CULTIC SACRIFICE

It is Paul, the earliest New Testament interpreter of the death of Jesus, who most frequently speaks of Jesus' death as "for others." Paul uses a variety of images, blending and conflating them even in the same verse. A classic example is Romans 3:23-26, where Paul asserts, "Since all have sinned and fall short of the glory of God, they are now justified by his grace, as a gift, through the redemption that is in Christ Jesus, whom God put forward as a sacrifice of atonement by his blood, effective through faith. He did this to show his righteousness, because in his divine forbearance he had passed over the sins previously committed; it was to prove at the present time that he himself is righteous and that he justifies the one who has faith in Jesus." In this text, considered by some to be the core of Pauline theology, the apostle combines metaphors from various realms—cultic sacrifice, economic redemption, and judicial acquittal—to speak of Jesus' death and its effects on humankind.[8]

One of the metaphors in Romans 3:23-26 comes from the cultic realm. Paul likens Jesus' death to the sacrificial offerings in the Temple.[9] Israel, like other ancient religions, offered sacrifices in the Temple to God as a gift or as a means of purification and forgiveness.[10] Several New Testament texts depict Jesus and his followers in the Temple,[11] but after its destruction, the notion of sacrifice is spiritualized in both Judaism and Christianity.[12] A number of New Testament texts speak of Jesus' death as accomplishing for his disciples what temple sacrifice had formerly done. In Romans 8:3, for example, Paul says, "For God has done what the law, weakened by the flesh, could not do: by sending his own Son in the likeness of sinful flesh, and to deal with sin (*peri hamartias*), he condemned sin in the flesh." The expression *peri hamartias* is an allusion to a sacrificial sin-offering.[13]

In Romans 3:25, while many modern translations render *hilastērion* as "sacrifice of atonement,"[14] the Greek word actually refers to the "mercy seat" itself rather than the sacrifice offered. The mercy seat was the top piece of the Ark of the Covenant that stood in the holy of holies, the innermost precinct of the Temple. It was made of gold and had two carved cherubim, one at each end, whose outstretched wings overshadowed the mercy seat (Exod 25:17-22; 1 Chr 28:18; Heb 9:5). On only one day a year, Yom Kippur, the Day of Atonement, did the high priest enter this chamber to sprinkle blood on the mercy seat. Blood, the life-force, was thought to have purifying power. Thus, this symbolic action effected a ritual cleansing of all the sins of Israel. A subtle but important distinction is that, in Romans 3:25, Paul does not equate Jesus with a sacrificial victim such as the animals ritually slaughtered and offered in the Temple (see Lev 16). Rather, here Paul speaks of Jesus as the new mercy seat itself, that is, the new place of encounter between God and humankind, where purification is effected. A better translation of *hilastērion dia tēs pisteōs* in Romans 3:25 would be "mercy seat of faith,"[15] not "expiation" or "sacrifice of atonement."

The New Testament writing that offers the most extended reflection on the death of Jesus as sacrifice is Hebrews.[16] The author makes Jesus both high priest[17] and sacrificial victim. He stresses Jesus' mercy and faithfulness (2:17; 3:2), his ability to sympathize with human weaknesses (2:17; 4:15; 5:2), and the efficacy of his sacrifice to expiate the sins of the people (2:17; 5:1, 3; 9:28; 10:12, 18). As high priest, Christ "entered once for all into the Holy Place, not with the blood of goats and calves, but with his own blood, thus obtaining eternal redemption (*lytrōsin*)" (9:12). The author contrasts the repeated sacrifices of the levitical priests with Jesus' perfect sacrifice (7:28; 10:14), made once and for all (7:27; 9:12, 25-26; 10:11-12, 18).

> "We offer sacrifice to ask permission of Pachamama, Mother Earth, to plant and harvest from her soil. We offer sacrifice to give thanks for these gifts. It is to maintain equilibrium in the cosmos and harmony in the community."
>
> —Berta, Centro Pachamama, El Alto, Bolivia 25 March, 2003

The First Letter of John contains two references to Jesus as *hilasmos*, "atoning sacrifice." The author is exhorting the community not to sin, but assures them, "If anyone does sin, we have an advocate with the Father, Jesus Christ the righteous; and he is the atoning sacrifice (*hilasmos*) for our sins, and not for ours only but also for the sins of the whole world" (1 John 2:1-2). Later, in an elaboration on God's love, he asserts, "In this is love, not that we loved God but that he loved us and sent his Son to be the atoning sacrifice (*hilasmos*) for our sins" (4:10). This offering of love from God is to be replicated in the lives of believers: "Since God loved us so much, we also ought to love one another" (4:11).

SACRIFICIAL LAMB

Several New Testament texts speak of Jesus' death in terms of the lamb who is sacrificed. Paul urges the Corinthians to "clean out the old yeast," since "our paschal lamb, Christ, has been sacrificed" (1 Cor 5:6-7). He calls on two images from the Exodus experience to exhort the Corinthians to expunge sin from their midst and to claim the freedom from sin they already have in Christ. Just as the blood of the lambs that was smeared on the doorposts of the Israelites averted the destroyer (Exod 12:7, 13, 22-23), so Christ's sacrificial blood effects liberation for his followers. And as leaven, a symbol of corruption,[18] is purged from the house at Passover, so must sin be purged from the community.

The Fourth Evangelist also makes use of the image of Jesus as Lamb of God. In the opening chapter, John the Baptist points to Jesus and declares, "Here is the Lamb of God who takes away the sin of the world" (John 1:29; similarly 1:36). Scholars debate the meaning of "Lamb of God" in John.[19] For some, it refers to the lambs offered twice a day in the Temple (Exod 29:38-46) or the lamb sacrificed as a sin offering that effects atonement for the people (Lev 4:32-35).[20] For others, it evokes the Suffering Servant in Isaiah: "He was oppressed and he was afflicted, yet he did not open his mouth; like a lamb that is led to the slaughter, and like a sheep that before its shearers is silent, so he did not open his mouth" (Isa 53:7). He was "stricken for the transgression" of his people (53:8), and his life was considered "an offering for sin" (53:10). But this image ill fits the Johannine Jesus,

"Our women identify strongly with the crucified Christ and his sufferings. When beaten or abused, we identify with Mary, the mother of Jesus, who kept all these sufferings in her heart. There is a strong sense of submission in our Aymara and Quechua cultures. Women submit to sexual abuse from their fathers, uncles, and husbands, with a strong sense of resignation. Women identify with the suffering servant in Isaiah; what we lack is a sense that we need to struggle against the causes of these sufferings. And women have the capacity to fight injustice. They are very strong. They can move the whole city to action when they put their mind to it. But in their own homes women are like meek doves who submit to their husband's beatings. What is necessary is space for women to reflect with other women. When they are united with others, then they can work for change."

—Sofía, La Paz, Bolivia
23 March, 2003

who is not silent before his accusers (John 18:19-24, 28-38). Others think more of the victorious lamb, as in the book of Revelation (7:17; 17:14), the lamb that will lead the flock of God's people. Most likely, it is the Passover symbolism the Fourth Evangelist intends, especially in view of the fact that Jesus is executed precisely as the lambs are being slaughtered in the Temple for the Passover sacrifice.[21] It is notable, however, that here the image of the sacrificial lamb is being used in a new way. Jesus is not a cultic offering of the people but is the Lamb *of God*. God is the one who enters the human story through Jesus and whose offering effects liberation for humanity.[22] Another important thing to note is that, in Jewish thought, the paschal lamb was not a sacrifice.[23]

Although the Gospel of Mark does not use the word *lamb* in reference to Jesus, many New Testament commentators relate the Marcan depiction of Jesus' passion to the Suffering Servant of Isaiah 52:13–53:12. Jesus' refusal to answer his accusers (Mark 14:60-61; 15:4-5) is seen as an allusion to the Servant, who, "like a lamb that is led to the slaughter . . . did not open his mouth" (Isa 53:7). Pilate's amazement (Mark 15:5) evokes Isaiah 52:14: "Just as there were many who were astonished at him." Jesus' words in Mark 10:45, "For the Son of Man came not to be served but to serve, and to give his life in ransom for many," have also been linked with the atoning death of the Servant. Here, the image of a sacrificial lamb whose death atones for sin is blended with the image of ransom, the metaphor we address next.

RANSOM, REDEMPTION

Another one of the metaphors Paul uses in Romans 3:23-26, "ransom," moves away from the realm of cultic sacrifice and takes us into the notion of economic exchange. Paul speaks of "the redemption (*apolytrōsis*) that is in Christ Jesus" (Rom 3:24).[24] The term *apolytrōsis* refers to the buying back of a slave or a captive, which makes such a one free by payment of a ransom.[25] A variation on the same root word is used in Mark 10:45 and its parallel in Matthew 20:28, where Jesus says he has come "not to be served but to serve, and to give his life in ransom (*lytron*) for many."[26] While *apolytrōsis* connotes the act of buying back a captive, *lytron* is the price of release, or the ransom money, used especially with regard to the manumission of slaves.[27] Another variation of the term is found in 1 Timothy 2:6, which speaks of Jesus as the one "who gave himself a ransom (*antilytron*) for all." Paul also uses the verb *agorazō* ("to purchase") and its compounds to speak of Christians being "bought with a price."[28]

The metaphor "ransom" or "redemption" makes Jesus' death the means of purchase of freedom for humanity. Several New Testament texts equate "redemption" with forgiveness of sin (Col 1:14; Tit 2:14; Heb 9:15). Some further elaborate that Jesus' blood is the means of payment: "You know that you were ransomed (*elytrōthēte*) from the futile ways inherited by your ancestors, not with perishable things like silver or gold, but with the precious blood of Christ, like that of a lamb without defect or blemish" (1 Pet 1:18-19).[29]

The ransom metaphor, often fused with sacrifice, is the one that dominates in the Deutero-Pauline letters (Eph 1:7; 1 Tim 2:6; Tit 2:14; 1 Pet 1:18-19) and is the one that becomes predominant in later Christian theologizing. As doctrines of atonement developed, three main theories emerged. One line of thinking, variously labeled as Christus Victor,[30] Ransom, or Rescue,[31] expands on the notion that God rescues humanity from the clutches of the devil, either by tricking the devil by raising Christ from the dead or by defeating him in a cosmic battle that ends in Christ's resurrection.[32] A second type of atonement theology, the Satisfaction Theory, advanced particularly by Anselm of Canterbury (1033–1109), envisions human sin as an affront to God's honor, which must be restored. Christ's death is satisfactory compensation that pays the debt. A third direction is the Moral Influence Theory, sometimes called the Subjective Theory of Atonement. It was advanced by Peter Abelard (1079–1142), who emphasized the change effected in the sinner by Christ's death. Moreover, he stressed that it was not only reflection on Jesus' death but on his

> "Jesus could endure the violence against him because he knew that through it would come the reign of God, with justice, love, and peace. But when my sister was abused, she could not count on such a vision. She was destroyed bit by bit. Her suffering could not bring about any love or peace."
>
> —Alicia, Chicago
> 26 October, 2002

whole life that would lead the Christian to become righteous and a greater lover of God.[33]

SCAPEGOAT

Another metaphor for speaking of Jesus' death "for us" is that of the scapegoat. This metaphor comes from the cultic realm, but differs from sacrifice. The scapegoat ritual does not involve an offering to God, but is an expulsion ritual.[34] On Yom Kippur, the Day of Atonement, in addition to offering sacrifices for sin, there was also the scapegoat ritual in which the sins of the people were symbolically transferred to a goat that was then driven into the wilderness (Leviticus 16). The expulsion of the animal from the midst of the people signifies the purging of their sins. In several places, Paul speaks of Christ's action for us in such terms. In Galatians 3:13, he says that "Christ redeemed us from the curse of the law by becoming a curse for us." In 2 Corinthians 5:21, he urges the Corinthians to become reconciled to God, who "for our sake he made him to be sin who knew no sin, so that in him we might become the righteousness of God." Just as the guilt of the people is transferred to the innocent goat and the purity of the scapegoat is transmitted to the people, so Christ has thus exchanged status with sinners.[35]

The Fourth Evangelist also evokes this image when describing a meeting of the council convoked by the chief priests and the Pharisees in the wake of Jesus' raising of Lazarus. Many of the Jews who had seen what Jesus did had begun to believe in him (John 11:45). The council deliberates about what to do, as their concern grows that if Jesus continues attracting more followers, "the Romans will come and destroy both our holy place and our nation" (11:48). Caiaphas, the high priest, wins the day with his declaration, "You do not understand that it is better for you to have one man die for the people than to have the whole nation destroyed" (11:50). In a narrative aside, the evangelist clarifies, "He did not say this on his own, but being high priest that year, he prophesied that Jesus was about to die for the nation, and not for the nation only, but to gather into one the dispersed children of God. So from that day on they planned to put him to death" (11:51-53). This scene is then reprised following Jesus' arrest. When Jesus is brought to Annas, the father-in-law of Caiaphas, the narrator recalls, "Caiaphas was the one who had advised the Jews that it was better to have one person die for the people" (18:14).

JUSTIFICATION

While the cultic and economic metaphors of sacrifice, scape-goat, and ransom speak of how the death of Jesus accomplishes salvation, other metaphors such as justification, reconciliation, and adoption focus on the effects of Jesus' death on humanity.[36] Justification is one metaphor that occurs frequently in Paul's letters. In Rom 3:23-26, it occurs four times, intermingled with metaphors of sacrifice and ransom: "since all have sinned and fall short of the glory of God, they are now justified (*dikaioumenoi*) by his grace, as a gift, through the redemption that is in Christ Jesus, whom God put forward as a sacrifice of atonement by his blood, effective through faith. He did this to show his righteousness (*dikaiosynēs*), because in his divine forbearance he had passed over the sins previously committed; it was to prove at the present time that he himself is righteous (*dikaiosynēs*) and that he justifies (*dikaiounta*) the one who has faith in Jesus." The verb *dikaioō* ("to justify, make upright") and the noun *dikaiosynē* ("justification," "righteousness") are judicial terms that refer to a verdict that results in acquittal. It is difficult to find a word in English that adequately expresses all that *dikaiosynē* conveys. At times, it is translated as "justice," but for many English-speakers, *justice* connotes something more akin to retribution, that is, everyone getting what they deserve, whether for good or for ill. Sometimes it is translated "righteousness"; other times, "justification." A problem with both terms is that they often call to mind *self*-righteousness, or *self*-justification, which is not the meaning of *dikaiosynē*. Another translation is "uprightness." None of these English renditions quite captures the biblical nuances. In this computer age, however, "justification" may say it best, as when one uses "full justification" for the margins of a document, all is lined up perfectly even.[37]

What Paul is trying to convey in Romans 3:23-26, and frequently in others of his letters, is that human beings are in right relation with God, not because of any actions of their own, but by the gift of God accomplished by Christ, in which believers participate through faith. However, Paul has created a tension by placing his statements of justification by grace alongside metaphors of sacrifice and ransom. He says that justification is a free gift, yet ransom implies there be a payment.[38]

MARTYRDOM AND HEROIC DEATH

Another image in view when New Testament writers use the formula "Christ died for us" is that of the hero who dies a noble death. From the Classical period forward, the notion of a heroic person dying for another person or for a noble cause was well known.[39] A noble person might die for his or her city or country, friends or family, or to uphold a philosophical truth. Aristotle considers virtuous those who are prepared to sacrifice themselves for their friends or their homeland.[40] Socrates dies to uphold the laws of the city.[41] The Greek tragedian Euripides frequently elaborates the theme of self-sacrifice. In *Phoenissae*, the town of Thebes is saved by the self-sacrifice of Menoeceus. In *Alcestis*, the title character is prepared to die to save her sick husband. And in *Iphigenia in Aulis*, Iphigenia asks to be led to the altar of sacrifice to die for Greece.

In Jewish sources, there are stories of heroic figures who are ready to die for their faith. Daniel and his companions, although spared death, were thrown into a fiery furnace for refusing to worship the golden statue set up by King Nebuchadnezzar (Daniel 3). And again, Daniel is saved after being thrown into a lion's den for continuing to pray to his God, acting against the decree of King Darius that only the king be the object of worship (Daniel 6). The Maccabean martyrs, by contrast, do give up their lives for the sake of their faith.[42] The aged priest Eleazar refuses to obey the decree of the Seleucid ruler Antiochus Epiphanes IV, who tries to force Jews to eat pork and food sacrificed to idols (4 Macc 5:2). As Eleazar is tortured, he exhorts, "Children of Abraham, die nobly for your religion!" (6:22). In his dying declaration, Eleazar interprets his death as "for the sake of the law"

> "Women endure all kinds of abuse from their husbands for the sake of their children. What would happen to me and to them, they ask, if I left my husband? And the church always reinforces that we must stay together."
>
> —María, La Paz, Bolivia
> 25 March, 2003

(6:27), and he prays that his blood be a purification (*katharsion*) for his people and that God takes his life "in exchange (*antipsychon*) for theirs" (6:29).

Similarly, seven brothers and their mother encourage one another to die nobly (2 Macc 7:5), dying for the sake of the law rather than transgress it (7:2, 9, 23, 37). The youngest brother interprets their deaths as a means to lead the king who executes them to repentance and as a way to bring an end to the wrath of God that has justly fallen on the whole nation (7:38). In 4 Maccabbees 17:21-22, their deaths are interpreted as purifying (*katharisthēnai*) the homeland, a ransom (*antipsychon*) for the sin of the nation, and an atoning sacrifice (*hilastēriou*) for Israel.[43] "You ought to endure any suffering for the sake of God," the mother exhorts her sons (4 Macc 16:19). She recalls for them how "our father Abraham was zealous to sacrifice his son Isaac, the ancestor of our nation; and when Isaac saw his father's hand wielding a knife and descending upon him, he did not cower" (16:20). She also reminds them of Daniel's courage when thrown to the lions and into the fiery furnace (16:21). A hymn of praise to the mother and the seven sons exalts them for nullifying the violence of the tyrant through their courage and faith (17:2). Similar to Paul's assertions in Romans 3:23-26, Eleazar's death and the deaths of the mother and her seven sons are seen as having purifying effects for the whole people.

Paul uses language that echoes this tradition of heroic death in various places in his letters. Most famously, in Romans 5:6-8 he says, "For while we were still weak, at the right time, Christ died for the ungodly. Indeed, rarely will anyone die for a righteous person—though perhaps for a good person someone might actually dare to die. But God proves his love for us in that while we still were sinners Christ died for us."[44] In other Pauline formulations, "for us" becomes "for our sins." One of the ancient pieces of kerygma embedded in Paul's first letter to the Corinthians asserts: "Christ died for our sins" (1 Cor 15:3). In Galatians 1:4, Paul elaborates that Christ's giving of himself "for our sins" was "to set us free from the present evil age." In Romans 4:25, Jesus' being "handed over to death for our trespasses" was for our justification.[45]

DANGEROUS DIRECTIONS AND LIBERATING POSSIBILITIES

Taking Metaphors Literally

The metaphors of sacrifice, ransom, scapegoat, justification, and martyr, despite having positive uses in speaking about Jesus' death, all have dangerous directions. As is evident in Pauline formulations, these metaphors are often mixed together, keeping fluid what is said of God and Christ. In many texts, Paul fuses images from cultic, economic, and legal realms to speak of how and what Jesus' death accomplished.[46] These varied formulations express how Christ's death brought cleansing for humanity, like sacrifice; restored order by casting sin out from our midst, like a scapegoat; purchased freedom for captive humanity, like ransom; or adjudicated the wrong incurred by sin, rectifying humanity's relationship with God by a verdict of acquittal. But later authors, both in the canon of Christian letters and the early Church Fathers, have tended to isolate, rigidify, and literalize the metaphors, especially those of ransom and sacrifice, to the exclusion of others, which increases the dangers these pose.[47]

Losing Sight of God's Gratuitous Love

It is important to examine the image of God presented in each metaphor and the corresponding dynamic implied in how humanity relates to God through Christ. In sacrificial and ransom metaphors, dangerous images emerge of a God or offended Lord who needs to be appeased, mollified, or paid off for human sinfulness. This has frightening consequences, especially for women for whom this image of God gives divine approbation to the ways in which they cower in submission before men who exercise this kind of power over them in their lives.

What is most problematic in many of the ways these formulations are elaborated is that they shift the emphasis away from God's love and make sin the center of attention.[48] Atonement theories find a basis in Pauline statements, but they have for the most part lost Paul's emphasis on God's initiative and the utter gratuity of God's gift to humanity in

> "What the cross is for us women today is the machismo in the church and in society. Women's work is not valued."
>
> —Beatríz, La Paz, Bolivia
> 25 March, 2003

the Christ event.[49] In Romans 5:8, for instance, God's love is to the fore: "But God proves his love for us in that while we were still sinners Christ died for us." As well, in Romans 3:23-26, it is God's freeing action that is stressed: it is God who put Christ forward as the new mercy seat, who shows righteousness, passes over sins previously committed (3:25), and justifies the one who has faith in Jesus (3:26). All this comes by God's "grace as a gift" (3:24). Likewise, in 2 Corinthinas 5:18, Paul insists, "all this is from God." Ephesians 2:4-5 puts it eloquently: "God, who is rich in mercy, out of the great love with which he loved us even when we were dead through our trespasses, made us alive together with Christ—by grace you have been saved." The author of 1 John also stresses God's love and initiative in sending Christ (1 John 4:10, 19) and tries to allay punishing notions of God, insisting that "there is no fear in love, but perfect love casts out fear; for fear has to do with punishment, and whoever fears has not reached perfection in love" (4:18).

Both the metaphors of sacrifice and ransom have at their base a fundamental psychology of exchange relations. In cultic sacrifice, one gives something to God in order to get something from God, either favor, cleansing, or restoration of order. Ransom denotes economic exchange, paying a price for the freedom of a captive. Both metaphors conflict with the notion that God's action in Christ is a free gift, as they advance a mechanistic or materialistic image of God. Instead of inviting believers into a freeing and fecund love relationship, they trap people in manipulative cycles of guilt and gratitude. Rather than experiencing release from the shame of sin as freeing, believers find themselves re-inscribed into indebtedness and submissive gratitude.[50]

God's Power

Ransom theories wherein God tricks or pays off the devil portray God as less than all-powerful in the face of a formidable opponent. How is God's omnipotence to be reconciled with this image? There is also the problem that an image of an embattled God who emerges triumphant over the devil fuels a dualistic conception of the world in which good is pitted against evil, leaving little room for ambiguity and shades of uncertainty that characterizes most of human reality. Moreover, it sanctions warlike human actions, which feeds cycles of violence. This militaristic imagery also overlooks the fact that what God's "victory" looked like was a failure. James Alison observes, "So great is the power behind Jesus' teaching and self-giving that he was able to fail, thus showing once and for all that 'having to win,' the grasping on to meaning, success, reputation, life, and so on, is of no consequence at all. . . . [I]f death can only get meaning by having victory, . . . then someone for whom it doesn't matter to lose is someone who is playing its game on totally different terms, and its potential for giving meaning collapses.[51]

Trivializing Suffering

Another danger in the theories that see Jesus' death as a trick is that the reality of the excruciating torture Jesus endured is obscured. This can lead to the trivialization of the real sufferings of abused and victimized persons today.[52] The Christus Victor approach, which understands Jesus' suffering as a prelude to triumph, can lead believers to interpret their own suffering as a something that simply needs to be endured as a preparation for new life beyond the present life. Such a stance can keep persons whose suffering arises from abuse or injustice from taking action toward stopping the abuse. Joanne Carlson Brown and Rebecca Parker assert, "The reality is that victimization never leads to triumph. It can lead to extended pain if it is not refused or fought. It can lead to destruction of the human spirit through the death of a person's sense of power, worth, dignity, or creativity. It can lead to actual death. By denying the reality of suffering and death, the Christus Victor theory of the atonement defames all those who suffer and trivializes tragedy."[53]

> "Our women too often follow Jesus' words about turning the other cheek. What they need is to be like Jesus who answered back to the policeman: 'Why do you strike me?'"
>
> —Consuelo, Centro Bartolomé de las Casas, Lima, Peru
> 10 April, 2003

Pitting God's Mercy and Justice against One Another

Another problematic aspect with these metaphors is that they pit God's loving mercy and divine justice against one another. There is danger in equating God's justice with punishment for sin. It reduces God's manner of setting all things in right relation to a simple equation and overlooks the whole process of conversion and transformation. When notions of atonement present forgiveness of sin as part of a "prepackaged deal," then what it evokes from us is a simple holding fast to what is right. This "bypasses the process of the breaking of heart in which we discover for ourselves, as part of real attitudes and patterns of heart and behavior in our lives, how we are sinfully involved, and what we are really called to be."[54] We will take up a fuller discussion of these dynamics of forgiveness, repentance, and reconciliation in chapter 4.

Restoring Offended Honor

There is also the difficulty that satisfactory atonement theories reflect and perpetuate medieval feudal modes of relating. Anselm, for example, in *Cur Deus Homo*, sees God as a lord whose honor is greatly offended by sin and must be restored. God is a tragic figure who remains estranged from humanity until Jesus, out of love for both alienated parties, makes the sacrifice required to effect reconciliation. From this perspective, just as Christ's suffering free God and humanity from their pain of alienation, dishonor, and shame, so it happens that a woman is particularly willing to endure suffering, thinking that her anguish will spare from pain another whom she loves. Such an equation of love with suffering encourages a woman who is being abused to be more concerned about the one victimizing her than about her own wellbeing.[55] Or, by equating suffering with love, women will say to their women friends, "I don't think my husband loves me anymore. He has not beaten me in a long time."

> "Many women identify suffering with love. They look at how Jesus showed his love for us by what he suffered on the cross. On Good Friday, the church is packed; no one comes for Mass on Easter Sunday. I've heard more than one woman say, 'My husband must not love me anymore because he doesn't beat me anymore.'"
>
> —Brígida, La Paz, Bolivia
> 24 March, 2003

Salvation through Suffering

Looking at Jesus' death from the moral influence tradition, such as that elaborated by Peter Abelard, also has its dangers. This line of theologizing sees that only an innocent, suffering victim, for whose suffering we are responsible, has the power to confront humankind with our guilt and move us to believe in and accept God's overwhelming mercy. From such a stance, women often interpret their sufferings as a way to "save" their husbands when they are abusive or violent. Rather than working to eradicate their suffering as innocent victims, they hope to cause change by inspiring evildoers to change.[56] This kind of change rarely happens.

In addition, a woman who takes this stance "moves with an undercurrent of hostility and arrogance. She is better, morally superior. She suffers righteously, indignantly. She languishes into misery, waiting for him to embrace her with humbled heart and passionate gratitude."[57] Her misery and his guilty gratitude become the forces that bind, instead of freely offered self-surrender in love.

> "Culturally, we are a people who suffer and who celebrate. But we don't celebrate suffering."
>
> —Amparo, Centro Bartolomé de las Casas, Lima, Peru
> 10 April, 2003

Scapegoating

Examining the nature of sacrifice, René Girard has put forth the theory that sacrifice encodes violence and perpetuates scapegoating.[58] He begins by reflecting on the dynamics of "mimetic desire," by which human beings learn to desire what others desire. From this arises rivalry and social violence. Societies around the world, says Girard, learned to preserve order by channeling violence onto a victim, or scapegoat, whose expulsion ensured peace for a time. However, the cycle repeats again and again, and new victims are always needed. Girard believes that sacrificial cult, universal to all religions, arose as a substitute for scapegoating and covers over the violence of the community through "ritual murder." The biblical story, as he sees it, exposes this violence and counters the prevailing myth of redemptive violence. The Old Testament[59] began to expose and counter mimetic desire with the mandates not to covet another's spouse or goods.

It is the crucifixion of Jesus that brings this violent pattern fully into the open. The cross is meant to expose and oppose it once and for all. As James Alison, a devotee of Girard, puts it, "By not having anything to do with sacrifice at all, Jesus was making available a perpetual and ongoing mode of presence of God as nothing-to-do-with sacrifice."[60] Building on Girard's insights, Walter Wink offers that the early church was not able to sustain the intensity of the revelation that God has nothing to do with violence and that Jesus, as the final sacrifice of atonement, liberates us from our internalized acceptance of violence as normal and from any further need of scapegoating.[61]

While Girard's theory has much to offer, it has too narrow an understanding of anthropology of religion. Religions and cultic rituals, as well as human patterns of violence, are more complex than the single issue to which Girard has reduced them. There is also a dangerous contradiction in Girard's theory. If God's intent is to expose and put an end to scapegoating violence, then how can it be reconciled with God participating in or allowing it in the death of Jesus? Does this not re-ensconce the scapegoat mechanism at the divine level?[62] With regard to Wink's hypothesis that Jesus is the final scapegoat, Nelson-Pallmeyer notes that Jesus' execution does not really fit the pattern of the scapegoat mechanism. In addition, while Wink sees Jesus' cross and resurrection as defeating oppressive powers, the empire and its oppressive policies and systems actually continued to thrive after Jesus' death. The cross exposes the brutality and violence, and Jesus' resurrection counters the system's ultimate sanction of death, says Nelson-Pallmeyer, but it does not end their rule. Jesus' death and resurrection free us to recognize evil for what it is and to challenge it, but it should not lead us to proclaim that evil is conquered.[63]

Self-Sacrifice

Another problematic aspect of sacrificial mentality is, as Joanna Dewey has pointed out, that "the understanding of sacrifice has shifted from that of a communal festival to an emphasis on individual self-sacrifice." The harmful effects of this include "legitimating hierarchy, encouraging violent behavior, and glorifying innocent victimhood."[64] To understand Jesus' death as sacrifice is to exalt his death as pleasing to God and meritorious for others. This contrasts with ancient notions of sacrifice: the victim was not exalted, nor did worshipers identify themselves with the victim. Christians, however, and especially Christian women, identify with Jesus as sacrificial victim and find their imitation of him in sacrificing themselves. This is seen as both pleasing to God and beneficial to others. Dewey observes that "self-sacrifice has been the most acceptable—often the only acceptable—means for women to take initiative in their lives."[65]

Dewey further notes how infrequent are the New Testament references to Jesus' death as sacrifice and how sacrifice is read into some texts that would not have been understood that way in the first century. As well, most scholars agree that Jesus did not view his death as sacrifice. Nor was the Eucharist originally understood in terms of sacrifice, as evident in the *Didache* (dating to approximately 100 C.E.). Ironically, Christians originally stood out from other peoples in that they refused to sacrifice.[66] Yet, sacrificial language began to enter into Christian meaning-making about Jesus' crucifixion in later New Testament writings, such as Hebrews, 1 Peter, and Revelation, and into the understanding of Eucharist. Cyprian, in the mid-third century, is the first to refer to the body and blood of Christ as sacrifice and to the bishop as *sacerdos*, "priest." He is also the first to "make a fully explicit transition from a universal apostolic heritage to a single line of apostolic descent attached to the episcopate."[67] Following his lead, Christian worship has, from the fourth century on, privileged the metaphor of sacrifice in its understanding of Eucharist.

> "Jesus died to teach us that we have to be humble and sacrifice, to let go of pride and self-centeredness, and to love others."
> —Anita, El Alto, Bolivia
> 28 March, 2003

Exclusion and Subordination of Women

One of the effects of this direction of meaning-making is the exclusion and subordination of women. In sacrificial systems, priesthood is the domain of men, whose control of the cultic taking of life stands in symbolic opposition to women's control of giving life by birthing. While blood of sacrificial offerings is viewed as holy and atoning, blood connected with birth is thought to be polluting. Consequently, women are excluded from the sanctuary of the holy and are dependent on men to share the benefits of the sacrifice with them. In addition, the sacrificial cult mirrored and legitimated hierarchical power relations in the ways that it delineated the roles of elite free men, freed men, slaves, and women. By refusing to sacrifice, Christians were also resisting the hierarchically ordered social structure of the empire. Dewey calls for a rejection of "sacrifice as a way to understand Christ's death" and a "return to the early church's categorical refusal of the practice of sacrifice."[68]

Similarly, James Alison advocates that we learn "to tell a different, a sustainedly non-sacrificial story," not only when speaking of the life and death of Jesus, but when speaking of our own struggles to recognize and renounce our involvement in violence and to learn to read texts and tell stories from the point of view of the random victim.[69] With regard to the Eucharist, he observes that "it is always in a sacrificial context as the antidote to that context."[70] It is the place where Christians who live in a violent world surrounded by sacrificial thinking are fed by the One who is "not-a-sacrifice-at-all" and are taught "how to stand up against that and begin, however tentatively, another way of living together."[71] As attractive as Alison's suggestion is, there is little in the way the Eucharist is presently celebrated to signal to worshipers that they are to take the sacrificial language as a contradiction to sacrificial mentality rather than a reinforcement of it.

> **"I never believed the priest when he would tell me that our life was about suffering and carrying the cross. It's about love and God's project for life for me."**
>
> —Carla, Torreón
> 9 November, 2002

Costly Self-Giving Love

Robert Daly argues for a proper understanding of the meaning of *sacrifice* when used with reference to the Eucharist. Common definitions of sacrifice are, "giving up what you love," or, "'a gift to God in which the gift is destroyed or consumed.' Symbolizing the internal offering of commitment and surrender to God, its purpose is to acknowledge the dominion of God, effect reconciliation with God and give thanks for blessings or petition for further blessings."[72] Although this is a good definition of ancient notions of sacrifice, Daly advances that it is disastrous as a definition of Christian sacrifice. He concurs with Girard, agreeing that Jesus did away with this kind of sacrifice.

Key to the Christian understanding is Trinitarian theology. There are three interconnected moments. "It begins not with us, but with the self-offering of God the Father in the gift of the Son. The second moment is the totally free, totally loving response of the Son in his humanity. The third moment—and only here does Christian sacrifice become real—takes place when the rest of humanity, in the Spirit, begins to be taken up into that self-offering, self-giving relationship of Father and Son."[73] This third moment is not something that the faithful do. "Rather it is what happens when, in the power of the same Spirit that was in Jesus, we are taken up into the totally free, totally loving, totally self-communicating, mutual love of Father, Son and Spirit."[74] Analogous to falling in love, it is something self-transcending that happens to us and transforms us.

Daly recognizes that "sacrifice" is not usually understood this way by most Christians and that it is freighted with many negative connotations. However, since it so permeates our liturgical language, he makes a pastoral suggestion that ministers help people reflect on their actual experiences of sacrifice for others that springs from self-giving love and that this can help correct false understandings of sacrifice. Mature people know from experience that "genuine self-giving love is not without its costs, costs that are sometimes very dear. And they know that it is the love and not the suffering that is the defining, eternal reality that will never pass away."[75] By analogy, Christians can see that it is "the self-giving love and not the suffering that accompanies it that is the essence of the sacrifice of Christ."[76] One difficulty remains with Daly's suggestion: what of those whose lives have been so marked by abuse and oppression that they have no genuine

"Jesus is always with me, helping me in my suffering and pain. I always feel he walks this way of the cross with me."
—Margarita, Chicago
26 October, 2002

experiences of free self-giving love? What if one has no real sense of self and no real power of choice to give that self in love?

Elisabeth Moltmann-Wendel attends to these questions when she speaks about replacing "sacrifice" with "the image of self-surrender, which includes not only passive suffering but also an element of self-determination."[77] In contrast to sacrifice, "self-surrender is an act of one's own free will; it is bound up with responsibility and love, and is interested in the preservation of life."[78] Jesus lived his entire life in self-surrender to God and to us; the self-surrender does not take place only in the moment of his death.

Jesus' Attitude toward Sacrifice

One other important consideration in evaluating the metaphors of sacrifice, ransom, scapegoat, and martyr is whether they cohere with Jesus' own understanding of his death, as reflected in the gospels. With regard to sacrifice, it is notable that Jesus is not a priest and that the gospels preserve traditions in which he utters words critical of sacrificial thinking. Like the prophet Hosea, who said, "For I desire steadfast love and not sacrifice, the knowledge of God rather than burnt offerings" (Hos 6:6), Jesus also speaks of God as one who does not require sacrifice but rather love and justice.[79] When the Pharisees grumble about Jesus eating with tax collectors and sinners, Jesus' response is, "Go and learn what this means, 'I desire mercy, not sacrifice'" (Matt 9:13). Jesus defends his disciples for plucking grain on the Sabbath when they were hungry, saying to the disapproving Pharisees, "If you had known what this means, 'I desire mercy and not sacrifice,' you would not have condemned the guiltless" (12:7). Jesus approves the insight of a wise scribe who concurs with him that love of God and love of neighbor are the greatest commandments and he adds, "This is more important than all whole burnt offerings and sacrifices" (Mark 12:33).

Jesus is also critical of those who use sacrifice to cover up injustice. Echoing God's word spoken through Amos, "Even though you offer me your burnt offerings and grain offerings, I will not accept them; and the offerings of well-being of your fatted animals, I will not look upon them. . . . But let justice roll down like waters, and righteousness like an everflowing stream" (Isa

5:22-24), Jesus denounces religious leaders who "have neglected the weightier matters of the law: justice and mercy and faith," while scrupulously adhering to minute ritualistic observances (Matt 23:23).

Although Jesus is not portrayed in the gospels as taking part in sacrificial cult, a number of passages take for granted the practice of sacrifice.[80] In the opening chapters of the Gospel of Luke, Zechariah is making an incense offering in the Temple (Luke 1:8-11), and after his birth, Jesus' parents make a purification sacrifice in the Temple (2:22-24). After healing a man with leprosy, Jesus instructs him, "Go, show yourself to the priest, and offer for your cleansing what Moses commanded, as a testimony to them" (Mark 1:44 // Matt 8:4 // Luke 5:14). He gives similar instructions to the ten people healed of leprosy in Luke 17:14. In the Sermon on the Mount, Jesus instructs his disciples, "When you are offering your gift at the altar, if you remember that your brother or sister has something against you, leave your gift there before the altar and go; first be reconciled to your brother or sister, and then come and offer your gift" (Matt 5:23-24). It is important to note, however, that the point of this saying is that reconciliation is acheived by an interpersonal forgiveness exchange, not through cultic ritual.[81] We will explore the topic of forgiveness and reconciliation in more depth in chapter 4.

Jesus' critique of the Temple is also evident in an episode depicted in all four gospels in which he performs a parabolic action of protest and utters a prophetic word in the Temple (Mark 11:15-19 // Matt 12:12-17 // Luke 19:45-48 // John 2:13-22). Each evangelist interprets the act slightly differently, and it is not clear that Jesus is challenging the notion of sacrifice per se. However, sayings such as, "I tell you, something greater than the Temple is here" (Matt 12:6) and the Johannine portrayal of Jesus embodying in himself what the Temple had previously signified (John 2:21) indicate a shift away from cultic sacrificial modes.

Jesus Forgives before His Death

It is also important to note that, in the gospels, Jesus freely offers forgiveness during his lifetime, apart from any cultic sacrifice and without any reference to his death.[82] In several episodes, faith is linked with forgiveness. In one instance, Jesus, upon seeing the faith of the friends of a paralyzed man, pronounces his sins forgiven and enables him to walk (Mark 2:12 // Matt 9:2-8 // Luke 5:17-26). In another episode, a woman who had been a sinner performs lavish deeds of love toward Jesus, an action that flows from having received forgiveness (Luke 7:36-50). At the end of the narrative, Jesus affirms, "Your faith has saved you; go in peace" (7:50). In the Fourth Gospel, there is an episode in which the scribes and the Pharisees bring before Jesus a woman caught in adultery (John 7:53b–8:11). Although the word *forgiveness* does not appear in the text, Jesus refuses to condemn the woman and says to her, "Go your way and from now on do not sin again" (8:11). In the Gospel of Mark, forgiveness also comes through responding to the word preached by Jesus. When Jesus explains the first parable to his disciples, he uses Isaiah's words (Isa 6:9-10) to describe how his prophetic speaking will lead some to repentance and forgiveness, while others will be closed to that gift (Mark 4:10-12).

> "Since it is women who have always carried the heaviest crosses—theirs and everyone else's—we should have all women do our Holy Week enactments of the Way of the Cross."
>
> —Silvia, Torreón
> 9 November, 2002

Salvation and Incarnation

Just as forgiveness is offered by Jesus during his lifetime, apart from his death, so too is salvation connected with his life and not only his death. It is the incarnate Christ who saves.[83] In the Gospels of Matthew and Luke, it is in relation to the birth of Jesus that the language of salvation first occurs. In the Gospel of Luke, the newborn Jesus is called *sōtēr*, "savior" (2:11), in the angelic announcement to the shepherds. Correspondingly, the pregnant Mary acclaims God as Savior (1:47), singing praise for the divine action on her behalf and that of the people through the child she bears. In the Gospel of Matthew, the angel tells Joseph that he is to name the son Mary will bear "Jesus, for he will save (*sōsei*) his people from their sins" (Matt 1:21). The Gospel of John also links Jesus' saving activity with the Incarnation and with faith. Jesus says to Nicodemus, "For God so loved the world that he gave his only Son, so that everyone who believes in him may not perish but may have eternal life. Indeed, God did not send the Son into the world to condemn the world, but in order that the world may be saved (*sōthē*) through him" (John 3:16-17; echoed also in 12:47). All of these texts associate salvation with Jesus' birth, not with his death.

Jesus' saving activity during his lifetime is profiled in a number of healing stories. It is important to note that in each of these instances, the verb *sōzein* has a double connotation: "to heal" and "to save." Like the stories of forgiveness, faith is central. On a stormy sea, the fearful disciples cry out to Jesus, "Lord, save (*sōson*) us!" His response is, "Why are you afraid, you of little faith?" (Matt 8:25-26). A woman suffering from hemorrhages for twelve years approaches him in a crowd saying, "If I only touch his cloak, I will be made well (*sōthēsomai*)." Turning and seeing her, Jesus replies, "Take heart daughter, your faith has made you well (*sesōken*)" (Matt 9:21-22 // Mark 5:28-34 // Luke 8:48). In another story, Peter becomes frightened when walking toward Jesus on the water, and as he begins to sink, he calls out, "Lord, save (*sōson*) me!" (Matt 14:30). Jesus reaches out his hand to him saying, "You of little faith, why did you doubt?" (14:31). In another episode, Jesus' healing of a man with a withered hand on a Sabbath provokes deadly opposition. Jesus confronts his opponents, "Is it lawful to do good or to do harm on the sabbath, to save life (*sōsai*) or to kill?" (Mark 3:4 // Luke 6:9). Another time, a Syrophoenician woman pleads with Jesus, "My little daughter is at the point of death. Come and lay your hands on her, so that she may be well (*sōthē*) and live" (Mark 5:23). In another episode, Jesus heals a blind man by the name of Bartimaeus, whom Jesus exhorts, "Go; your faith has made you well (*sesōken*)" (Mark 10:52 // Luke 18:42). Another man who had been possessed by a legion of demons was healed (*esōthē*) by Jesus (Luke 8:35). To those who come to report the death of Jairus' daughter, Jesus assures, "Do not fear. Only believe, and she will be saved (*sōthēsetai*)" (8:50). To the man who had been healed of leprosy who returns to thank Jesus he responds, "Get up and go on your way, your faith has made you well (*sesōken*)" (17:19). Midway through Jesus' Galilean ministry, Mark summarizes, "Wherever he went, into villages or cities or farms, they laid the sick in the marketplaces, and begged him that they might touch even the fringe of his cloak; and all who touched it were healed (*esōzonto*)" (Mark 6:56). In an ironic twist, at the crucifixion of Jesus, the chief priests, scribes, and elders mock Jesus: "He saved (*esōsen*) others; he cannot save himself" (Matt 27:42 // Mark 15:31 // Luke 23:35). In these instances, salvation is linked with faith and is manifest through Jesus' deeds of healing during his lifetime, without any overt reference to his death.

There are also passages in which Jesus' words are associated with salvation. In the discourse following the healing at the pool of Bethesda of a man who was paralyzed, Jesus asserts, "I say these things so that you may be saved (*sōthēte*)" (John 5:34). Later, he declares, "I do not judge anyone who hears my words and does not keep them, for I came not to judge the world, but to save (*sōsō*) the world" (12:47). In the Lucan explanation of the parable of the sower and the seed, Jesus also links belief in the Word with salvation: "The seed is the word of God. The ones on the path are those who have heard; then the devil comes and takes away the word from their hearts, so that they may not believe and be saved (*sōthōsin*)" (Luke 8:11-12). In the climax of the story of Jesus' encounter with the woman of Samaria, the villagers first come to faith on the basis of her word (John 4:39) and then, after hearing Jesus firsthand, they declare him "Savior (*sōtēr*) of the world" (4:42). Not Jesus' death, but his words and his faith in them are associated with salvation.

In the Marcan appendix, faith and baptism lead to salvation. The risen Christ stresses to the disciples, "The one who believes and is baptized will be saved (*sōthēsetai*); but the one who does not believe will be condemned" (Mark 16:16). A similar image appears in John's Gospel, when Jesus declares, "I am the gate. Whoever enters by me will be saved (*sōthēsetai*)" (John 10:9). Jesus' seeking out of those on the margins manifests his saving mission. The chief toll collector, Zacchaeus, who gives half his possessions to the poor and repays fourfold anyone he has defrauded, is assured by Jesus, "Today salvation (*sōtēria*) has come to this house, because he too is a son of Abraham. For the Son of Man came to seek out and to save (*sōsai*) the lost" (Luke 19:9-10).

Jesus' Interpretation of His Death
at the Last Supper

It is important, as well, to look at the gospel accounts of the Last Supper, where Jesus' final words and deeds interpret the meaning of his death. The synoptic Gospels make the final supper a passover meal,[84] underscoring themes of joyful remembrance of the deliverance from Egyptian bondage and eager anticipation of the coming deliverance.[85] As with all meals, the act of eating together symbolizes life shared in communion. Jesus' practice of including outcasts and sinners at table with him signifies God's embrace of such persons in the heavenly realm. The Last Supper is the culmination of many such meals.[86]

Mark and Matthew tell that, while Jesus and his disciples were eating, "he took a loaf of bread, and after blessing it, he broke it, gave it to them, and said, 'Take: this is my body'" (Mark 14:22 // Matt 26:26).[87] There are no interpretive words concerning the bread as there are with the cup. Although the phrase, "gave it to them," repeated in the words over the cup, underscores that Jesus' impending death is a free act on his part and one of total self-giving.[88] Luke makes this explicit, as he elaborates, "This is my body, which is given for you." He also adds: "Do this in remembrance of me" (22:19).[89] The present imperative *poiete* ("keep doing") is a directive to continue what is already being done. The disciples are to continue the Passover remembrance of liberation (Deut 16:3) through remembrance of the liberating life and death of Jesus. The word *anamnēsis* ("remembrance") means, not simply calling to mind, but making truly present. Although some scholars read a sacrificial connotation into the verbs *didonai* ("give") and *poiein* ("do"), these meanings do not accord with Lucan theology.[90]

The offer of the cup and an explanatory word follow the gift of the bread.[91] "Then he took a cup and after giving thanks, he gave it to them, and all of them drank from it. He said to them, 'This is my blood of the covenant, which is poured out for many'" (Mark 14:23-24; similarly Matt 26:27-28). "Cup" is not only the vessel for the wine, but a metaphor frequently used in the scriptures to refer to the suffering of Israel.[92] In its two other instances in the gospels, it refers to the suffering borne by Jesus. When James and John request privileged places with Jesus "in your glory" (Mark 10:37 // Matt 20:21), Jesus asks if they can "drink the cup" that he is about to drink (Mark 10:38-39 // Matt 20:22-23). In Gethsemane, Jesus implores the Father to let "this cup" pass from him (Mark14:36 // Matt 26:39 // Luke 22:42).

Jesus' interpretive words over the cup bring together two powerful symbols: blood and covenant. Blood signifies the life-force (Gen 9:4; Deut 12:23; Lev 17:14) over which only God has power. In the Old Testament, the term *blood* is not often associated with "covenant," but the expression "blood of the covenant" occurs when Moses ratifies the Sinai covenant by sprinkling blood on the people and on the altar (Exod 24:1-8; see also Heb 9:19-21; 10:28-30). In Mark and in Matthew, Jesus interprets the shedding of his blood as the ratification of the covenant.[93] His own blood seals again God's covenant with God's people, just as Moses did with blood sprinkled on the people (Exod 24:8).[94] The Lucan Jesus interprets the cup as "the new covenant in my blood" (22:20).[95] This is an allusion to Jeremiah 31:31, where the "new covenant" does not signify a rupture with the old covenant. Both the former and the new covenant are initiated by God made with the entire people of Israel, and the desired response from them is obedience to the Law. What is different in the "new covenant" envisioned by Jeremiah is the internalization of the Law; God puts it within the people and writes it on their hearts (Jer 31:33).[96] This is the only instance in which the expression "new covenant" is found in the Old Testament. In addition to Luke, Paul and the authors of Hebrews and Revelation use it to express their experience of a new relationship with God through Jesus.[97]

To "pour out blood," *haima ekchein*, is a way of expressing death, as in Genesis 9:6; Ezekiel 18:10; and Isaiah 59:7.[98] In each of the synoptic Gospels, Jesus says the pouring out of his life-blood is for others. In Mark and Matthew, it is "for the many," (*hyper pollōn*, Mark 14:24; *peri pollōn*, Matt 26:28). As in Mark 10:45 and Matthew 20:28, where Jesus says he has come to give his life as a ransom "for many" (*anti pollōn*), "many" (*pollōn*), has a comprehensive sense, reflecting a Semitic expression in which "many" is the opposite of "one," thus the equivalent of "all."[99] In the Gospel of Luke, Jesus says the cup is poured out "for you" (*hyper hymōn*) (22:20).[100] As Christian liturgical tradition has confirmed, "you" refers not only to the disciples present at the Last Supper, but to all who are bound to God through Jesus.

Many scholars see in this phrase as an echo of Isaiah 53:12, in which the Suffering Servant "poured out himself to death, and was numbered with the transgressors; yet he bore the sin of many [*pollōn* in the LXX], and made intercession for the transgressors." However, Sharyn Dowd and Elizabeth Struthers Malbon have argued convincingly that neither Mark 14:24 nor Mark 10:45 is meant to be read in light of Isaiah 53:12. Neither the verb *lytroō* nor the nouns *lytron* or *lytra* appear in LXX Isaiah 52:13–53:12. The only link between Mark 10:45 and Isaiah 53:12 are two phrases: *hē psychē autou* ("his life") and *pollōn* ("many"). Both the Isaian servant and the Marcan Jesus lost their lives, and this was a benefit to many, but the nature of the benefit is different in Isaiah than it is in Mark. In Mark, Jesus' death is not linked to forgiveness of sin.[101]

While Matthew (26:27) and Luke (22:17) include Jesus' invitation to the disciples to partake of the cup, only Mark relates that "all of them drank from it" (14:23). By accepting Jesus' invitation to drink from the cup, Jesus' disciples accept the suffering that befalls them as a consequence of following him and living the gospel.[102] At the same time, partaking of the blood signifies acceptance of the life-force of God, which empowers disciples to endure and overcome suffering and evil. In the Gospel of Matthew, this power is explicitly linked with forgiveness. Only Matthew adds "for the forgiveness of sins" to the words over the cup (26:28). I propose that Matthew is referring not only to Jesus' death as effecting forgiveness of sins, but also to Jesus' whole way of life. Matthew particularly stresses how Jesus lived and taught forgiveness throughout his ministry as a means of breaking cycles of violence and leading to reconciliation. Jesus has accepted "the cup" of opposition that such a life has engendered, which will culminate in his death. The phrase "for the forgiveness of sins" (26:28) not only interprets Jesus' death as effecting forgiveness for all, but also signifies an invitation into a way of life in which practices of forgiveness release all from the bondage of violence. The topic of forgiveness, healing, and reconciliation will be taken up in more detail in chapter 4.

In sum, there is little in the synoptic Gospels to support an understanding of the death of Jesus as sacrifice or as atonement for sin.[103] Jesus freely offers forgiveness for sin during his lifetime without cultic sacrifice and without any reference to his death. Forgiveness is more often linked with faith than with Jesus' death. Jesus' words at the Last Supper interpret his death as a freely offered gift to all that renews and seals again the covenantal relationship of God with God's people. Although many scholars see the "pouring out of blood" as a reference to sacrificial offerings to atone for sin,[104] this is a false association. The context of the Last Supper is a Passover meal, which celebrates God's powerful deeds in liberating Israel from Egyptian bondage and looks forward to God's future freeing acts. The paschal lamb was not a sacrifice for sin. The pouring out of Jesus' blood is not evocative of sacrifices for sin, but rather of the blood poured out on the people and the altar (Exod 24:8) that ratifies the covenant. It signifies the life-force that binds the people to God and seals their relationship. At the core is the freely offered love of God, who initiates and sustains this covenantal bond now embodied in the gift of Jesus.

A FRIEND WHO LAYS DOWN HIS LIFE FOR HIS FRIENDS OUT OF LOVE

In the Gospel of John, there are no words of Institution at the Last Supper. Rather, Jesus conveys to his disciples the meaning of his death by washing their feet, an acted parable that he then explains (John 13:1-20).[105] This is not an isolated action; it crystallizes the theme that weaves throughout the Gospel: Jesus is a friend who freely lays down his life for his friends out of love.[106] In many ways, this image of "a life for others" is different from those we have already examined and offers more liberative possibilities. In John 10:11-18, Jesus first speaks to his disciples about laying down his life for them when he likens himself to a shepherd who lays down his life for his sheep. Unlike a hired hand who runs away at the first sign of danger because he cares nothing for those under his care, Jesus will go to calamity's depths for the ones entrusted to him because he knows them intimately and is one with them.

As the Last Supper scene opens, the evangelist provides an interpretive clue that ties the foot washing to the crucifixion. "Having loved his own who were in the world, he loved them to the end (*telos*)" (John 13:1). The word *telos* points ahead poignantly to Jesus' final word on the cross, which comes from the same root, *tetelestai*, "it is finished" (19:30). The Johannine Jesus is fully self-aware and self-directed. He takes up the basin to wash his disciples' feet, "fully aware that the Father had put everything into his power and that he had come from God and was returning to God" (13:3). His action is a totally free self-gift, which can be accepted or rejected.

After washing the feet of each disciple, Jesus interprets his parabolic action: it is the example, or model (*hypodeigma*, v. 15),[107] for them to follow. He speaks to them about servants not being greater than their masters (v. 16) and invites them to emulate the kind of service he performs for them. It is not the kind of service that a slave must render to a master nor the kind whereby a doctor, for example, serves the needs of a patient. Both of these types of service imply inequality of status and obligation. The sort of service Jesus exemplifies and enjoins his disciples to perform is of a third kind. It is that which a friend renders for a friend, freely and out of love. This kind of service supersedes inequities. Acts of self-giving to a friend not only evoke a response in kind but also reach beyond, forming communities of friends. The missionary dimension comes to the fore as Jesus continues to interpret the foot washing. He speaks of an *apostolos*, "apostle" or "messenger" (v. 16),[108] not being greater than the one sending and of how the one who receives the messenger receives the sender (v. 20).[109]

As the Last Supper discourse continues, Jesus makes it clear that, as he lays down his life for his friends out of love, so are his disciples to do for one another. They are not servants but friends of him and of one another (John 15:15). Jesus commands them to love one another (13:34), and he speaks of the witness that their love bears: "By this all will know that you are my disciples" (13:35).

The metaphor of friend who goes to calamity's depths for his friends offers an interpretation of Jesus' death with much potential to interrupt cycles of violence and victimization. The Johannine Jesus is not a silent bearer of every kind of suffering that befalls him. When Jesus can alleviate suffering, he does so through healing, forgiveness, and confrontation with those who oppose his purpose to bring life in abundance for all (John 10:10). The cross is not his purpose or goal but the means by which he brings his friends to life eternal.[110] His purpose is to befriend humanity so as to draw all persons to himself and unite them with God (12:32; 17:21). He is obedient, not to a Father who sent him to die, but to the One who sent him to bring life. There is no language in John of Jesus dying for our sins.[111] Rather, Jesus is a friend who, out of love freely chooses to go to calamity's depths for his friends. He undergoes crucifixion as the labor pangs that precede the new life he will continue to nurture (16:21; 19:34).[112] Those who accept Jesus' offer of friendship enter into this relationship with freedom, autonomy, mutuality, responsibility, and joy. They form an ever widening community of friends who are willing to lay down their lives for one another (13:12-20, 34-35; 15:12-17), living in and giving to others hope in God's ultimate triumph over suffering and death. From the Johannine Jesus, friends learn to stand with those who are victimized, support their journeys to safety and healing, and break cycles of violence by refusing to replicate or cooperate with them.[113]

BIBLICAL AND CONTEMPORARY WOMEN WHO GIVE THEIR LIVES FOR OTHERS

In the New Testament, it is not only Jesus who is depicted as laying down his life for others. A number of female figures also emulate Jesus' loving self-gift. These provide for women icons of Christ-like action in female form that validate women's bodies and women's experiences as a locus of revelation of the divine and depict women as capable of emulating Christ in every way. We will look at three such biblical examples and then at liberating ways in which contemporary women have appropriated these images.

A Widow Who Gives Her Whole Life (Mark 12:41-44)

In the Gospel of Mark (similarly, Luke 21:1-4), after Jesus has performed a provocative act of protest in the Temple (Mark 11:15-19) and after having engaged in debate with chief priests, scribes, and elders (11:27); Pharisees and Herodians (12:13); Sadducees (12:18); and scribes (12:28), he observes a woman who puts two small copper coins into the treasury (12:41-44). Their monetary value was negligible. Jesus calls his disciples and says, "Truly, I tell you, this poor widow has put in more than all those who are contributing to the treasury. For all of them have contributed out of their abundance but she out of her poverty, has put in everything she had, all she had to live on (*ton bion autais*)" (12:43-44).

There is ambiguity about how the evangelist intends us to see this widow. The most common interpretation is that she is an example of supreme generosity, giving her last pennies. This may be so. But another interpretation is possible. In the passage immediately preceding, Jesus denounces the scribes because they "devour widows' houses" (Mark 12:40). Whatever this expression means,[114] it is clear that the scribes are exploiting widows, and Jesus warns his disciples not to imitate them. In this context, Jesus' remark about the widow's gift may be heard as a lament for the ways in which some religious leaders take advantage of the gullibility and generosity of those in their care.[115] Moreover, the Marcan Jesus considers the Temple a doomed institution, conveyed by the withered fig tree episode that frames his protest in the Temple (11:12-25). The widow not only contributes to a system that exploits her, but her gift is a waste, for, as Jesus tells his disciples, "not one stone will be left here upon another; all will be thrown down" (13:2).

This interpretation provides an important warning, not only to leaders who might be tempted to emulate scribes who bilk the poor, but also to women who would think they are doing a godly thing when they pour out their whole life in service to others to such an extent that they have no life of their own or who are so oppressed that they have no true freedom from which to give of themselves. The last line of the text is significant. The word *bios* means, not only "all she had to live on," but "life" itself.[116] If the widow's gift of self is given with free choice out of love, then we can find in her a female counterpart of Jesus, the friend who freely lay down his life for his friends out of love.

A Woman Who Pours out Lavish Love (Luke 7:36-50)

Each of the Gospels tells the story of a woman who anoints Jesus. In Mark, Matthew, and John, this occurs just before the passion narrative, and it is an anointing for burial—a foreshadowing of Jesus' death.[117] The Lucan version of the story is different. It occurs in the midst of the Galilean ministry (7:36-50) and has another connotation entirely. A woman, who had been a sinner and who had experienced forgiveness, enters the home of a Pharisee who is hosting Jesus. She weeps at Jesus' feet, pours expensive ointment on them, continues to kiss his feet, and dries them with her hair. This action provokes criticism from Simon, the host, who insists that, if Jesus were a prophet, he would know "who and what kind of woman this is who is touching him—that she is a sinner" (v. 40). Jesus then tells Simon a parable in which a creditor forgives two debtors who cannot repay: one debtor who owed a large amount and another who owed a much smaller sum. Jesus poses the question: "Which of them will love him more?" (v. 42). Simon easily grasps the correct answer when it is put to him in the form of a story. But the real question is the one Jesus asks next: "Do you see this woman?" (v. 44). The issue is whether Simon can accurately read what Jesus knows to be true: the woman's lavish demonstrations of love flow from her experience of having been forgiven her many sins.[118]

That the woman was forgiven prior to the dinner episode is evident from the perfect tense of the verb *apheōntai*, "have been forgiven," in verse 47, which indicates a past action whose effect endures into the present.[119] The challenge is whether Simon, who, like the person in the parable, has less to be forgiven, can open himself to seeing and receiving what is plainly before him: a prophet who frees people from whatever binds them and the resultant love and joy that such a liberated one experiences. The parable is open-ended, not saying how Simon will respond to Jesus' challenge to look again at this woman, let go his preconception of her as a sinner, and see a lavish lover. If he can do that, then he too may be able open himself up to the gift Jesus offers. The story invites us also to see in the woman a female icon of

Jesus, one who emulates his self-giving. Just as Jesus pours himself out in love, ultimately allowing his body to be broken and his blood to be poured out, so the woman pours out her love, breaking the delicate alabaster flask and pouring out its precious contents. As Jesus washed the feet of his disciples as a symbol of this self-gift (John 13:1-20), so she gives herself in love, bathing Jesus' feet with her tears of joy.[120]

A Mother Pleads for Her Daughter (Matt 15:21-28)

Many women will not take action for their own wellbeing; they continue to "carry their cross" rather than rock the boat. But when it comes to their children, they summon a boldness and strength from deep within, and no price is too high to pay. Such is the mother who pleads with Jesus to heal her daughter (Matt 15:21-28). The story opens with Jesus going into the district of Tyre and Sidon.[121] A woman from the region, a Canaanite, approaches Jesus and cries out, "Have mercy on me, Lord, Son of David, my daughter is tormented by a demon" (15:22). Designating the woman as Canaanite (in contrast to Mark, who says she was a "Gentile of Syrophoenician origin" [7:26]) recalls the original struggle between the Hebrews and the indigenous people of the land.[122] Though not a Jew, she seems to know all the right Jewish formulas. She implores Jesus with the identical words of the two blind men in Jericho (Matt 20:31) who moved Jesus to compassion and whom he healed. She uses words from the Psalms (Pss 51:1; 123:3),[123] *eleēson me* ("have mercy on me"), as do another pair of blind men (Matt 9:27) and the father of a boy with epilepsy (17:15) whom Jesus also heeded and healed. She addresses Jesus as "Son of David," an important Christological title in the Gospel of Matthew.[124] Yet her only response from him is icy silence. She refuses to be ignored and continues to shout after him, at which point Jesus' disciples urge him to send her away. Jesus does not want to engage her; he is steadfastly focused on his mission "only to the lost sheep of the house of Israel" (15:24).[125]

But she will not give up. She blocks him from going any further, kneeling at his feet and begging him once again to help her. Now he cannot avoid speaking to her. His biting reply is, "It is not right to take the children's food and throw it to the dogs" (Matt

15:26). What more can this gutsy mother do? She has poured out her every resource for her daughter: she has expended her voice calling out to Jesus, she has given up her own religious language as she addresses him with his own prayer forms, she has sacrificed her dignity by begging at his feet, and all she has received is a scurrilous insult.[126] Yet she has one more thing to say: "Even the dogs eat the crumbs that fall from their master's table" (15:27). In Mark's version of the story, it is her cleverness with words and her victory in the verbal sparring that finally wins Jesus over (Mark 7:29). As Matthew tells the story, it is the woman's great faith that Jesus at last recognizes that causes him to grant what she has asked (15:28). This stands in contrast to the "little faith" of his disciples, for which Jesus is consistently upbraiding them.[127] Not only do we see a woman of tenacious faith, but we see one who, like Jesus, is willing to go to extremes to pour out herself from love for her daughter, unwilling to relinquish the struggle until her daughter's wellbeing is achieved.[128]

Women of CODIMUJ

Many modern-day stories can be told of those who lay down their lives for others out of love. One that I've heard several times in Chiapas concerns a woman who lives in a small rural village. She had been discovering a new life through the women's Bible study groups sponsored by CODIMUJ. Like most of the women who had joined, she first agreed to come to a meeting at the invitation of a friend. The kinds of things the

> "Men have laid crosses on our backs, when we aren't given the right to study or opportunities for empowerment. But this is changing. We keep trying to overcome these crosses that they have laid on us."
>
> —Mónica, La Paz, Bolivia
> 25 March, 2003

women talked about were exhilarating, if not also a bit frightening. So many things that she and the others had always accepted as the way things were, were being challenged as they were learning to read the Bible through the mind, eyes, and heart of a woman. Had God really decreed that wives need to be submissive to their husbands in all things? Or was that a culturally conditioned value that now needed to be reexamined? Looking at Jesus' interaction with women in the gospels, they began to understand their value as women and grew in self-esteem. They began to reason that, if Mary Magdalene could leave her home to learn about the good news and to help spread it with Jesus, then they should be able to do the same. The women began to question whether they should be willing to suffer abuse as their way of "carrying the cross." They had been learning in their study of the gospels that "carrying the cross" (Mark 8:34) did not refer to willingness to suffer abuse or injustice, but rather that it meant accepting the possible negative repercussions of discipleship.[129] Maybe, they reasoned, "the cross" would mean the hardships they endured in order to participate in the Bible study groups. Some walked long hours through rugged terrain to come to a meeting. Some scrimped and scraped to find bus fare to attend the zonal meetings. Some would arise at 3:00 A.M. to prepare all the meals in advance for their family while they attended a meeting. Some of the women endured gossip and slander from their neighbors, "Where is she going? She must be having an affair. What kind of wife and mother would leave the children in the care of others while she traipses off to a church meeting?"

Working together to confront these personal challenges, the women were growing in their ability to solve problems in the family and in the community and to look for the root of the problems. They were learning how to analyze reality at the local, zonal, national, and global levels and to how to make their voices heard in all spheres: social, cultural, political, economic, and ecclesial. They began to teach their children differently from the way they were educated. All this they were trying to share with their husbands, but it was not always easy.

> "Women here need to learn to hear the Word as subjects of their own theological reflection, not as servants."
> —Adelaida, Centro Bartolomé de las Casas, Lima, Peru 10 April, 2003

One day, upon returning from a meeting of the women's Bible study group, one woman found her husband drunk and in a rage that she had not been there to serve him his coffee when he wanted it. He beat her badly, as he had done many times before. The next morning when her friends saw her battered face and bruised body, they decided it was time to act. About thirty of them gathered and, together, descended upon the husband, threatening him that if he ever touched her again, it would be he with the battered face and bruised body.[130] The husband was shocked. Never had he been so confronted. It moved him to receive the help he needed to stop drinking and to convert from his battering habits. One wishes that all such stories could end so well. This community of friends took the chancy action of laying down their lives for their friend out of love, risking reputation and possible reprisals from their own husbands.[131]

> "What does us in is when we say, 'We can't do anything.' We become empowered when we have our own money, when we are able to sell what we make in the market, and when we have access to education. What we need are leaders that remind us, 'Yes you can do it,' and who call us together so we aren't alone in our struggles."
>
> —Rosa, El Alto, Bolivia
> 28 March, 2003

María Elena Moyano

María Elena Moyano was only thirty-three years old when she was brutally murdered by the *Sendero Luminoso* ("Shining Path") in the Villa El Salvador neighborhood of Lima, Peru. A mother of two boys, ages eleven and twelve, María Elena Moyano had been an activist since her teens. In 1984, at the age of twenty-four, she was elected president of the Federación Popular de Mujeres Villa El Salvador, a federation of women whose work encompassed community kitchens, efforts for improved health care and education, programs to supply milk for children, and programs to help generate income for this shantytown populated mostly by people who had migrated from the sierra. Six years later, she was elected deputy mayor of Villa El Salvador, during the time when the terrorist threat from *Sendero Luminoso* was on the rise.

By mid-1991, *Sendero* began openly targeting women leaders in Lima. The women's strong support among the grassroots and their vocal denunciations of the violence of *Sendero* made these women a threat to the terrorist organization. María Elena did not desist from her efforts even as Juana López, coordinator of the

Vaso de Leche ("Glass of Milk") program for children, was murdered and as Emma Hilario, director of the National Federation of People's Kitchens, survived a shotgun blast inside her own home. María Elena moved about, not sleeping at home or even in her own neighborhood. Her friends provided what protection they could but finally convinced her to leave the country as the death threats increased. Ten days later, she returned, saying she would rather lose her life struggling against *Sendero* than die with feelings of anguish and impotence away from the country.[132] On February 15, 1992, she was present at a fundraiser in Villa El Salvador, when men from *Sendero* burst in and machine-gunned her in front of her children and other women and then blew up her corpse with dynamite. Her community of friends for whom she lay down her life does not think it was in vain. As one of them declared,

> We believe Peru to be a viable country, a place for women and men of all ages, races, classes, and conditions to live in. This is what María Elena lived for. Presently in Peru we, as women, have taken on a political role of more importance than ever before in the history of the country. We are leaders, citizens, women's rights activists, organizers, and mobilizers of the grassroots efforts to survive, to overcome the crisis, and to protect life and livelihoods, as well as the democratic spaces and values that have cost us so much effort to construct.[133]

CONCLUSION

In this chapter, we have looked at diverse aspects of the image of Jesus' death as the culmination of a life lived for others. We have analyzed the biblical roots of metaphors such as atoning sacrifice, ransom, redemption, justification, scapegoat, lamb, martyr, and friend, examining both the deadly directions in which they can be taken and the liberating possibilities. We have seen the problems that arise when these metaphors are isolated, rigidified, or taken literally or when sin displaces love as the central

"The thing is that you don't go looking for the cross; it is those things you have to confront and against which you have to fight, joined with Christ, looking at him, and at his example."

—Brígida, La Paz, Bolivia
24 March, 2003

focus. We have seen how some of these metaphors can lead to the glorification of suffering and to attitudes that prevent those who are abused from taking action toward their wellbeing instead of continuing to "carry their cross." One particularly promising metaphor is that of Jesus as friend who lays down his life for his friends out of love. We have seen that, not only Jesus, but a number of biblical and contemporary women exemplify what it means to live a life for others in ways that are freely chosen and motivated by love. In the next chapter, we turn to the question of what it meant for Jesus to be obedient to God's mission for life that culminated in his death on a cross.

CHAPTER TWO

Obedient to God[1]

"My whole life I was taught to obey: first of all, my father and mother. At age twelve my father decided who I would marry. My future husband had come one day to pay his respects to my father and mother, and presented them with a bottle of aguardiente. My father and his father made the agreement. I had no say. I could not object that I didn't even know the man to whom my father had promised me. My only choice was to do my father's will. My father and mother told me this: 'Now you will leave the home of your birth because we desire and permit it. Now your parents will be those of your husband. And so, my daughter, behave well, do not gossip or lie, do not criticize your in-laws. Obey the commands of your father-in-law and your mother-in-law and your husband. Never act high-handed. Listen carefully to what they say to you so that you can obey well. You will only be happy if you obey. If you complain or criticize or speak ill of them, if you do not respect your husband, then sickness and evil will come upon you and the family. Please, daughter, do not let in the devil. If you listen and obey well you will be happy and no shame will come upon the family.'

After I was married, I tried to obey my husband in everything. He would never ask my opinion on anything. He was the one who always made the decisions. I had to ask permission of my husband to do anything or to go anywhere. The only places I was permitted to go were to do what was necessary to take care of the household: carry water, wash clothes, haul firewood, grind the corn, or to go out to the field to work with my husband. I would ask to go visit my mother, and my husband would refuse. In addition, I had to obey my father- and mother-in-law, especially my mother-in-law. We lived in their home, waiting for the day when my father-in-law would give my husband his own piece of land. It seemed like that day would never come. I tried to be an obedient daughter and wife, but my father was wrong. I was not happy. My heart was always sad. I would cry out to God in my prayers, but the only answer I got was that God ordained that it should be this way."

—Women of CODIMUJ in Chiapas[2]

AN EXPLANATION FOR THE DEATH of Jesus that often goes hand-in-hand with "He died for my sins" is "God sent Jesus to die." Jesus is said to go obediently to his death, following God's will. Images of Jesus as an obedient Son who faithfully carries out God's will give a powerful underpinning to submissive responses by women to the rule of fathers and husbands. The biblical texts that most explicitly validate such obedience and submission for women are the household codes in Colossians 3:18—4:1; Ephesians 5:21—6:9; and 1 Peter 2:18–3:7.[3] In these texts, Paul and the authors writing in the names of Paul and Peter[4] adapt and Christianize the prevailing patriarchal codes of conduct. These texts prescribe strict lines of authority and obedience for the smooth running of a household: wives must be submissive to their husbands, children to their parents, and slaves to their masters, "as is proper in the Lord" (Col 3:18). When a literal reading of these texts is coupled with a reading of Genesis 3:16 as divine prescription for rule over women by men, the results can be deadly. In this chapter, I will take up an examination of these texts, as well as others that depict Jesus' obedience unto death.

The language of obedience and submission is found in a number of New Testament texts that explain the death of Jesus in terms of his obedience to God. The early Christian hymn found in Philippians 2:6-11 sings of the way Jesus emptied himself, becoming incarnate as a human being, and then humbled himself "and became obedient to the point of death— even death on a cross" (2:8). In a similar vein, the letter to the Hebrews asserts, "Although he was a Son he learned obedience through what he suffered" (5:8). The synoptic Gospels play out this image of obedient Son who goes to his death in two particularly vivid texts: the parable of the wicked tenants and Jesus' prayer in Gethsemane. We turn first to the parable of the murderous tenants.

OBEDIENT SON SENT TO THE VINEYARD (Mark 12:1-12)

In the parable of the wicked tenants (Mark 12:1-12),[5] the vineyard owner, usually understood as a figure for God, repeatedly sends servants to gather his produce. The wicked tenants beat and kill servant after servant. Finally, the owner has one left: "a beloved son" (12:6), whom he sends. The son's fate is the same. They "seized him, killed him, and threw him out of the vineyard" (12:8). The parable ends with the decision of the vineyard owner to destroy the wicked tenants and to give the vineyard to others. A quotation from Psalms 118:22-23 concludes the parable: "The stone that the builders rejected has become the cornerstone. This was the Lord's doing and it is amazing in our eyes" (Mark 12:10-11).

The allegorical nature of the parable is evident. The repeated sending of servants by the landowner recalls God's persistent sending of prophet after prophet, habitually called "servants," to Israel (Jer 7:25; 25:4; Amos 3:7; Zech 1:6). While only two prophets are said to be killed in the Hebrew scriptures,[6] the killing of prophets is a frequent theme in the New Testament.[7] That the final servant in the parable is meant to be understood as Jesus is clear from his designation as "beloved son" (Mark 12:6), which echoes the voice from heaven at Jesus' baptism (1:11) and at his transfiguration (9:7).

The main point of the parable is to confront the religious leaders who have murderous intentions toward Jesus (Mark 12:12) and to offer them one last chance to recognize Jesus' true identity as Son.[8] The metaphor of an unproductive vineyard is a familiar one. The synoptic parable initially follows the contours of Isaiah 5:1-7 quite closely. However, the ending is not the same. In Isaiah 5, the disappointed owner destroys the vineyard. In the Gospel parable, the vineyard is still capable of producing a good harvest. It remains while the tenants are replaced. While the "others" to whom the vineyard will be entrusted are not specified, it is clear that the current tenants are the Jerusalem authorities (Mark 12:12). The quotation of Psalm 118 (in Mark 12:10), which recalls God's unlikely choice of David as king and messianic prototype, points toward the new leadership of God's vineyard as coming from the followers of the rejected Jesus.[9]

Although the focus of the parable is not so much on the obedience of the son, troubling questions arise. After seeing that servant after servant is abused or killed, why would the son obey the vineyard owner? Why would he not protest or insist on a different plan? And what kind of father would knowingly send his beloved son to such a fate? These disturbing questions are left unanswered in the parable itself, which focuses on ensuring productivity of the vineyard by entrusting it to faithful tenants. As Stephen Finlan points out, the vineyard owner sends the son to collect the produce, not to be killed. Moreover, the owner "is not happy nor even sadly resigned when the tenants kills his son; he is angry. Clearly, this killing was not what he intended."[10] Some of the questions raised by this parable can be better answered when we see how the Gospel as a whole, not just this parable, depicts Jesus' obedience to God. It is a choice Jesus makes to be faithful throughout his whole life to God's mission to bring healing and wellbeing to all, a choice that impels him to continue to offer God's love to all, even to those who will reject him and put him to death.

> "'God sent his son to die'—this is the way almost everyone here speaks of Jesus' death. But when confronted with the question: 'Would you, as a parent do such a thing?' The answer is always an emphatic 'No!,' which then opens the way into a new consideration of God."
>
> —Sr. Patricia Dieringer, CSC,
> Lima, Peru
> 16 April, 2003

NOT MY WILL, BUT YOURS (Mark 14:32-42)

The questions that surface in the parable of the murderous tenants become even more acute in the Gethsemane scene, as portrayed in the synoptic Gospels.[11] In Mark's and Matthew's versions, Jesus is "deeply grieved, even unto death" (Mark 14:34; Matt 26:38) and goes apart from his companions, Peter, James, and John. He falls prostrate on the ground and prays three times, "Abba, Father, for you all things are possible; remove this cup[12] from me; yet not what I want, but what you want" (Mark 14:36; similarly Matt 26:39). There is no reply. There is no voice from heaven to give divine assurance, no ministering angel,[13] no inner sense of calm. Does God turn a deaf ear to the pleas of the Son, such as the women in Chiapas perceived when they cried out to God in their suffering? Is there a conflict between Jesus' will and

God's will? Does being an obedient Son demand simple acquiescence to the divine will? Does God have a foreordained plan by which this suffering will serve a greater good?

"IF YOU ARE THE SON OF GOD"

While the revelation of the identity of Jesus as Son of God is a feature of all four Gospels, there is a unique emphasis on this in the crucifixion scene in Matthew's Gospel (27:38-43). For this reason, we will focus on the Gospel of Matthew in the next sections. The theme of Jesus as God's Son builds throughout the Gospel. Early in the story, we glimpse an intimate scene between God and Jesus, as Jesus goes out to the desert to receive John the Baptist's water baptism (3:13-17).[14] In this profound religious encounter, Jesus experiences no distance between himself and God. He senses that "the heavens were opened to him" (3:16), that no obstacles stood in the way of communication with the divine Lover.[15] He feels a gentle descent of the Spirit of God on him (3:16), moving powerfully within him. This is the same Spirit by whose power creation came forth (Gen 1:2) and who inspired prophets and judges,[16] impelling them to speak God's Word and to make decisions for the good of God's people. At his baptism, Jesus comes to know that this same Spirit of God is within him, giving him power to heal and transform God's broken creation and to preach and teach with authority (Matt 7:29). As signs of God's presence enfold him, a heavenly voice affirms, "This is my Son, the Beloved" (3:17).[17]

> "There is a strong sense of guilt in our culture. When a woman is victimized, she often assumes the blame. It is a psychological mechanism by which she submits in order to survive. Suffering with Jesus liberates her a little from the guilt."
>
> —Adelaida, Centro Bartolomé de las Casas, Lima, Peru
> 10 April, 2003

In the next scene, the Spirit leads Jesus into the desert to be tempted by the devil (4:1-11). Twice the devil taunts Jesus, "If you are the Son of God . . ." (Matt 4:3, 6). First, he tempts Jesus to feed his own hungers rather than attend to God's hungry people. Then he urges Jesus to display flashy manifestations of God's power, thus convincing people of his true messianic identity. Finally, he tries to get Jesus to worship him rather than God.

Throughout the trial, Jesus is sustained by a palpable presence of the divine: "angels came and waited on him" (4:11). Jesus' temptations do not end when he leaves this period in the desert. Jesus was fully human and experienced temptations throughout his life, as all people do, though he did not succumb to them (Heb 4:15). Like us, he had to make the decision to be true to God's will at every turn. A life of faithful choices reaches its climax in the Gethsemane scene, where his struggle to know and to choose God's will for life is particularly excruciating, making him "deeply grieved, even to death" (26:38).

Between the initial temptation scene in the desert and the struggle in Gethsemane, Matthew continues to unfold Jesus' identity as "Son of God." During Jesus' Galilean ministry, two men possessed by demons identify him thus (Matt 8:29). On another occasion, the frightened disciples in the boat exclaim, after Jesus walks on water, "Truly, you are the Son of God!" (14:33). When Jesus asks the disciples who people say that he is, Peter declares, "You are the Messiah, the Son of the living God" (16:16). Another turning point comes at the Transfiguration, where Jesus discerns that he is to leave his ministry in Galilee to confront the seat of religious and imperial power in Jerusalem.[18] Once again, he has the assurance of a heavenly voice, "This is my Son, the Beloved" (17:5).

The portrait of Jesus as obedient Son of God continues to build in the Gethsemane scene (Matt 26:36-46). Jesus twice addresses God as "my Father" (26:39, 42) and prays, "If it is possible, let this cup pass from me; yet not what I want but what you want" (26:39; similarly 26:42). But now there are no ministering angels as in the temptation in the desert. Here is no heavenly voice, no palpable response from God—only silence, terror, and the uncertainty of *how* God will accomplish the divine will to heal and save through this gruesome death. As he goes forward in faith, trusting in the God he has known to be faithful, he faces more insidious taunts about his sonship. At the interrogation before the Sanhedrin, the high priest demands, "Tell us if you are the Messiah, the Son of God" (16:63). At the crucifixion, the passersby who deride Jesus not only taunt him about the Temple but also say, "If you are the Son of God, come down from the cross" (27:40).[19] As the chief priests, scribes, and elders continue the mockery, Matthew alone adds, "He trusts in God; let God deliver him now, if he wants to;

for he said, 'I am God's Son'" (27:43). These references to Jesus as "Son of God" in Matthew 27:40, 43, are unique to the first Gospel. The theme climaxes when the centurion and those with him keeping watch over Jesus declare at his death, "Truly this man was God's Son!" (27:54).

OBEDIENCE AND LISTENING

Throughout the gospels, Jesus is depicted as going apart to pray, often in discerning prayer, to listen to God to know the next step in his faithful journey with God. In his letter to the Romans, Paul captures well how obedience entails faithful listening. As Paul struggles to explain why his beloved fellow Jews have not accepted the gospel, he says, "But not all have obeyed (*hypēkousan*) the good news; for Isaiah says, 'Lord, who has believed our message (*akoē*)?' So faith comes from what is heard (*akoēs*), and what is heard (*akoē*) comes through the word of Christ" (Rom 10:16-17). The wordplay with the verb *hypakouō*, "to hear," and the noun *akoē*, "message, what is heard," makes clear the intimate link between the message, the hearing, and obedience. Obedience flows from a discerning heart that listens intently to God's word and to where the Spirit is leading in the present circumstances.

There are several key passages in the gospels in which Jesus, using the verb *akouō*, "to hear," gives instructions about discipleship, with the implication that hearing leads to obedience. In the parables discourse, the emphasis on hearing is particularly acute.[20] Repeatedly, Jesus admonishes, "Let anyone with ears listen (*akouetō*)!" (Matt 11:15; 13:9, 43). Luke places special emphasis on hearing that leads to obedient responding. Jesus says that his mother and brothers and sisters are "those who hear the word of God and do it" (Luke 8:21). To a woman in a crowd who raises her voice to bless the womb that bore Jesus and the breasts that nursed him he replies, "Blessed rather are those who hear the word of God and obey it!" (11:28).

As Matthew builds his portrait of Jesus as obedient Son of God, he depicts Jesus himself as one who listens to God in prayer.[21] In Matthew 14:23, Jesus goes apart by himself to pray. He also prays when children are brought to him (Matt 19:13). His prayer of thanks in Matthew 11:25 highlights the oneness between himself and the Father. He utters prayers of blessing and thanksgiving when feeding the crowds (14:19; 15:36) and over the bread and cup at the Last Supper (26:26-30). Jesus speaks of prayer numerous times to his disciples (5:44; 6:5, 6, 7, 9; 21:22; 24:20; 26:36, 41). Thus, Jesus' prayer in Gethsemane (26:39, 42, 44) and his final cry to God from the cross (27:46, using Ps 22:2)[22] should be seen as the culminating moments of a lifelong communion with God by which Jesus discerns how to be the obedient Son. Matthew also builds the theme of Jesus' obedience to God with his motif of fulfillment of scripture and with his use of the noun *thelēma*, "will," and the verb *thelō*, "to will," in relation to Jesus' mission.

FULFILLMENT OF SCRIPTURE

Matthew is more emphatic than other evangelists that Jesus died in fulfillment of the scriptures. In the arrest scene, the Matthean Jesus twice interprets what is happening as fulfilling the scriptures (Matt 26:54, 56).[23] This theme appears frequently throughout the Gospel, to interpret major moments: Jesus' birth (1:22), his rescue as an infant from Herod's murderous intentions (2:15), the massacre of other children in Bethlehem (2:17), the settling of the holy family in Nazareth (2:23), Jesus' baptism by John (3:15), Jesus' making his home in Capernaum at the beginning of his public ministry (4:14), his declared intent to fulfill the Law and the prophets (5:17), his healing ministry (8:17, relating it to the servant in Isa 53:4) and the opposition it provokes in the Pharisees (12:17, relating it to Isa 42:1-4), his use of parables (13:35), his entry into Jerusalem (21:4), and the buying of the potter's field (27:9). These incidents, along with Jesus' arrest in Gethsemane (26:54, 56), mark important movements in the narrative related to Jesus' mission. By explicitly naming each of these as fulfillment of scripture, Matthew creates an aura of obedience around Jesus' life and actions.[24]

GOD'S WILL

Matthew's frequent use of the noun *thelēma*, "will," always referring to God's will, also contributes to his construction of Jesus as obedient Son. In addition to the Gethsemane scene, in which

Jesus prays, "Your will (*theléma*) be done" (Matt 26:42), there are five other instances. Jesus teaches his disciples to pray to "Our Father, your will be done" (6:10) and says that his true kindred consists of "whoever does the will of my Father in heaven" (12:50). Jesus tells parables that commend obedient responses of *doing* "the will of my Father," not just saying so (7:21; 21:31). And at the conclusion of the parable of the lost sheep, Jesus pronounces, "It is not the will of your Father in heaven that one of these little ones shall be lost" (18:14).

That Jesus' will is consonant with the will of God to heal and save is emphasized in the instances of the verb *theló* that refer to Jesus' will.[25] A leper pleads with Jesus, "Lord, if you choose (*theló*), you can make me clean," to which Jesus responds, "I do choose (*theló*)" (Matt 8:2-3). When criticized for eating with tax collectors and sinners, Jesus articulates his will, "I desire (*theló*) mercy, not sacrifice" (9:13; similarly 12:7). Facing a hungry crowd of four thousand, Jesus says, "I do not want (*theló*) to send them away hungry" (15:32). He laments over Jerusalem, "How often have I desired (*ethelésa*) to gather your children together as a hen gathers her brood under her wings, but you were unwilling (*ouk ethelésate*)!" (23:37). In two instances, *theló* refers to the will of one petitioning for healing. A Canaanite woman pleads for healing for her daughter, to which Jesus finally responds, "Let it be done for you as you wish (*theleis*)" (15:28). Jesus asks two men who are blind, "What do you want (*thelete*) me to do for you?" (20:32). That it is Jesus' will to heal them is evident when he does so.[26]

Jesus instructs his disciples about how they should follow his example in what they should will: "If any want (*thelei*) to become my followers, let them deny themselves and take up their cross and follow me. For those who want (*thelé*) to save their life will lose it, and those who lose their life for my sake will find it" (Matt 16:24-25). To the one who had many possessions, Jesus says, "If you wish (*theleis*) to enter into life, keep the commandments" (19:17) and "if you wish (*theleis*) to be perfect, go, sell your possessions, and give the money to the poor" (19:21). To the ten who were indignant with James' and John's desire to sit at Jesus' right and left in his kingdom, Jesus responds, "Whoever wishes (*thelé*) to be great among you, must be your servant, and whoever wishes (*thelé*) to be first among you must be your slave;

just as the Son of Man came not to be served but to serve, and to give his life a ransom for many" (20:26-28).

CHOOSING TO BE FAITHFUL

Through his emphasis on Jesus' sonship, his prayer, the fulfillment of scripture, and his use of the verb *thelō* and the noun *thelēma*, Matthew builds a portrait of Jesus as beloved and obedient Son whose will is to do God's will. Jesus enacts this divine will as he heals and saves the lost and teaches his disciples adherence to Torah and relinquishment of possessions, and even of life itself, for the sake of those made poor. Thus, in Gethsemane, when Jesus prays, "not what I want, but what you want (*ouk hōs egō thelō all' hōs sy*)" (Matt 26:39), and, "your will (*thelēma*) be done" (26:42), we have not a sadistic God who is deaf to the pleas of the Son, nor a struggle between the will of Jesus and the will of God, nor a puppetlike compliance on the part of Jesus. Rather, Jesus is seen as one who has lived his whole life discerning the will of God and responding obediently to the divine will to save and to heal. This divine will does not change in Gethsemane. What Matthew does in the passion narrative is to situate Jesus' suffering and death within God's saving will; Jesus' death does not occur outside God's saving will and power. This is underscored when the chief priests, scribes, and elders taunt the crucified Jesus: "He trusted in God; let God deliver him now, if he wants (*thelei*) to; for he said, 'I am God's Son'" (27:43). The reader of the Gospel knows that this portrayal of God and God's will on the lips of Jesus' opponents is false, having echoes of the words of the tempter, "If you are the Son of God, throw yourself down; for it is written, 'He will command his angels concerning you,' and 'On their hands they will bear you up, so that you will not dash your foot against a stone'" (4:6). Jesus' choice to go forward without signs of assurance and without knowing how God's will for life will be accomplished is not an isolated act of blind acquiescence, but rather the final obedient act of a life spent listening to and responding to God's will. This is the kind of obedience Jesus' followers are also asked to emulate, as the divine voice indicates at the Transfiguration: "Listen to him," (17:5).

Jesus' final choice in his lifelong pursuit of God's will is a free one. He is not forced or coerced to "drink the cup." He chooses to do so, not because he seeks to suffer or because God wills his death, but because it is the means to life for God's people. At the final Passover meal with his disciples, Jesus explains to his disciples his choice to "drink the cup." Just as Moses sprinkled blood, the symbol of life (Deut 12:23), on the altar and on the people to seal the covenant (Exod 24:8), so his death is the ratification of a renewed life in covenantal fidelity for all (26:28).[27]

DEADLY DIRECTIONS AND LIBERATING POSSIBILITIES

When any of the aforementioned texts are read in isolation from the rest of Jesus' lifelong discernment of and choice to be faithful to God's will to heal and save, obedience can take on deadly connotations. Literal readings and typological applications are also problematic, as we will see.

A Greater Good

Many Christians resolve the tensions in the Gethsemane scene by imagining that God knows the greater good that will result for humankind from Jesus' death, and so God allows, or even desires, the death of the beloved Son, to which Jesus obediently accedes. Such an interpretation of Jesus' obedience can feed attitudes of acceptance and uncritical compliance by dominated persons, particularly women, to those in authority over them. They may reason that their husbands or their leaders act with God's authority and so must be obeyed. Or they may believe the suffering they endure will bring about a greater good for their children or their families. Such thinking can also lead Christians to reason that the sacrifice of some obedient sons and daughters is necessary in war, for example, for the sake of a greater good and that they need to trust their leaders to know what is that greater good. Such unthinking compliance discourages any critical study or prayerful discernment to determine whether a person in authority should be obeyed.

Contemporary examples of U.S. citizens and even military officers who are now questioning their former obedient compliance with the summons to war in Iraq that George W. Bush launched in March 2003 are illustrative of this point. At the time of this writing, the war was entering its fifth year. And only now that the bloodshed has reached unspeakable proportions, with no end in sight and no real progress toward peace, is the question being more widely raised whether, indeed, the deaths of so many men and women is accomplishing the supposed greater good. One mother, Lila Lipscomb of Flint, Michigan, encouraged her son, Michael Pedersen, to enlist in the army. "I grew up with the understanding that you support the president, no matter who he is," she explained. Likewise, Michael "had a clear commitment to fulfilling his oath for this nation."[28] It was only after receiving Michael's letters from Iraq questioning why he was there and following his death in April 2003 that Lila's trusting compliance crumbled. She now questions why her son died and why we are at war in Iraq as she travels around the country speaking with antiwar groups.

> "We always have to ask our husband's permission to leave the house. Some women are afraid to come to the women's group because they think it will awaken the wrath of God or of their family because they are not obeying what they were taught when they got married."
> —CODIMUJ, 49

While Lila Lipscomb frames her experience in terms of misguided patriotism and unquestioning willingness to obey the elected leader, one might ask whether a theology of obedience might also be at play in the decisions of Christians who trustingly follow leaders who take them into war. Casey Sheehan, son of Cindy, who has become a vocal antiwar activist, grew up in a devout Catholic home. He was an altar server at the Palm Sunday Mass on April 4, 2004, the day he was killed in Baghdad. Immediately after Casey returned from mass, his sergeant called for volunteers to be part of a quick reaction force to aid fellow Americans under attack by Muqtada al'Sadr's forces in Sadr City, Iraq. "Where my chief goes, I go," Sheehan immediately responded.[29]

The case of Ehren Watada offers a different example of obedience. He enlisted in the army in the spring of 2003, just as the United States was going to war with Iraq. He initially supported the war because he believed that Iraq had weapons of mass destruction and he wanted to do his part for his country. After having completed his training and having studied further, Watada concluded that "we have been lied to and betrayed by this administration."[30] On June 7, 2006, Lt. Watada announced at a news conference that he had refused orders for deployment to Iraq on the grounds that he is bound to uphold the U.S. Constitution and not to follow illegal orders. He stated, "Today I speak with you about a radical idea . . . born from the very concept of the American soldier. The idea is this, that to stop an illegal and unjust war, the soldiers can choose to stop fighting it."[31] Watada is now facing court-martial for refusing to deploy to Iraq, as well as for making statements deemed contemptuous of the president and other top government officials. David Krieger's editorial about Watada in the *National Catholic Reporter* is entitled, "Honor above Obedience." However, from the perspective of obedience as portrayed in the Gospel of Matthew, Watada's stance does not put obedience in a subordinate place, but rather exemplifies an even more radical sense of obedience than the kind displayed by those who blindly obey superiors, trusting that they know the greater good.

As many women are discovering, the greater good is not served when any of God's beloved daughters or sons are sacrificed for a supposed greater good. When anyone is subjected to unjust pain or death, whether in abusive relationships or in war, all suffer. True obedience requires hard, analytical work, a discerning heart, and a freeing of the imagination to discover the ways to break cycles of violence through creative acts of self-gift that result in wellbeing for all.

Testing Faithfulness

Another deadly misdirection is when suffering or death is thought of as being sent by God as a test of one's faithfulness. Such is the case when the story of the near-sacrifice of Isaac by Abraham (Genesis 22) is related to the death of Jesus. Every year at the Easter Vigil, the second reading is Genesis 22:1-18. For those Christian churches that follow the three-year common lectionary cycle, this text is also read on the second Sunday of Lent, along with the gospel reading of the Marcan version of the Transfiguration (Mark 9:2-10). The link between Abraham's willingness to sacrifice his beloved son Isaac and God's willingness to "give up" Jesus is forged in these liturgical contexts.[32] When the Johannine Jesus carries his own cross (John 19:17), a connection is readily seen with Isaac, who carries the wood for the sacrifice (Gen 22:6). This story, foundational for both Jews and Christians, as well as Muslims, presents Abraham as the supreme example of faith.[33] He proves his obedience to God by being willing to sacrifice Isaac when he thinks this is what God is asking of him. Many Christians satisfy themselves with the explanation that God was only testing Abraham. In their own trials and suffering, Christians will often speak of God as testing their faith. This chilling interpretation makes God into a sadistic character who toys with the affections of devoted followers and who seemingly derives pleasure from watching them squirm until God calls off the dastardly game. As Rita Nakashima Brock has observed, this is tantamount to divine child abuse and gives approbation to humans to do likewise.[34]

One way to confront the deadliness of this interpretation is to ask believers if they themselves, as parents, would do such a sadistic thing to their own children. The answer is always an emphatic, "No!" Carol Delaney questions further, "Why is the willingness to sacrifice one's child *the* quintessential model of faith, why not the passionate protection of the child?"[35] It is horrifying, observes Delaney, that Abraham is "revered not for putting an end to the practice [of child sacrifice], but for his willingness to go through with it. *That* is what establishes him as the father of faith. *That* is what I find so terrifying."[36] She ponders why it is that the story of the woman who is willing to relinquish her son to another woman who claims him as her own, rather than let the child be cut in two (1 Kings 3:16-28), is not our foundational story.[37]

As an anthropologist, Delaney is concerned with the social implications of religious myth. "People continue to derive their identity, orient their lives, and interpret the meaning of life from the patterns first charted by the story."[38] She invites us to ponder what would be the shape of our society if the supreme model of faith and commitment were not the sacrifice, but the passionate protection of the child.[39] She analyzes how the Abraham story advances a particular definition of the family and gender roles that derive from an outmoded theory of procreation in which the male is thought to be the creative one who begets, while the female role is to nurture his "seed." Correspondingly, just as God, whose power to create implies the concomitant power to destroy, so men, who were thought to bestow life, also claimed power over it. And so God, envisioned as male, interacts only with Abraham, who has power over Isaac. There is no involvement of Sarah or Hagar.[40] This scenario is played out in parallel ways in contemporary contexts, such as those described at the beginning of this chapter by the women of CODIMUJ in Chiapas. Raising critical questions about the origins and consequences of such religious myths that keep patriarchal structures of authority and obedience in place is a first step toward dismantling them.

The Abraham story also raises questions concerning the power to command and the role of choice in religious obedience. "What allowed Abraham to assume the child was *his* to sacrifice?" asks Delaney.[41] "If Abraham had wanted to prove his devotion and obedience, why didn't he offer to sacrifice himself?"[42] Here is where the story of Jesus is fundamentally different from that of Abraham and Isaac.[43] As the Johannine Jesus insists, he freely lays down his life of his own accord; no one takes it from him (John 10:17-18). Authentic obedience is not blind acquiescence, nor does it deliver up the life of another. Delaney wonders why Abraham did not object to God's command: "Why didn't he argue with God as he did when Ishmael was to be banished, or as he did to try to save Sodom and Gomorrah from destruction?"[44] Or why did Abraham not doubt whether or not he had perceived correctly God's command when it seemed so opposite to God's previous revelations of love and promise? Some of the rabbis opine that God did not test Abraham at all—Abraham misunderstood God. "What, do you think I meant for you to slay him? No! I said only to take him up . . . and now I say take him down" (*Gen. Rab.* 56:8).[45] Here we might raise the question of the role of the larger community in discerning God's will and in deciding together what actions in the current situation constitute faithfulness to God. An alternative model of leadership would be to include the voices of the whole body in the discernment and not rely on the decisions of a solitary man who might misunderstand what God has said. Obedience is incumbent on all in the community and emerges as assent to faithfulness found in shared wisdom of the whole.

Similar questions to those that arise concerning Abraham and Isaac can be raised about Jephthah's daughter who was sacrificed by her father after his rash vow (Judges 11). Although there are differences in the plot, the same kind of rigid understanding of obedience and its deadly consequences undergirds the story. This time it is not God who tells a father to sacrifice his child, but the sacrifice comes after Jephthah makes a hasty vow to God. It is curious how the parallels are so often seen between Isaac and Jesus when, in truth, there are more similarities between the daughter of Jephthah (Judges 11) and Jesus. Jesus and Jepthah's daughter both actually die, both go up to a mountain with friends, neither is spared, both accept and know their fate, and both are powerless to avert their deaths at the hand of a father or imperial power.[46] We might ask why God does not intervene to prevent the death of Jephthah's daughter, as with Abraham's son. Is the life of a daughter any less precious to God? One of the ways this story can function is to cause us to question whether God is involved at all in such human violence.[47] Like Josephus, who claimed that Jephthah's sacrifice was not acceptable to God, and the rabbis, who point out that Jephthah had alternatives and that he ought not to have sacrificed his daughter,[48] we, too, need to tell the story in such a way as to expose the senseless violence, causing us to vow, "Never again!"

An alternative reading of the story of Abraham and Isaac is offered by Don C. Benjamin, who sees it not as a test of Abraham's obedience at all.[49] What is at issue is the question of who will be the heir of Abraham. Benjamin understands the story to be about God's choice between Abraham's two sons. When Abraham orders his slaves, "Stay here with the ass; the boy and I will go over there" (Gen 22:5), he is instructing the slaves to stay with Ishmael, who was described as a "wild ass of a man" (16:12) while he takes Isaac forward for the ordeal. In the end, Yahweh accepts both Ishmael and Isaac; both are given land and children (21:13, 18; 22:17-18). Yahweh is not testing Abraham to see how he will react. It is not a story that celebrates blind obedience, but one that depicts God as covenant partner who helps resolve the conflict as to who should be heir. "These ancestor stories celebrate Abraham, Sarah, and Hagar for their faith and perseverance in moving their households from slavery to freedom—from being slaves without land and children, to being free or Hebrew, blessed by Yahweh with the children of Ishmael and Isaac and the lands of Beersheba and Moriah."[50]

These ways of confronting the disturbing questions presented by the story of Abraham and Isaac, related to the death of Jesus, can help to undo the myths that God tests faith or that one learns obedience through suffering (Heb 5:8). They can open up new directions toward experiencing God as one who does not need proof of obedience, but who desires to give love freely, drawing all into that loving embrace so as to empower beloved daughters and sons to share that love with others.

Mythic Roots of Disobedience

Just as the story of Abraham and Isaac has become a founding myth, so has the story in Genesis 3 enshrined the mythic beginnings of sin as rooted in human disobedience. Although in the story both the man and woman are present in the garden, and both disobey and suffer the consequences, popular interpretations place the blame on the woman. She is the source of all temptation, sin, and evil.[51] The remedy, as this interpretation goes, is that God puts man in charge of woman so as to restore order to creation. New Testament admonitions such as, "Wives, be subject to your husbands, as is fitting in the Lord" (Col 3:18),[52] fuel the patriarchal notion that it is man's place to rule over woman.

Phyllis Trible, using rhetorical criticism, was one of the first feminist biblical scholars to reinterpret this founding myth.[53] She notes that it is the serpent, not the woman, who is the tempter. Contrary to most cultural stereotypes, the woman is the stronger one in the story. She is the spokesperson; she theologizes in the dialogue with the serpent and correctly interprets God's commands. Though in the man's presence, she acts independently and not secretively. The man, by contrast, is silent and passive. He does not theologize; he simply acquiesces. When confronted by God, he is defensive, trying to blame God and then the woman, before he finally accepts responsibility for his transgression. What the story conveys is that both man and

"Woman carries the blame for all that is wrong in the world. This springs from the story of Adam and Eve—she is the one who brought sin into the world. From this, women even think of themselves as deserving to be punished."

—Verónica, La Paz, Bolivia
24 March, 2003

woman sinned, although in different ways; both were responsible and both suffer the consequences. As a result, they experience hardship, opposition, and tension. The woman's desire for her husband, while once mutual, will no longer be reciprocated (Gen 3:16).[54] The man's work, while once creative, now becomes alienated labor. Divine, human, animal, and plant worlds are all adversely affected. Where once there was unity in diversity, now there is opposition. The domination of man over woman is not God's intent; it is part of the disarray in God's creation caused by the disobedience of both.

An alternative interpretation is offered by Carol L. Meyers based on sociohistorical study of Israel before the monarchy.[55] She understands Genesis 3:16 not as articulating the woman's punishment, but as describing the hardships that existed for women in premonarchic Israel when increased population and harder work were necessary. It is not the pain in childbearing that increases, but the number of births, along with the amount of work needed to produce goods for subsistence. Meyers translates the last half of the verse: "to your man is your desire, and he shall predominate over you."[56] The "desire" speaks about a relationship between the woman and the man that goes beyond the sexual process of reproduction. The last phrase is not a prescription for male dominance, but a statement that man's share of the subsistence work will be greater than that of the woman. In these interpretations of Genesis 3, there is no justification for the subordination of women to men, nor is there blame of woman for introducing disobedience into creation.

"Wives Be Submissive to Your Husbands"

By a similar token, the New Testament admonitions to wives to be subordinate to their husbands must also be understood in their historical contexts. These texts are Christianized versions of household codes that were commonly known from the teachings of philosophers, moralists, and political thinkers from the time of Aristotle onward. They prescribe lines of authority and obedience, not only between husband and wife, but also between parents and children, masters and slaves. In the New Testament versions of the code, the harmonious household not only is a microcosm of society as a whole, but also symbolizes the relationship between humanity and the divine (in Eph 2:19, the church is explicitly referred to as "the household of God"). However, these codes enshrine not divinely assigned roles, but rather, culturally determined mores of the ancient world.[57] Even in antiquity, there may well have been women and some men who regarded these as outmoded or banal, given the reality that women such as Phoebe (Rom 16:1-2), Prisca (Rom 16:3-5; Acts 18), Junia (Rom 16:7),[58] Mary Magdalene (Luke 8:1-3; John 20:1-2, 11-18), and Nympha (Col 4:15) were leading house churches and taking on roles of preaching,

> "I remember one wedding I attended when the priest gave an hour-long discourse on how the woman needed to submit to her husband. This attitude of submission is thoroughly internalized in Andean culture. We are trying to change that by talking about the complementarity there is in all the relations, and to struggle for the harmony that there is in nature."
>
> —Sofía, La Paz, Bolivia
> 24 March, 2003

teaching, evangelizing, and various other ministries as deacons, apostles, and widows. They may have quietly ignored the efforts to align them into traditional roles inscribed in the household codes.[59] Moreover, "the household code was probably addressed to many women who would have been anything but the model *matrona* of elite Greco-Roman literature, whose idealized life underlies these traditional ethical exhortations: slave women, divorced and abandoned women, women disobeying their pagan husbands on account of Christian allegiance."[60]

Efforts to understand such texts in their original contexts are one approach to dismantling their power to keep women trapped in attitudes of submission to males who exercise abusive power over them. It is a misuse of the Bible to justify abuse of wives by their husbands through texts that prescribe ideal roles in the ancient household or that tell of the mythic origins for the way things are presently experienced.[61] These are deeply ingrained attitudes, however, that will take much time to replace. One mother who confided in a minister that she had known for some time that her husband had been sexually abusing their daughters never tried to stop him. Her husband had convinced her that it was not really wrong. She had been indoctrinated with the belief, based on a faulty reading of Genesis 3:16, that women are more easily misled than men and need to trust men to make moral judgments for them.[62]

As Gilbert Bilezikian states, "Any religious teachings that imply woman's moral inferiority to man, that infer she is created less in the image of God than is man, and that cause her to trust man's judgment more than her own are not only a heretical distortion of the gospel message, but are tragically dangerous to her and her children."[63] By countering faulty interpretations of biblical obedience, we may be able to put an end to sacrificing women to abuse and children to poverty, sexual abuse, and war. There are viable alternatives to the myths by which we currently live.

"The church has been a strong force in reinforcing the image of the submissive woman. Mary is presented as the model, as the passive carrier for God's action, not as an actor in her own right. She is veiled, covered up, letting whatever God wants to be done to her. Consequently, many women, when they have difficulties, pray: 'Virgencita, save me!' The attitudes of dependency and submission make them feel incapable of solving their problems. And the worst part is when women themselves help perpetuate these attitudes in their children."

—Magdalena, La Paz, Bolivia
25 March, 2003

AUDACIOUSLY OBEDIENT BIBLICAL WOMEN

The Gospels give us portraits not only of Jesus as obedient hearer and doer of God's will but also of many female figures who do likewise. Prominent among them are Jesus' mother and his relative Elizabeth. From his people's history, there are the audacious midwives who listen to God and not to Pharaoh. In the figure of Martha is also an obedient disciple who struggles against opposition. We turn first to her.

Martha (Luke 10:38-42; John 11:1–12:1-11)

Martha has long been seen as the one who has not "chosen the better part." The prevailing image of her is as the busy-bee or workaholic who is too concerned about all that needs to be done to give proper attention to listening to Jesus as her sister Mary does. This image is derived from Luke 10:38-42, where the two sisters are thought to represent the tension between action and contemplation. Many Christians find themselves identifying with the overly busy Martha, longing to sit contemplatively at the feet of Jesus as does Mary. The message many derive from Luke 10:38-42 is that one can only serve actively after having sat quietly listening to Jesus. One problem with this interpretation is that Luke's story of Martha and Mary does not speak of integrating the two poles; rather, the sisters are pitted against one another, and only "hearing" is approved by Jesus. This is problematic when we observe that throughout the Gospel of Luke, discipleship is formulated in terms of both hearing the word of God and acting on it (Luke 6:47; 8:15, 21; 11:28). In recent years, scholars have questioned the traditional interpretation of Luke 10:38-42 and offer other possibilities. Martha can be seen as a leader in the believing community who has been obedient to her call to discipleship and ministry but who has to struggle against disapproving males, who consider such roles improper for women.[64] The vignette in Luke 10:38-42 shows that even her own sister is being persuaded to accept this attitude.

Rather than reading Luke's story of Martha and Mary as representative of an event in the life of Jesus, it may be that the evangelist has used this episode to resolve tensions in his own community over the roles of women. He puts a definitive answer on the lips of Jesus, hoping to settle the issue. Both women welcome Jesus; Martha welcomes Jesus into her home (v. 38),[65] and Mary sits at his feet and listens (v. 39). The difficulty is over what each does with what she hears. While many think that the conflict concerns a meal and its preparation, the greater likelihood is that the problem is a ministerial one. The translation of Martha's complaint and the description of how it has affected her in verse 40 is crucial. The Greek expression *periespato peri pollēn diakonian* has been rendered "burdened with much serving" (*NAB*), "distracted by her many tasks" (*NRSV*), "busy with all the details of hospitality" (1970 edition of *NAB*), and "distracted with all the serving" (*NJB*). First is the question of the meaning of *diakonia* rendered in these translations as "serving," "tasks," and "details of hospitality." While many think of it as domestic service, *diakonia* more often refers to ecclesial ministry, especially in the Lucan writings. In Jesus' words to his disciples at the Last Supper, the noun *diakonia* and the related verb *diakonein* refer to Jesus' mission, which is to be emulated by his disciples: ". . . the greatest among you must become like the youngest, and the leader like the one who serves (*ho diakonōn*). For who is greater, the one who is at the table or the one who serves? Is it not the one at the table? But I am among you as one who serves (*ho diakonōn*)" (22:26-27). In Acts 1:25, where the successor for Judas is chosen, *diakonia* refers to apostolic leadership. The conflict concerning the widows of the Hebrews and those of the Hellenists in Acts 6:1-7 is resolved with a division of labor among those who will take charge of the *diakonia tou logou*, "ministry of the word" (Acts 6:4) and those who dedicate themselves to the "ministry of the table," *diakonein trapezais* (6:2).[66] In Luke 8:3, *diēkonoun*, "serving, providing for," refers to the financial ministry that Mary Magdalene and the other Galilean women render to Jesus and the other disciples.[67] Similarly, the relief money collected by Paul and Barnabas for the church in Jerusalem is referred to as *diakonia* in Acts 11:29; 12:25. All the various kinds of ministries that Paul exercises are summed up in the term *diakonia* in Acts 20:24; 21:19. While *diakonia* can refer to serving a meal (as in the parable of the slave serving his master at table in Luke 12:37), the preponderance of instances of *diakonia* in the Gospel of Luke and Acts points toward a ministerial connotation in Luke 10:40.[68]

A second problem is how to understand *periespato*. Translations such as "burdened," "distracted," and "busy" have led commentators to conclude that the problem is Martha's attitude and that the solution is for her to become centered on Jesus and to lighten up her serious or anxious stance. However, another meaning is possible. The preposition *peri* has the sense "about," or "concerning." Martha is burdened about or with reference to her numerous ministerial works, not *by* or *with* them. In addition, the primary meaning of the verb *periespaō* is "to be pulled or dragged away."[69] Martha's

> "In spite of all the suffering, we keep moving forward, happy, leaving behind those things that enslave us, sharing with and animating other women, never giving up. We are strong and we know how to survive and help others survive any crisis."
>
> —Rosa, La Paz, Bolivia
> 24 March, 2003

distress, then, is *about* the much ministerial work and the efforts of some in the community to pull her and other women away from such roles and to leave them to the men. Even her sister has been persuaded to back away from their former partnership in ministry.[70] Martha complains to Jesus, "Do you not care that my sister has left me to do all the work (*diakonein*) by myself? Tell her then to help me" (v. 40).

From this perspective, Martha has obediently heard and welcomed the Word and has put it into action through her leadership in ministry. But, like Jesus himself, she experiences opposition even from her own brothers and sisters. Luke, who consistently portrays women in silent and passive roles,[71] sides with those who would restrict ministerial leadership to men and portrays Jesus as authoritatively siding against Martha. While Luke may think the issue settled, the reality of women's ministerial leadership has never been obliterated.[72] With Martha, who hopes that Mary can be persuaded to respond actively again to what she hears in her contemplative listening, so women continue to advance the mission by obedient listening and action.[73]

A very different portrait of Martha emerges in the Gospel of John. There, she is the disciple who utters the most profound articulation of faith as she dialogues with Jesus after the death of her brother Lazarus. As always in the Fourth Gospel, such conversations move deeper and deeper, as Jesus and his interlocutor gradually reveal themselves to one another. The exchange climaxes with Martha's recognition, "Yes, Lord, I believe that you are the Messiah, the Son of God, the one coming into the world" (John 11:27).[74] In the synoptic Gospels, this acclamation of faith is placed on the lips of Peter.[75] Martha's faithful listening is expressed in *diakonia*, as she is seen serving in the following chapter (12:2).[76]

Jesus' Mother (Luke 1:26-36; John 2:1-12)

In the Gospel of Luke, Jesus' mother is depicted as one of the first examples of one who hears God's Word and obeys it.[77] Mary is first presented as a young girl making wedding plans—plans that are turned upside down by God (Luke 1:26-36). As with Jesus in his passion, God asks an extraordinary act of obedience on her part—one that entails great struggle and suffering, without knowing how God will be able to bring forth blessing and goodness from it. All that Mary knows is that God is with her and that she is a beloved daughter, "favored" by God (1:28, 31). Despite her perplexity and fear, she obediently responds "Amen," believing that God can bring salvation and blessing from what seems an impossibly shameful situation. While our religious imagination usually envisions this as a beautiful, prayerful scene, with Mary wrapped in a joy-filled aura, the reality is that in her first-century

> "I think of the women in the Old Testament who were so valiant in the way they carried out God's plan for salvation against the powers of their day. And Mary, how strong she had to be to have a child out of wedlock. It is not easy to do this. But God gave her the strength to keep following the way."
>
> —Lidia, La Paz, Bolivia
> 24 March, 2003

Palestinian Jewish village, she is in a horrendously difficult situation. In her culture, a woman found to be pregnant before starting to live with her husband would be regarded as sinful and adulterous.[78] How can it be that God's reign will be furthered and salvation[79] for God's people will come forth from this situation? Without knowing the answers to these questions, Mary freely assents. She is not forced nor coerced, but, as her son does in Gethsemane, she chooses to follow God in faith. Like her son, she lives her life seeking to know and do God's will, treasuring and pondering what she hears in her heart (2:19, 51).

Another vignette from the Gospel of John gives us an additional view of Mary's obedience to God. At the wedding feast at Cana (John 2:1-12), Jesus' mother[80] knows the time for Jesus to manifest himself publicly. We can surmise that this is because she lives her life so attuned to God that she is able to discern the correct timing, just as later in the Gospel, Jesus "knew his hour had come to depart from this world and go to the Father" (13:1), because he is in intimate union with the Father (10:30; 12:50). Jesus' mother instructs the servants at the wedding to be obedient to Jesus, "Do whatever he tells you" (2:5). Jesus, in turn, is obedient to her prompting and performs the first of his "signs," which brings the disciples to believe in him (2:11). Mary's obedience to God comes full circle when she keeps vigil at the cross with her sister, Mary, the wife of Clopas, and Mary Magdalene.[81] In a neat Johannine inclusio, she faithfully witnesses to Jesus' obedience to God from the start of his earthly ministry to its finish. His obedience to God is encircled by her own.

In popular piety, Mary's obedience is more often than not depicted as docile acceptance of all that befalls her. Her response, "May it be done to me according to your word" (Luke 1:38, *NAB*), can be taken to reinforce passivity and endurance rather than active discernment of how God's will is expressed in present circumstances and how to respond obediently. In these interpretations, we see Mary, instead, as one who models this active and faithful engagement with God toward transformation. Father Michael Gilgallon, writing from La Paz, Bolivia, notes the contradictions between devotions to the Blessed Virgin and the real lives of oppressed women in Latin America. He questions, "Why does Catholic machismo take pride of place in homes and offices and real life in the streets? Why is the real live Latina woman degraded and physically victimized daily while pious, but not always relevant, devotions and processions in honor of the Virgin Mary take place in parishes, schools and countless Marian shrines all over the continent? The contradictions are plain for all to see."[82] Understanding the biblical Mary as one to be emulated, who actively chooses obedience to a God whose will is for life, helps to dislodge passive acceptance of victimization by women.

Elizabeth (Luke 1:5-7, 23-24, 39-45, 57-66)

In the opening verses of the Gospel of Luke, we find Elizabeth, who is a descendent of Aaron and the wife of Zechariah (1:5). Elizabeth's very name emphasizes her reliance on and obedience to God. In Hebrew, *Elîšeba'* means "My God is the one by whom to swear," or "My God is satiety, fortune." Her name signifies that she depends utterly on God and is filled to satisfaction by God. Luke describes both Elizabeth and her husband as "righteous[83] before God, living blamelessly according to all the commandments and regulations of the Lord" (1:6). This flawless, lifelong obedience of Elizabeth is what prepares her to make further obedient responses to God in the extraordinary events surrounding the birth of John the Baptist. The note that Elizabeth is barren[84] and that both she and her husband were "getting on in years" (1:7) serves, not only to highlight the miraculous nature of John's conception, but also to accent Elizabeth's long years of faithful relationship with God. Elizabeth's faithful obedience, although seemingly long unrewarded, is unshakable. In this, she prefigures Jesus, who resolutely trusts in God even as he is confronted with his passion and death.

There is a strong contrast between the response of Elizabeth and the response of her husband to the impending birth of John. Zechariah is fearful, disbelieving, and mute (Luke 1:8-23), while Elizabeth recognizes God's favor and grace upon her. She does not question or object, but acclaims God's action toward her in removing the disgrace she has endured from her childlessness (1:24-25). Her lifelong relationship with God has enabled her to recognize God's action even when it seems impossible. She understands God's will is not that she suffer, but that God desires life and delight for her and for God's people, concretely manifest in the child she carries.

While Zechariah is left unable to speak until he comes to a fuller understanding of and acquiescence to God's ways, Elizabeth obediently speaks God's Word in the gathering of family and friends at John's circumcision and naming (Luke 1:57-66). Ordinarily, it was the prerogative of the father to name the child (Matt 1:21).[85] When the relatives are about to name the child "Zechariah, after his father" (1:59), Elizabeth intervenes, declaring, "No; he is to be called John" (1:60). Being faithfully attuned to God, she rightly conveys God's intended name for her son. The name *Yôhānān* expresses both Elizabeth's experience

> "From the moment she is born, a woman begins to experience discrimination, as they say,'Ah, it's only a girl.' From then on she carries her cross. She can't go to school or inherit land from her father. But I'm a rebel and I decided I am not going to go along with this. I snuck off to school, unbeknown to my father. I did weaving and sold it to pay for school supplies. By the time my father found out, there was nothing he could do about it. It's when we women claim our rights then we can go forward and make a difference in this life."
>
> —Berta, Centro Pachamama, El Alto, Bolivia 25 March, 2003

of God and God's desire for the people: "Yahweh has given grace (ḥnn)." Elizabeth's obedience opens the way for her husband's obedient response and that of the whole people (1:63).

Shiphrah and Puah (Exod 1:15-21)

In Jesus, we see that obedience to God often puts one in mortal opposition to ruling powers. Such was the case of the Hebrew midwives, Shiphrah and Puah, in Exodus 1:15-21. Their story is situated in the time after Joseph's death and after the passing of the generation who had known some measure of favor in Egypt with him. A new pharaoh arose who did not know Joseph (1:8). He feared the increasing numbers of the Hebrews and "became ruthless in imposing tasks on the Israelites, and made their lives bitter with hard service in mortar and brick and in every kind of field labor. The Egyptian taskmasters were ruthless in all the tasks that they imposed on them" (1:13-14).

The brutality of Pharaoh then takes the form of orders to the midwives to kill all male infants as they emerge from the womb (Exodus 1:15-16). With an extraordinary act of courage and resistance, the midwives, who "feared God" (1:17), decided that they must obey God and not the murderous Pharaoh. The details of how they prayed, how they decided on their course of action, are now lost to us. All we are told is that their faithfulness to God moved them to risk their own lives to continue their work of bringing forth new life. Astonishingly, when Pharaoh called them to give an account for their disobedience, their clever words dissuaded Pharaoh from murdering them as well (1:19). While God rewarded their faithfulness by multiplying and strengthening the people (1:20-21), Pharaoh devised a new deadly tactic: he would drown every Hebrew boy in the Nile (1:22). The story continues with the collaboration of three more women obedient to God while resisting Pharaoh: Moses' mother, his sister, and Pharaoh's daughter, whose subversive actions save Moses' life (2:1-10).[86]

CONCLUSION

When texts such as the Gethsemane scene and the parable of the vineyard are read in the context of the whole Gospel, Jesus' obedience to God in his passion can be seen as the culmination of a life spent seeking to understand and to faithfully follow God's will for all to live fully. Jesus' choice is not to follow a divine will that is opposed to his own but to complete his lifelong mission that carried the consequences of a brutal death. He was faithful even unto death,[87] not faithful to a God who wanted him to die. God did not send Jesus to die but, out of love, sent him in human form to gain life for all (John 3:16). Being human necessarily entails death. Jesus' death, then, is God's will only in the sense that God willed for Jesus to live a truly human history.[88] God did not send Jesus to die but to fulfill a mission that culminated in death.[89] Jesus obediently offers God's love to all and, with God, longs for a positive response to that love.

It is a perversion of the Gospel when women are socialized to believe that their lives are meant to be ruled by their fathers and husbands and that obedience to these men embodies obedience to God. Such long ingrained attitudes, sustained by misreadings of texts such as Genesis 3:16 and Colossians 3:18, for example, will not die quickly, however. As a number of the women of CODIMUJ in Chiapas found when they began to break out of such patterns to gather in Bible study, "At first we felt guilty all the time; we felt we were disobeying what had been inculcated into us. We thought we were disobeying the law of God. It's been a long process, but one way or another, we talked and listened to one another and we kept moving ahead. Now we know that it is not God who commands it to be so, but it is a matter of culture and education. We were not born to be subservient as they had made us believe."[90]

> "At first we felt guilty all the time; we felt we were disobeying what had been inculcated into us. We thought we were disobeying the law of God. It's been a long process, but one way or another, we talked and listened to one another and we kept moving ahead. Now we know that it is not God who commands it to be so, but it is a matter of culture and education. We were not born to be subservient as they had made us believe."
>
> —CODIMUJ, 96, 138

Obedience to God, as exemplified by Jesus, not only puts one at odds with prevailing cultural mores, but it also calls for resistance to ruling human powers when these are opposed to God's designs for life to the full for all. Jesus' challenges to those with power and privilege, who benefited from domination over others, brought on mortal opposition. Obedience to God takes precedence over obedience to human rulers. One instance in which Jesus' followers do likewise is depicted in Acts of the Apostles. The high priest brings Peter and the apostles before the council, reminding them, "We gave you strict orders not to teach in this [Jesus'] name, yet here you have filled Jerusalem with your teaching and you are determined to bring this man's blood on us." Peter and his companions, like the Hebrew midwives Shiphrah and Puah, respond, "We must obey God rather than any human authority" (Acts 5:29-30).

Obedience to God also entails a willingness to go forward in trust, even when it is impossible to see how God will bring blessing and goodness out of horrendous suffering. Poet and artist Mary Horn, a Dominican Sister from Aotearoa/New Zealand, captures the sense of this:[91]

> so what has it been about
> this life
> that sometimes passed us by
> at the gate of our possibility
>
> while we hesitated
> on the threshold
> afraid to venture
> along the twisted path
> out into the unknown road
> that would take us
> we know not where
>
> can we endure
> to know not where
> and set out even so

In the next chapter, we take up the image of Jesus as prophetic martyr, whose ministry not only gave hope and healing to the poorest and most marginalized people but also provoked hostility and deadly animosity toward him that would ultimately cost him his life. As we explore this image, we will also see how biblical women, such as Elizabeth, Mary, Miriam, Huldah, Noadiah, Anna, a Samaritan woman, and a widow who confronts an unjust judge, embody Christ's prophetic mission in female form. We also take up questions of how to discern when is the propitious time to confront unjust rulers and systems in speech and action.

CHAPTER THREE

Prophetic Martyr

THE SETTING IS AMATENANGO DEL VALLE.[1] The newly painted walls of the sixteenth-century church glisten white in the afternoon sun. Colorful streamers from the roof of the church and poinsettias blooming in the yard bid us welcome. In the community room, sixteen Tzeltal women are gathered to watch a video on domestic violence. The women range in age from very young to quite elderly. Padre Carlo, an Italian missionary, pours coffee. Unlike the majority of men in Amatenango, he seems comfortable in this untraditional role of servant to the women. His presence is unobtrusive, as the women continue their meeting. For several years, with the help and encouragement of CODIMUJ, the women's group has been meeting to study the Bible. The struggle has been hard, but the effects have been revolutionary. In the voice of Angelina, a catechist:

> "When we first began to meet, many of the men felt threatened. Some of the women were beaten by their husbands, who wanted them to stay at home and make tortillas and do the washing and take care of the children. Men have the right to leave the house whenever they want, but they don't want us women to leave the house. They are suspicious that we are meeting someone else, that we will find another husband. So the first obstacle to overcome was to be able to leave our houses to meet together.
>
> Another difficulty is that traditionally, women were never given the right to speak; we were not allowed to have an opinion. All the decisions were to be made solely by our husbands, without even consulting us. Almost all of us were illiterate, and most of us could speak only Tzeltal, not Spanish. No one thought it was important for us to go to school. Knowing how to cook and sew and clean and make clay figurines to sell

was enough of an education for us. In public we would never voice what we were thinking.

Some of us began to question these attitudes, and we began meeting quietly to study the Bible. There we encountered valiant women who overcame their fears and followed Jesus. We saw how brave was Mary, Jesus' mother, who went to see her son when he was murdered. We saw how Mary Magdalene, Joanna, and Susanna followed Jesus and ministered with him, and we said, if they could leave their homes to learn to be disciples, then so can we. And when we saw how Mary Magdalene was sent to proclaim the gospel, we learned that we, too, could speak out and share the Word with others as catechists and teachers and evangelizers. This is a long, slow, process, though, because we are not used to claiming our own voice; we are not used to thinking we have rights or that we have any dignity or value in ourselves, or that what we have to say is important.

The cross that women carry is the burden of preaching and proclaiming the gospel. We base this on the fact that the risen Jesus presented himself to the women; it was the women who had the strength to be there. It is dangerous to carry this cross, just as it was for Jesus. The reason they put Jesus to death is because he had compassion on the people and he defended the poor. In so doing he denounced the powerful, and that is very dangerous. In particular, he freed women, like the woman who was bent over, and he enabled them to know their rights and their worth. One of the rights of women is to preach. But when women know their rights and struggle to obtain them, much suffering comes from those who oppose them. Women suffer greatly because they are not allowed to speak. It is the work of both women and men to carry the cross, but men think that they are the ones that have the right to do it, that they are the stronger ones. But it was the women who went to the tomb of Jesus; the men were at home, afraid to go out. The women were the ones who gathered their strength to hand over their lives just as Jesus gave his life for them."[2]

The women of Amatenango del Valle, along with many others in the Diocese of San Cristóbal de las Casas, have arrived at a very different understanding of Jesus and his cross than the one they held previously. Formerly, they had said, "Jesus died for my sins,"and their own self-understanding as sinful and deserving of punishment fed into such a theology. A Jesus who was a silent, suffering servant who uttered nary a word in protest during his passion walked with them in their sufferings but gave them no encouragement whatsoever to question or to speak up.

With the advent of grassroots Bible study groups in Latin America that engaged the perspectives of liberation theology, Jesus emerged as the prophet who raised up the poor and was rejected by the powerful. It took the prophetic vision of Don Samuel Ruiz to help bring forward this profile of Jesus in the Diocese of San Cristóbal de las Casas and, in turn, to call forth the prophetic gifts of the women of this diocese.[3]

Don Samuel's efforts brought him both the love and devotion of the poor of his diocese and deadly opposition from the rich and powerful. The death threats against him have been numerous. Not only does he exercise the ministry of prophet himself, but he also calls forth the prophetic gifts of others, both women and men.

PROPHET JESUS

In all four Gospels, the theme of Jesus as prophet is present,[4] but most prominently so in the Gospel of Luke.[5] In the opening episode of his public ministry, the Lucan Jesus takes up the mantle of Isaiah, applying the prophet's words to himself: "The Spirit of the Lord is upon me, because he has anointed me to bring good news to the poor. He has sent me to proclaim release to the captives and recovery of sight to the blind, to let the oppressed go free, to proclaim the year of the Lord's favor" (Luke 4:18-19; Isa 61:1-2; 58:6).

> "It was to be expected that they would put Jesus to death for his alliance with the poor."
> —Magdalena, El Alto, Bolivia
> 27 March, 2003

As the narrative continues, Jesus then aligns himself with the prophets Elijah and Elisha. He speaks of Elijah's attention to the widow of Zarephath (Luke 4:25-26) and Elisha's cure of Naaman the Syrian (4:27). He then proceeds to imitate these very deeds. When Jesus heals the slave of a centurion (7:2-10), the resemblance to Elisha's healing of Naaman (2 Kgs 5:1-14) is unmistakable.

And when he restores the widow's son to life at Nain (Luke 7:11-17), there is a clear echo of Elijah's raising of the widow's son at Zarephath (1 Kgs 17:17-24) and of Elisha's resuscitation of the Shunammite woman's son (2 Kgs 4:18-37). Indeed, the onlookers at Nain exclaim of Jesus, "A great prophet has arisen among us!" (Luke 7:16). Jesus' feeding of the multitudes (9:10-17)[6] is also reminiscent of Elisha's provision for his followers (2 Kgs 4:42-44), as well as of God's provision of manna for the Israelites in the wilderness under Moses' prophetic leadership (Exod 16:4-36).

Like Elijah and Elisha (Luke 4:26-27), Jesus also reaches beyond the confines of his own people as he heals and preaches to people who are not Israelites. He heals a Roman centurion's son (7:2-10) and a Samaritan leper (17:11-17). And he wants to evangelize Samaria on his way to Jerusalem (9:52). When the Samaritan villagers rebuff Jesus' messengers, the latter want to "command fire down from heaven and consume them" (9:54). But here Jesus rejects the pyrotechnics for which Elijah was famous (1 Kgs 18:36-38; 2 Kgs 1:9-14)[7] and peacefully proceeds to another village (Luke 9:55). Like the prophets before him, Jesus also knows from the outset that he will be rejected. He declares in Nazareth, "No prophet is accepted in the prophet's hometown" (4:24).[8]

One other identification with Elijah is alluded to at the beginning of Jesus' journey to Jerusalem. Luke begins the travel narrative with the statement, "When the days drew near for him to be taken up he set his face to go to Jerusalem" (Luke 9:51). Just as Elijah was "taken up" to heaven in a whirlwind (2 Kgs 2:11), so Jesus will be "taken up" into heaven at his ascension (Luke 24:51; Acts 1:9).

Jesus is also cast as the expected "prophet like Moses" (Deut 18:15) in the Third Gospel. At the Transfiguration (Luke 9:28-36), Jesus' face becomes radiant, as did that of Moses after his encounter with God on Mount Sinai (Exod 34:29-35). Moses and Elijah converse with Jesus about his *exodos*, which is about to be accomplished in Jerusalem (Luke 9:31). The Greek word *exodos*, meaning "way out," has a double connotation. It refers to Jesus' "death" and it alludes to the Exodus, God's liberation of the Israelites from Egyptian bondage. Jesus' death, then, is to be understood as the means by which God's new act of liberation will be accomplished. The admonition of the voice from heaven, "Listen to him" (9:35), echoes the directive to Israel, "You shall heed such a prophet" (Deut 18:15), reinforcing the identification of Jesus with the expected prophet like Moses.[9]

The identity of Jesus as prophet is solidified in Luke 7. The imprisoned John the Baptist, after hearing reports from his disciples about Jesus, sends two of them to ask Jesus whether he is "the one who is to come" (7:19; see also 3:16). This is an allusion to the expectation that the prophet Elijah would come again as precursor of the Messiah (Mal 3:1-23). Jesus replies that they should tell John what they have seen and heard: "The blind receive their sight, the lame walk, the lepers are cleansed, the deaf hear, the dead are raised, the poor have good news brought to them" (Luke 7:22). Then to the crowds, Jesus asks what they went out to the desert to see: "A prophet?" (7:26). He answers his own question, "Yes, I tell you, and more than a prophet," and then makes it clear that it is John the Baptist who is the Elijah-like precursor (7:26-30).[10] The scene closes with Jesus telling a parable that illustrates how both he and John, Wisdom's prophets, experience what is common to all prophets: some accept their message and repent, but others reject them out of hand.[11] Those who close themselves off from God's messenger find fault with John's asceticism as well as with Jesus' banqueting habits. Yet in the end, "Wisdom is vindicated by all her children" (7:31-35).[12]

In the next episode (Luke 7:36-50), Jesus' identity as prophet is once more central. In the scene at the home of Simon the Pharisee, when a woman who had previously been forgiven weeps at Jesus' feet and anoints them, Simon declares, "If this man were a prophet, he would have known who and what kind of woman this is who is touching him—that she is a sinner" (7:39). The irony is great, as the reader knows clearly that Jesus is, indeed, a prophet and that the woman has already been released from her sins. Jesus tells Simon a parable about how being forgiven much leads to great love (7:41-42), but at the end of the episode, it remains unclear whether Simon is persuaded that Jesus is a prophet or whether his other dinner guests who question Jesus' identity (7:49) hold sway over him.[13]

The question of Jesus' identity as prophet surfaces again in Luke 9. Herod has heard about Jesus, and "he was perplexed because it was said by some that John had been raised from the dead, by some that Elijah had appeared, and by others that one of the ancient prophets had arisen" (9:7-8).[14] And so Herod kept trying to see Jesus, a desire finally fulfilled when Pilate sends Jesus to him after he has been arrested (23:6-12). But Herod and his soldiers only treat Jesus with contempt and mock him (23:11) before sending him back to Pilate. Likewise, those who were holding Jesus after his arrest mocked him, saying, "Prophesy! Who is it that struck you?" (22:64). As the drama of the passion unfolds, Jesus' words to the Pharisees who tried to warn him about Herod are fulfilled: "It is impossible for a prophet to be killed outside of Jerusalem" (13:33; see also 11:49). Yet even as Jesus is aware of the inevitable fate of the prophet,[15] he deliberately sets his face to Jerusalem (9:51) and still longs for acceptance on the part of his beloved people, as he says, "Jerusalem, Jerusalem, the city that kills the prophets and stones those who are sent to it! How often have I desired to gather your children together as a hen gathers her brood under her wings and you were not willing!" (13:34). Even as he embraces his own death as a consequence of his prophetic ministry, he also speaks of the devastating repercussions for those who reject him: "See, your house is left to you. And I tell you, you will not see me until the time comes when you say, 'Blessed is the one who comes in the name of the Lord'" (13:35). These are the words on the lips of the multitude at Jesus' entry into Jerusalem (19:38), echoing Zechariah 9:9; Isaiah 40:9; and Malachi 3:1, and reinforcing Jesus' identity as the expected eschatological prophet.

The image of Jesus as prophet who is rejected by the powerful but vindicated by God is brought to completion in the final chapter of Luke's Gospel. Cleopas and his companion, not yet recognizing the risen Christ, tell him that Jesus of Nazareth was "a prophet mighty in deed and word before God and all the people" (24:19). As they continue to recount the events of the previous days, Jesus admonishes them for their slowness of heart to believe "all that the prophets have declared" (24:25). And then, "beginning with Moses and all the prophets, he interpreted to them the things about himself in all the scriptures" (24:27). Earlier in the Gospel, Jesus had used the image of the prophet Jonah, who spent three days in the belly of a whale before emerging alive, to speak of his death and resurrection and the urgent need to repent in the face of this sign (11:29-32).[16]

THE DEATH OF THE PROPHET

When Jesus is seen as a prophet, his death is understandable as the consequence of his prophetic praxis throughout his life.[17] He has responded to God's call to take up the work of a prophet, that is, one who embodies the hope that a different way is possible in God's realm. His prophetic ministry involves both denunciation and annunciation: he confronts evil and evildoers, and he heals, forgives, and raises up all those in need. He offers freedom to people from anything that binds them. Such a ministry always has dual results: he is loved by those who become liberated in the embrace of God, but he is hated by those whose power, privilege, and status he threatens with his alternate vision of how life is to be lived in the realm of God. His execution is no accident; it is the foreseeable outcome of the prophetic mission he has freely accepted.

MISSTEPS

One of the important aspects of understanding Jesus' death as the expected outcome of a prophet who speaks truth to power is that it keeps us from losing sight of the concrete historical and political situation in which Jesus was executed. In this interpretation, we do not lose sight of the historical reasons while searching for spiritual meaning. Yet there are some missteps that disciples of the prophet Jesus can make in attempting to follow in his footsteps. Several of these are signaled in the scriptures, with questions of how to discern a true prophet from a false one.[18]

Self-Appointment

True prophets are called by God and are usually reluctant to do what they perceive God is calling them to do. Jeremiah objected that he was too young and that he did not know how to speak (Jer 1:6). Moses demurred, "Who am I that I should go to Pharaoh, and bring the Israelites out of Egypt?" (Exod 3:10). He further objected that he was "slow of speech and slow of tongue" (4:10). Jonah tried to flee from God by boat (Jonah 1:3-4). Reluctance usually characterizes the true prophet. We should be wary of those who too easily claim the mantle of "prophet."

Side-Stepping Pain

Another misstep is when a supposed prophet announces good news but is not ready to bear the cost of what it will take to bring about the liberating vision. This may take the form of a prophet who presents a rosy vision but discounts the fact that any true transformation toward it will be costly. Or, such as these may try to have others pay the price, while they themselves simply speak the vision. They ask others to take risks they themselves are not willing to shoulder. Authentic prophets live what they preach and derive their power to lead from the coherence of their lives with their words. They are willing to give their lives, if necessary, to witness to the truth of the gospel.

Compulsion to Speak

False prophets can sometimes be identified by their compulsion to speak out at every opportunity. Authentic prophets know that timing is all-important. They have the virtues of prudence and patience. They know that the propitious moment to speak or act must be discerned carefully. They calculate when is the moment that the prophetic word will be able to be heard and be most effective. They have inner freedom. They are "free to speak the hard message for the right reasons and free not to speak it for the wrong reasons or at the wrong time because of some compulsion that is ultimately selfish."[19]

This is the kind of inner freedom we see in Jesus as he discerns whether to leave his ministry of healing and teaching in the Galilee to confront the powers in Jerusalem, the hub of religious and political power. Luke tells that Jesus went up a mountain to pray, along with three of his disciples. There, he prayed to know the next step in following God's will. Should he stay in Galilee? There was much good he could continue to do there. Or should he go to Jerusalem? As he prayed, the answer became clear, and his face lit up.[20] Like Moses, whose face became aglow after his encounter with God on Mount Sinai (Exod 34:29-30), and Hannah, whose face was no longer downcast after receiving an answer to her prayer for a son (1 Sam 1:18), Jesus' face reflected the radiance of his experience with God. The dialogue with Moses and Elijah (unique to Luke's account) explains that Jesus came to understand that the time was right to go to Jerusalem and that, paradoxically, it would mean his death; however, his death would not be the end of his mission, but would open the way forward for all, as a New Exodus for God's people. What Jesus, Moses, and Elijah discuss is Jesus' *exodos*, "which he was about to accomplish at Jerusalem" (Luke 9:31). The Greek word *exodos* both connotes death[21] and calls to mind the paradigmatic saving event of Israel's history. After this discerning prayer, Jesus sets his face resolutely toward Jerusalem (9:53).

Driven by Anger

Anger at injustice is the right response that helps galvanize energies toward transformative change.[22] But prophets who do not experience and embody God's love and who do not demonstrate love either for the people whom they are trying to lead or for the ones they consider opponents are not entirely authentic. True prophets have a wisdom that comes from the pursuit of truth in love. They have a wideness in their horizons; there is a place for all. They can see that those who disagree with them also have a piece of the truth. They can see the large picture and do not limit their concern to a single issue.

Courting Martyrdom

True prophets know there is a high price for the vision of peace and justice they proclaim, and they are willing to suffer, even to pay with their lives if necessary, to bring it about. But they are not reckless nor suicidal, nor do they seek to become martyrs for a cause. They are different from protesters who sacrifice themselves for a cause. Prophetic martyrs are those who "[accept] death rather than give up their beliefs; they are witnesses," not "people seeking death to force others to change their practices."[23] They work, as Augustine envisioned, to "create a world where people can live peacefully with their beliefs instead of dying for them."[24] In chapter 4, we will explore some of the dynamics by which such becomes possible.

The flip side of the danger posed by the prophet who courts martyrdom is that posed by those who glorify martyrdom. As

Rebecca Ann Parker observes, "The violence directed against activists and revolutionaries must evoke grief not adulation."[25] When the pain of backlash and repression is presented as something positive, this can cloak perpetrators. Perpetrators of violence "should not be hidden by language that praises the death of martyrs as nourishment for the world."[26] In remembering martyrs, there must be a dual dynamic: both an exposing of the "darkness, the *mysterium iniquitatis,*" the unspeakable horrors wrought by evil and violent acts, and at the same time, a "luminosity, the *mysterium salutis,*" that sheds light on the paradoxical healing love of God in Christ that becomes transparent in the self-surrender of the martyr.[27]

THE RESURRECTION OF THE PROPHET

The mission of the prophet does not fizzle out at his death. Jesus' opponents could not succeed in silencing him. By raising him up, God confirms Jesus, his message, and his way of living. Moreover, resurrection is a reality already visible in Jesus in the way he lived. As Dorothee Sölle says, "Jesus rose and continues to rise wherever prophets arise, breaking through the system of lies, and offering a glimpse of the true God of life who stands against the evil systems of worldly power."[28] Jesus' tenacity for life continues to rise in those who are victimized, who refuse to accept the power of the rulers to silence the prophets.[29] Christ's power and spirit for life lives on in the community of believers, as Msgr. Oscar Romero, Archbishop of El Salvador, martyred in 1980, expressed so well. His words, uttered just days before his assassination, are inscribed on the outside of the Chapel of La Universidad Centro Americana in San Salvador: "If they kill me, I will rise again in the Salvadoran people."[30]

PROPHETIC DISCIPLES

That followers of Jesus are likewise to exercise a prophetic ministry is clearest in the Gospel of Luke.[31] In the Sermon on the Plain, Jesus assures his disciples, "Blessed are you when people hate you, revile you and defame you on account of the Son of Man. Rejoice in that day and leap for joy, for surely your reward is great in heaven; for that is what their ancestors did to the prophets"

(Luke 6:20).[32] In explaining the parable of the sower, Jesus warns them of not falling away in a time of testing, but rather, they are to bear fruit through patient endurance (8:13, 15).[33] When Jesus sends his followers on mission, he advises that when they are not welcomed, they are to shake the dust from their feet (9:5; 10:11; see Acts 13:51).[34] After speaking of his own passion, he then says quite explicitly that the disciples' fate will be the same as his: "If any want to become my followers, let them deny themselves and take up their cross daily and follow me" (9:23; see also 14:27).[35] Luke's addition of the word *daily* to this saying reinterprets the cross as the daily readiness and willingness of a disciple to undergo persecution for the sake of the gospel, not just the preparedness to pay the ultimate price in martyrdom.[36] There is also a saying unique to Matthew in which Jesus tells the disciples, "Whoever welcomes a prophet in the name of a prophet will receive a prophet's reward" (10:41). The "reward of a prophet" is ambiguous. On the one hand, the reward of or from prophets is hearing the message they speak from God, thus opening themselves to the blessings that entails, both in the present and in the age to come.[37] On the other hand, prophets are often "rewarded" with persecution. Those who host a prophet are also opening themselves up to possible negative repercussions.[38]

Alongside these sober admonitions, Jesus also reassures disciples that they will be given divine protection when they are opposed and that nothing will harm them (Luke 10:19). They have nothing to fear from those who can kill the body but after that can do nothing more (12:4-12; 21:12-19).[39] Even though all hate them because of Jesus' name, not a hair of their head will perish (21:17-18). When they are brought before synagogues, rulers, and authorities, they are not to worry; the Holy Spirit will teach them what to say (12:11-12).

The Acts of the Apostles recounts abundant instances in which these promises of Jesus are fulfilled.[40] It also depicts at the outset the descent of the Spirit upon all the disciples gathered in the upper room, who are then emboldened to prophesy. Peter interprets these happenings with the words of the prophet Joel:

> In the last days it will be, God declares,
>
> that I will pour out my Spirit upon all flesh,

and your sons and your daughters shall prophesy,

and your young men shall see visions,

and your old men shall dream dreams.

Even upon my slaves, both men and women,

in those days I will pour out my Spirit;

and they shall prophesy.

(Acts 2:17-18 citing Joel 3:1-5)

It is ironic, however, that while the second volume of Luke gives the justification for women prophets, this evangelist does not give any further encouragement to women to exercise their discipleship and ministry in this manner. In Acts, those who are explicitly said to be filled with the Spirit, directed by the Spirit, or mediating the power of the Spirit are all men: Peter (Acts 4:8; 10:19, 44; 11:12, 15; 15:8); David (4:25); Stephen (6:3, 5, 10; 7:55); Philip (6:3; 8:29, 39); Prochorus, Nicanor, Timon, Parmenas, and Nicolaus (6:3-5); Barnabas (11:24; 13:1-2, 4); Symeon, Lucius, and Manaen (13:1-2); Paul (9:17; 13:4, 9; 16:6, 7; 19:21); Judas (15:32); Silas (15:32; 16:6, 7); Timothy (16:6, 7); Agabus (11:28; 21:11); the apostles and presbyters (15:28); twelve men in Ephesus (19:6-7); and the Ephesian elders (20:22, 23, 28). No women are so depicted. The only mention of women prophets is a passing reference to Philip's "four unmarried daughters who had the gift of prophecy" (21:9). Nothing further is known about their ministry; none of the words of their prophetic utterances is preserved.[41]

Such a diminishment of prophetic speaking by Spirit-filled women is also evident in the Third Gospel. In the infancy narrative, almost all the characters are said to be filled with the Spirit: Elizabeth (Luke 1:41), Zechariah (1:67), John the Baptist (1:15, 80), Mary (1:35), and Simeon (2:25-27). Noticeably absent from the list of Spirit-filled characters is Anna. Although designated a prophet (2:36), her specific words are not preserved in the form of a canticle, as are those of her counterpart Simeon (2:29-35). Moreover, in contrast to the amazement that Simeon's words evoke (2:33),[42] no reaction to Anna's speaking is related. The effect is that Luke discourages his readers from giving Anna much notice. In the remainder of the Gospel, Jesus is the only one depicted as empowered by the Spirit.[43] As for speaking, in the Third Gospel, women rarely speak and when they do, they are corrected.[44] When Martha speaks to Jesus about her concerns about ministry,[45] she is rebuffed, and her silent, passive sister is said to have chosen "the better part" (10:38-42). A woman in a crowd who raises her voice, exclaiming, "Blessed is the womb that bore you and the breasts that nurse you!" is corrected by Jesus, "Blessed rather are those who hear the word of God and obey it!" (11:27-28).[46] And when Mary Magdalene, Joanna, Mary the mother of James, and the other women tell the eleven and the rest the message they have received at the empty tomb, Luke reports, "These words seemed to them an idle tale, and they did not believe them" (24:10-11).

Other books in the New Testament also give evidence of attempts to silence and marginalize women prophets. Two texts in the first letter to the Corinthians show that there were controversies involving women prophets. The nature of the problem in 1 Corinthians 11:2-16 remains enigmatic, but the fact that women pray aloud and prophesy in the assembly is not the issue. In 1 Corinthians 14:34b-36, however, Paul admonishes, "Women should be silent in the churches."[47] In this same vein, we find 1 Timothy 2:11-12, "Let a woman learn in silence with full submission. I permit no woman to teach or to have authority over a man; she is to keep silent." Despite the controversies over women's exercise of prophetic speaking in the early church, there are yet strong portraits of women prophets on which disciples can still rely, as we will explore next.

IN THE COMPANY OF WOMEN PROPHETS

While Jesus plays a unique role as eschatological prophet, biblical tradition makes it clear that he is not a sole heroic envoy but rather, is shaped by a long tradition of prophetic ancestors and, in turn, forms his disciples to continue in this vein. In thinking about Jesus' ministry as prophet, we might see him not so much as a singular indi-

"What we have to do is to reclaim the important roles that women have played in our history, which will animate us to speak of how God is operative in our lives. We are very capable of proclaiming the risen Jesus."

—María, La Paz, Bolivia
24 March, 2003

vidual who continues a linear progression of divine messengers and whose disciples take up his mantle after his death. Rather, we can envision that, even in his lifetime, the movement begun by Jesus was one of shared prophecy in which women and men participated in a common spirit and understood themselves as being and bringing the reign of God.[48]

When the evangelists directly cite or allude to Jesus' prophetic predecessors, they generally refer to the well-known male prophets, especially Isaiah, Jeremiah, Jonah, Moses, Elijah, Elisha, Malachi, Zechariah, and Joel. Yet there are also powerful women prophets among Jesus' antecedents and with whose ministry Jesus' life and mission aligns. The Gospel of Luke, in particular, portrays Jesus' relative Elizabeth and his mother Mary with prophetic characteristics evocative of the female prophets in the Hebrew scriptures, especially Miriam, Hannah, Huldah, and Deborah. Significant also is Anna, whose prophecy greets the eight-day-old Jesus, for whom she has waited expectantly for eighty-four years. A parable Jesus tells about a widow who persists in raising her voice against injustice and the example of a woman who anoints him in preparation for death illustrate women's exercise of prophetic ministries. Philip's four daughters (Acts 21:9) and women in Corinth (1 Cor 11:2-11) are among those who fulfill the Pentecost promise that both Spirit-filled women and men will prophesy (Acts 2:18, citing Joel 2:28-29). We will now explore some of their stories.

Elizabeth (Luke 1:39-45, 57-66)

In chapter 2, we explored Elizabeth's obedience, an essential virtue of a prophet. Although not explicitly designated as "prophet," Elizabeth is clearly portrayed as a woman with prophetic characteristics: she is in intimate relationship with God (Luke 1:5, 24), is filled with the Spirit (1:41), and makes prophetic utterances that lead others to God (1:59-66). Different from the prophet who suffers as a result of the mission God entrusts to her, reference to Elizabeth's suffering comes before her prophetic speaking. She has endured childlessness (1:7), a condition that, in her culture, would have made her the object of scorn (1:24). While others may have speculated that her barrenness was a punishment for sin, the evangelist makes it clear that Elizabeth is completely upright. Moreover, she continues to believe in God's goodness and desire for life for all, even when there are no tangible results to her faithfulness. In this, she prefigures Jesus' continued trust in God even as he undergoes crucifixion without knowing how God will bring forth new life from this horror. When new life begins to grow within Elizabeth, she immediately recognizes this as God's doing and exclaims, "This is what the Lord has done for me when he looked favorably on me and took away the disgrace I have endured among my people" (1:24). She knows God's delight is not in the suffering of the just ones, but in their vindication and fullness of life.

Luke then provides two vignettes that feature prophetic speaking by Elizabeth. In the Visitation scene (Luke 1:39-45), when she hears Mary's greeting, Elizabeth is filled with the Holy Spirit and exclaims a blessing on Mary and the child she carries in her womb (1:41). She affirms the faithfulness of Mary who, like her, has trusted the divine Word spoken to her (1:45). In her final appearance in the Gospel, Elizabeth again gives a prophetic utterance. At the circumcision of her son, her neighbors and relatives are about to name the child Zechariah after his father (1:59). But Elizabeth announces, "He is to be called John" (1:60), in accord with the divine instruction to Zechariah (1:13). Her prophetic declaration is effective, leading an ever-widening circle of people to a recognition of God's gift and grace (the name *John* literally means "gift/grace of God"). After nine months of muteness from disbelief and incomprehension of God's ways, Zechariah is enabled by her to affirm, "His name is John" (1:63). Hearing this, amazement (*thaumazō*, v. 63) and fear (*phobos*, v. 65) come upon all their neighbors. These same words are used to describe the awestruck reaction of people to the prophetic words and works of Jesus.[49] The scene concludes with the Word going out "throughout the entire hill country of Judea," leading people to ponder the meaning in their heart (1:66; see also 2:19, 51). The same language is used of Jesus to speak of the universal acclaim he receives in the early stages of his prophetic ministry.[50]

Mary and Miriam (Luke 1:46-55; Exod 15:1-21; Num 12:1-16)

Jesus' mother is also cast in prophetic terms by the Third Evangelist. She has a visionary encounter with the holy (Luke 1:26-38), is filled with the Spirit (Luke 1:35; Acts 1:14; 2:1-12), and articulates an alternate ordering of life in God's realm by means of prophetic song (Luke 1:46-55). In this way, she also prefigures the prophetic nature of Jesus' own ministry.

Like many of the prophets, Mary experiences God's call[51] through an angelic messenger (Luke 1:26-38). So too, her son comes to a deeper understanding of his prophetic call through encounters with angelic messengers (9:28-36; 22:43-44). Gabriel's opening address, *chaire*, is not only the common Greek greeting "Hail!" but also means "rejoice," recalling prophecies of restoration that begin with a call to rejoice (Zeph 3:14; Joel 2:21; Zech 9:9). Jesus, when calling his disciples to a prophetic ministry, also encourages them to rejoice when people hate them on his account, because their "reward is great in heaven; for that is what their ancestors did to the prophets" (Luke 6:23; see also 10:20).

Mary's designation as "favored one" (*kecharitōmenē*, Luke 1:28, 30) aligns her with figures from Israel's past who found favor with God: Noah (Gen 6:8), Moses (Exod 33:12-17), Gideon (Judg 6:17), and Samuel (1 Sam 2:26). Jesus is also characterized as God's favored one. After being presented in the Temple, Luke notes, "The child grew and became strong, filled with wisdom; and the favor (*charis*) of God was upon him" (2:40). And at the conclusion of the story of the 12-year-old Jesus in the Temple, "Jesus increased in wisdom and in years, and in divine and human favor" (*charis*, 2:52). After Jesus' inaugural proclamation of his prophetic mission (4:18), the crowd is amazed at his gracious words (*logois tēs charitos*, 4:22). One might think that a person "favored" by God would be spared suffering and distress, but quite the opposite is true. All who are so designated in the Bible are people of whom God asks a great deal. Their special relationship with God is for the

> "The prophet announces and denounces. It is very difficult to be a prophet—they crucify prophets."
>
> —Adriana, Surco, Lima, Peru
> 10 April, 2003

sake of the people, for whom they lay down their lives. But like Mary, they are reassured that "[t]he LORD is with you" (Luke 1:28; Judg 6:12) and that God's Spirit gives them the power to carry out the mission entrusted to them. Just as God's presence settled upon (*episkiazein*) the tent of meeting (Exod 40:35, LXX), so does the "power of the Most High overshadow (*episkiazein*)" Mary (Luke 1:35). With the assurance of God's power and presence, Mary, like Elizabeth, chooses freely to trust in God despite the incomprehensibility of divine ways (1:38). This is a foretaste of Jesus' similar choice in his final prayer on the Mount of Olives (22:42) and of his assurance to his disciples of divine power and protection (12:11-12; 21:12-19).

Mary is also cast as prophet when she sings of God's triumphs in the Magnificat (Luke 1:46-55). The similarities between her hymn and Hannah's song of praise (1 Sam 2:1-10) have often been noted, but there are also strong parallels with the prophet, Miriam, Mary's namesake, who led the Israelites in singing and dancing after their escape from the Egyptians (Exod 15:1-21).[52] Both women begin by celebrating what God has done for them personally. Miriam sings, "The LORD is my strength and my might, and he has become my salvation; this is my God, and I will praise him" (Exod 15:2). Similarly, Mary proclaims that God "has looked with favor on the lowliness of his servant . . . the Mighty One has done great things for me" (Luke 1:48-49). Both speak of the might of God's arm by which God's powerful deeds are done (Exod 15:6, 16; Luke 1:51). Both exult in God's mercy and steadfast love (Exod 15:13; Luke 1:50).[53] Both acclaim God as mighty (Exod 15:16; Luke 1:49) and holy (Exod 15:11; Luke 1:49). Both celebrate how God brings down the powerful who oppose God's plans (Exod 15:4, 7, 14, 15; Luke 1:52) and how God has helped Israel (Exod 15:16-17; Luke 1:54). Both sing of the expectation that God's reign and the divine promises will last forever (Exod 15:18; Luke 1:55).

Singing such a hymn and leading the dance are not the activities one might first think of as associated with a prophet. But this is, indeed, one of the ways in which prophets are identified. When Samuel anoints Saul as ruler, he tells Saul that he will meet a band of prophets "coming down from the shrine with harp, tambourine, flute, and lyre playing in front of them; they will be in a prophetic frenzy. Then the spirit of the LORD will possess you, and you will be in a prophetic frenzy along with them" (1 Sam 10:5-6). It is notable that Miriam is identified as a prophet in Exodus 15:20, precisely at the point when she takes a tambourine in hand to lead the singing and dancing.[54] As prophet, Miriam is a messenger for God, leading the people to understand their present experience as God's gift of new life and to imagine—and thus be able to achieve—a new future in the land of God's promise.[55] Similarly, Judith led her people in such a victory hymn following her daring deed against Holofernes (16:1-16), as did Deborah after leading the successful campaign against the Canaanite King Jabin (Jdg 5:1-31). Deborah is celebrated as both prophet and judge (Jdg 4:4). In rabbinic tradition, her judging is remembered as prophetic, as she is said to have "judged according to the word," that is, according to divine inspiration.[56] Like Hannah, Miriam, Judith, and Deborah, Jesus' mother also sings of reversals and of a hope-filled future for those who have been oppressed, a frequent theme in prophetic preaching. She exults in how the proud are scattered, the powerful dethroned, the lowly lifted up, the hungry filled, while the rich are sent away empty (Luke 1:52-53).[57] A theme of reversal continues throughout the Gospel of Luke, as her son devotes himself to this very program (4:18-19).

In the victory hymns of women prophets, the dominant note of joy overshadows the suffering that accompanies their vocation. In the case of Miriam, Numbers 12:1-16 recounts the repercussions she suffers when she, along with her brother Aaron, challenges the leadership of Moses, saying, "Has the LORD spoken only through Moses? Has he not spoken through us also?" (Num 12:2). As happens to prophets whose message is unwanted, she suffers terrible consequences. She is struck with a skin disease and is cast out of the camp. In the experience of being cast out, there is an echo of Jesus' parable of the landowner's son who is cast out of the vineyard

> "Reading the Bible helps us interpret our lives and recognize our gifts. Some of us have the gift of evangelization. We can spread the gospel, even if it is only to five other persons."
>
> —Anita, El Alto, Bolivia
> 28 March, 2003

and killed by the wicked tenants (Luke 20:15 // Matt 21:39// Mark 12:8). Miriam's ostracism is replicated in Jesus' rejection by his opponents. Yet Miriam's power is such that the community will not move forward without her. They wait for her restoration before they continue their journey (Num 12:15).[58] When she dies and is buried at Kadesh (a name that means "sacred") the place is remembered (Num 20:1), much as Jesus' women followers will see and remember where he is buried (Mark 15:47; Matt 27:61; Luke 23:55). The lasting memory of Miriam's prophetic leadership is reflected in the fact that she is named alongside Moses and Aaron by the eighth-century prophet Micah (6:4).[59]

As for Mary, there is also a high cost for her participation in the prophetic life to which God has called her and for which God has empowered her. The opening chapters of Luke mask her suffering by highlighting, instead, the theme of joy (1:14, 44, 58; 2:10). This keeps from view the distressing and shameful situation in which Mary finds herself as an unmarried young woman who is with child before she and Joseph have begun to live together. In a tight-knit community of friends and kin, there would be rumors, suspicion, false conclusions, gossip, and ostracism. The glorious praise of the angels and the shepherds at the birth of Jesus (2:8-20) overshadows the great hardship endured by Mary of being made to travel from Nazareth to Bethlehem by imperial decree in her last days of pregnancy, with no proper accommodations or female family members at hand to help at the birth of her son (2:1-7).

The price of embracing her prophetic vocation becomes more explicit when she and Joseph present the child Jesus in the Temple. There, the prophet Simeon tells her, "This child is destined for the falling and rising of many in Israel, and to be a sign that will be opposed so that the inner thoughts of many will be revealed—and a sword will pierce your own soul too" (Luke 2:34-35). With words that echo Isaiah 8:14, 18; 28:16, Simeon describes the effects of the ministry of her prophet son: those who heed his call to justice will be raised up; those who reject him stumble and fall. Any mother wishes only success and joy for her child; the rejection experienced by her son cuts her spirit to the quick as well. The Gospel of John captures her anguish by placing her at the foot of the cross in the company of her sister, Mary the wife of Clopas, and Mary Magdalene (19:25).[60]

In the Gospel of Luke, however, Mary is not explicitly said to be present at the crucifixion. However, it is possible that she is implied as part of the scene. Luke, unlike the other evangelists, does not name any of those who witness the crucifixion. To the anonymous "women who had followed him from Galilee" who "stood at a distance watching these things," he adds all Jesus' acquaintances as well as crowds who had gathered for the spectacle (23:48-49).[61] When Luke next mentions the women followers in Acts 1:14, Mary, the mother of Jesus, is explicitly named as being among those gathered in Jerusalem awaiting the promised Spirit. It is possible, then, to envision Jesus' mother among the nameless women in Luke's Gospel who witness Jesus' execution and his pain matched by her own.

Simeon's reference to a sword piercing Mary's own soul likely refers to the sword of discrimination spoken of in Ezekiel 14:17, dividing some for mercy and some for judgment. What Simeon is prophesying is that Mary is not immune from having to struggle to understand God's ways.[62] Some of what God asks seems utterly impossible to her (Luke 1:26-38). Yet she continues to ponder everything in her heart (2:19, 51) and remains faithful, even when God's ways seem incomprehensible.[63]

Huldah, Noadiah, and Anna (2 Kgs 22:3-20; 2 Chron 34:8-28; Neh 6:14; Luke 2:36-38)

Among the women prophets who are part of Jesus' heritage are three who have ties to the Temple in Jerusalem. Huldah, who lived in the holy city during the reign of King Josiah in the seventh century B.C.E., was the prophet to whom the priest Hilkiah brought the scroll found in the Temple during the renovations (2 Kgs 22:3-20 and 2 Chron 34:8-28). It is notable that the prophets Jeremiah, Zephaniah, and Nahum were active at the same time, yet it is Huldah who was asked to authenticate and interpret the scroll. Perhaps this was because she was literate and they were not. The fact that Jeremiah needed a scribe, Baruch, to write down his message (Jer 36:4, 32) may indicate that he himself was not able to read and write.[64] Huldah verifies that the message in the scroll is from God, and she proceeds to interpret it. Huldah's role is most unusual; prophets ordinarily spoke oracles and performed parabolic acts—they were not interpreters of scrolls.[65]

Moreover, Huldah begins the process that results in the formation of a canon of scripture, as the scroll she authorizes and interprets comes to form the core of the book of Deuteronomy.[66] The extent of Huldah's influence is evident in the triple gates named for her at the southern entrance to the Temple. In addition, the rabbis thought that she conducted an academy in Jerusalem.[67] They made this conclusion based on the word *bamishneh*, which describes where Huldah lived in 2 Kings 22:14. The root *sh-n-h* means "to repeat," translated as "Second" Quarter in 2 Kings 22:14. But *sh-n-h* is also evocative of the main means of learning in antiquity: oral repetition.[68] The association of this word with Huldah, who is literate, leads to the proposition that Huldah operated a school.[69]

Noadiah the prophet is named in Nehemiah 6:14, along with Tobiah, Sanballat, and "the rest of the prophets," as an opponent of Nehemiah in his work of rebuilding the Temple. Tobiah was an Ammonite official, and Sanballat was the governor of Samaria. We know nothing further about Noadiah, nor do we know anything of the nature of her dispute with Nehemiah. We can deduce, however, her importance and status, in that she is named along with two highly influential figures. Also important to note is that the other female prophets named in the Hebrew scriptures, Miriam, Deborah, and Huldah, belong to the pre-exilic period. The mention of Noadiah supplies evidence that women exercised official prophetic ministry in post-exilic times as well.[70]

Another female prophet associated with the Temple is Anna, who, along with Simeon, prophesies when the infant Jesus is presented in the Temple (Luke 2:36-38).[71] She is advanced in years (2:36), making her a reliable figure of maturity and wisdom. That she had lived with her husband seven years evokes the image of an ideal wife (seven being the number for perfection or completeness in biblical symbolism). She worships in the Temple night and day with fasting and prayer, prefiguring Jesus' nights of communion with God (6:12), his fasting (4:2), and his frequent prayer,[72]—practices that are continued by Jesus' disciples.[73] Anna typifies those who, like the widow of Luke 18:1-8, call out day and night and are heard by God.

There are strong parallels between Anna and Judith, who was also a widow (Jdt 8:4), who "fasted all the days of her widowhood"

(8:6), and who prayed for the rescue of Israel while the incense was being offered in the Temple of God in Jerusalem (9:1). Echoes of Judith urging the rulers of Bethulia to pray while they waited for deliverance from God (8:17) can be heard in Anna's prophesying to "all who were awaiting the redemption of Jerusalem" (2:38). Finally, Anna's age can be calculated to be the same as Judith's. If Anna were married at fourteen, lived seven years with her husband, and eighty-four more as a widow,[74] she too had reached one hundred and five years (16:23).[75]

That Anna is a widow provides an interesting lens on her prophetic ministry. The Greek term for "widow," *chēra*, means "forsaken," "left empty." Instead of being "forsaken," she forsakes her home in Asher, in the north of the country, to take up residence in Jerusalem. Rather than one "left empty," she fills her days with fasting and prayer and prophecy. The Hebrew word for "widow," *'almanah*, has at its root the meaning "unable to speak"; a widow is one "not spoken for." Ironically, as one "not spoken for," she speaks as God's mouthpiece for her people.[76]

The Anointer of the King (Mark 14:3-9)

All four of the Gospels contain a story of a woman who anoints Jesus. We have already examined in chapter one the Lucan version (7:36-50),[77] which depicts a woman who was forgiven much and who in turn pours out her love for others. This rendition is distinct from the other three Gospels, in which a woman anoints Jesus before his passion.[78] We will examine Mark's version, which depicts the action of this woman as prophetic.[79]

The scene is set at a table at the home of Simon, a leper, a character not previously introduced in the narrative. A woman who remains nameless[80] enters with "an alabaster jar of very costly ointment of nard" (Mark 14:3), breaks the neck of the tiny flask to release its precious contents, and anoints Jesus on the head. Anointing the head is mentioned in Psalms 133:2 as a symbol for peace and unity. And in Proverbs 27:9, oil is something that makes the heart glad. Psalms 23:5 and Ecclesiastes 9:7-8 associate anointing of the head with banqueting. Egyptian paintings of banquet scenes show guests with cones of oil that drip on their heads to cool and refresh them.[81] Jesus tells his disciples to anoint their heads even when fasting (Matt 6:17-18).[82] But the anointing of Jesus in Mark 14:3 has a much deeper significance. In the Old Testament, anointing of the head was primarily associated with the consecration of kings, priests, and prophets.[83] The prophet Samuel anoints Saul as king (1 Sam 9:15—10:1) and then David (1 Sam 16:12-13). The priest Zadok anointed Solomon as king (1 Kgs 1:38-40). Elijah was appointed by God to anoint Hazael as king over Aram, Jehu as king over Israel (1 Kgs 19:15-16), and Elisha as prophet to replace himself (1 Kgs 19:16). Just so, the woman who anoints Jesus performs a prophetic role. She is not simply providing a comforting gesture. She has recognized that the time has come for the anointing of the king. The kingship of Jesus is a major motif in the Marcan passion narrative. Jesus is acclaimed "king" as he enters Jerusalem (Mark 11:1-10), and his kingship is the focus of his trial before Pilate (15:2). The title occurs five more times: in Pilate's exchange with the crowd (15: 9, 12), in the mockery of Jesus by the soldiers (15:18), in the inscription placed on the cross (15:26), and in the mockery of the chief priests and scribes (15:32).

Jesus defends and interprets the woman's action over the protests of others at the meal. When they object to the extravagance of the ointment poured out, they echo the protest of Peter when Jesus first speaks of his death (Mark 8:31-33). They do not understand the prophetic foreshadowing in her deed. In her breaking the vial and pouring out its precious contents, she mirrors the brokenness of Jesus' body and his blood poured out. The costliness of the nard signals the costliness of Jesus' prophetic mission and the costliness of following him (Mark 8:35; 10:17-31).[84] In the next meal scene, his last with the disciples, Jesus uses broken bread and wine poured out to say the same thing (14:22-25). Those without understanding deem the extravagant self-gift of the prophet Jesus and of the woman as a waste. Jesus' words of approval for the woman's act are important. He says, literally, "What she had she has done (*epoiēsen*)" (14:8). As Susan Miller points out, one would expect Jesus to use the verb *didōmi*, "to give," rather than *poieō*, "to do." "The verb *poieō*, however, places emphasis on the woman's action and recalls the teaching of Jesus that his family consists of whoever does (*poieō*) the will of God" (3:35).[85] He further affirms that what she has done is to anoint his body for burial and that this "will be told in remembrance of her" (14:9). Elisabeth Schüssler Fiorenza observes ironically, "The woman's prophetic sign-action did not become a part of the gospel knowledge of Christians. Even her name is lost to us. Wherever the gospel is proclaimed and the eucharist celebrated another story is told: the story of the apostle who betrayed Jesus. The name of the betrayer is remembered, but the name of the faithful disciple is forgotten because she was a woman."[86] As contemporary Christians remember her story, if not her name, we find her act repeated myriad times in countless women who keep emulating the prophet Jesus, anointing the world with their costly witness, releasing its perfume to invade the most putrid spaces of death.[87]

Because of Her Testimony (John 4:4-42)

In the opening declaration in the Gospel of John, John the Baptist testifies that he himself is not the Messiah, nor Elijah, nor the prophet (John 1:21), and he points to the one who comes after him (1:25-27). While most Jews awaited a messianic figure, there was no uniform expectation at that time. The "prophet" alludes to Moses' promise, "The LORD your God will raise up for you a prophet like me from among your own people; you shall heed such a prophet" (Deut 18:15). The first person in the Fourth Gospel to identify Jesus as a prophet is the woman whom Jesus meets at a well in Samaria (John 4:4-42). Likewise, the people who witnessed the sign of the feeding of the five thousand acclaim, "This indeed is the prophet who is to come into the world" (6:14). At the Feast of Tabernacles, when people hear Jesus speak about rivers of living water that flow from his and the believer's heart,[88] some affirm, "This is really the prophet" (7:40), and others, "This is the Messiah" (7:41). The man who was blind from birth and who was healed by Jesus also identifies Jesus as a prophet (9:17). In each case, "prophet" is a correct identification of Jesus, but in this Gospel, one not fully adequate to convey who Jesus is.

The Samaritan woman engages in a lengthy theological discussion with Jesus in which the two gradually disclose their identities to one another. She first probes whether Jesus is greater than Jacob (John 4:12); he responds with the promise of living water that gushes up for eternal life (4:14), a gift for which she then asks (4:15). Her recognition of Jesus as prophet (4:19) comes as he speaks about her lack of a husband. As the entire dialogue takes place on a highly symbolic and theological level, the discussion of the five husbands that the woman has had should also be understood to be symbolic.[89] Like many of the characters in the Fourth Gospel, she is a representative character for her whole people.[90] Jesus is inviting the people of Samaria into the renewed people of God and is remarking on their present lack of relationship with the Jewish deity. Like the prophet Hosea, Jesus uses a marital metaphor[91] to speak about religious fidelity. He is referring to Samaria's infidelity to the Mosaic covenant, occasioned by the acceptance, by remnants of the northern tribes who returned from Assyrian captivity, and of the worship of the false gods of five foreign tribes (see 2 Kgs 17:13-34).[92] Jesus is not displaying knowledge of the woman's sexual history, nor is he exposing her as a sinner. He is speaking about the religious situation of her people. She recognizes that, as did the prophet Hosea, Jesus is extending an invitation to her and her people, which she continues to explore in terms of place of worship. As that portion of the dialogue progresses, she moves to the recognition of Jesus as "messiah" (John 4:25-26).

As with everyone who comes to believe in Jesus in the Fourth Gospel, the woman goes to bring others to him. Leaving her jar at the well as did the fishermen leave their nets when called by Jesus in the synoptic Gospels (Mark 1:18 and pars.), she goes to the city and says to the people, "Come and see a man who told me everything I have ever done! Is this not the Messiah?" (John 4:29).[93] The question does not indicate that the woman is unsure; rather, it is a rhetorical device of the evangelist that allows the villagers and the reader of the text to hear the woman's words as an invitation into relationship with Jesus. Her bidding, "Come and see," is the same response Jesus offers the first disciples whom John the Baptist has directed to him (1:39). One of them is Andrew, who then finds his brother Simon Peter announcing to him, "We have found the Messiah" (1:41). The same dynamic of bringing others to Jesus is repeated when Philip conducts Nathanael to Jesus (1:44-52) and Mary Magdalene brings the other disciples to the risen Christ (20:1-18). The effect of the Samaritan woman's testimony is that "many of the Samaritans from that city believed in him" (4:39), and they ask him to remain with them (4:40). Remaining or abiding with Jesus is a key theological theme in this Gospel.[94] The final verses tell that many others came to believe in Jesus because of his Word,[95] and they tell the woman, "We know that this is truly the Savior of the world" (4:42).

From her encounter with the prophet, the woman herself becomes a prophet, testifying in word and deed. She stands in contrast to Nicodemus, the teacher who, in the previous chapter, came to Jesus at night, but remained unsure and unable to commit himself at the end of the encounter.[96] She, however, comes at noon,[97] the time of day when the light is strongest, a symbol of her coming to full faith. In this Gospel, there is no account of the call or the sending of the Twelve.[98] In the Fourth Gospel, this woman is the paradigm of mission. Her prophetic testimony results in bringing many others to the light.[99]

Mary Magdalene: Apostle to the Apostles (John 20:1-18)

We explore in chapter four how Mary Magdalene, a woman healed of a severe infirmity, in turn ministered to Jesus and his followers (Luke 8:1-3). We turn to her now to see her prophetic role as the first to encounter the risen Christ and to announce this to the other disciples. In the Gospels of Mark and Matthew, Mary is named first in the list of the women who are present at the crucifixion (Mark 15:40; Matt 27:55), who see where his body is laid (Mark 15:47; Matt 27:61), and who discover the tomb empty (Mark 16:1; Matt 28:1). Luke does not give individual names of the witnesses at the crucifixion, but notes that "all his acquaintances, including the women who had followed him from Galilee, stood at a distance, watching these things" (Luke 23:49). The Galilean women also watch where Jesus' body is laid (23:55), but it is not until the end of the account of the empty tomb that their names are supplied, with Mary Magdalene at the head of the list (24:10). In the Fourth Gospel, Mary Magdalene is clustered with Jesus' mother, his mother's sister, and Mary, the wife of Clopas.[100]

The four accounts of the empty tomb and of Mary's prophetic witness vary widely. In the Gospel of Mark, the women do not encounter the risen Jesus directly, but are told by the angelic figure to go to Galilee and there they would see him (Mark 16:7). The ending of this Gospel is paradoxical, as the women flee from the tomb in terror and amazement, but say "nothing to anyone, for they were afraid" (16:8). This Gospel remains open-ended, inviting the hearers to complete the story with their witness to the risen Christ. In the Gospel of Matthew, after receiving the message from the angel that Jesus has been raised from the dead and having been instructed to tell this to the disciples, the women go forth and meet the risen Jesus on the way.

"How can we follow Mary Magdalene's example and preach the good news? We have to throw off the old garments of anything that holds women back. And when you are on this mission, it feeds you and you learn. You speak differently, as you gain courage to go about preaching."

—Adriana, Surco, Lima, Peru
10 April, 2003

He himself reassures them not to be afraid and reiterates the command to go to the other disciples and tell them "to go to Galilee, there they will see me" (Matt 28:10). That the testimony of the women was received and their instructions were followed can be seen in the introduction to the final scene of the Gospel, which reports that the disciples did go to Galilee as Jesus had directed them (28:16).

In Luke's version, when the two angelic figures tell the women that Jesus has risen, they do not commission the women to tell the others. Rather, they invite them to remember what Jesus had said to them about being crucified and about rising. And so they do.[101] They do not encounter the risen Christ directly, nor are they commissioned by him to tell the others. Nonetheless, returning from the tomb, "they told all this to the eleven and all the rest" (Luke 24:9). The response of the apostles is disbelief: "These words seemed to them an idle tale" (24:11). At this, Peter runs to the tomb, sees the linen cloths, and goes home amazed (24:12). Luke consistently portrays women as silent and passive; they only speak to be corrected or disbelieved.[102] This evangelist portrays Elizabeth, Jesus' mother, and Anna as prophets, but they belong to the period of the Law and the prophets.[103] They are not disciples of Jesus nor, in Luke's mind, do they provide a model for women followers of Jesus. In the debate about whether women should exercise visible, public roles of leadership, Luke sides with those who applaud the silent Mary who sits at Jesus' feet rather than the vocal Martha (10:38-42).[104]

It is the Fourth Gospel that gives the strongest portrait of Mary Magdalene as apostle to the apostles.[105] In this account, she appears alone as a representative character.[106] The question of where to encounter Jesus pervades the story. This is an important theme throughout the Fourth Gospel. The first disciples who follow Jesus ask, "Rabbi, where are you staying?" (John 1:38). Key to understanding Jesus' identity is to know from where he comes and to where he is going. Jesus knows this, but his enemies do not (8:14). In the Last Discourse, a central question is, "Where are you going?" (14:5). "Where" connotes inner communion with Jesus, not geographical space.

The answer to where the risen Jesus is to be encountered comes in two parts. In verses 3-10, as Peter and the Beloved Disciple enter the empty tomb and see the burial cloths, the reader understands that Jesus has returned to the Father, as he has said he would (John 17:5). In the second part (vv. 11-18), Jesus' dialogue with Mary reveals that he has also returned to his own, as he promised (14:28). Mary turns from her grief-filled weeping and insistent searching for her beloved[107] as she recognizes Jesus when, like the Good Shepherd (10:3-5), he calls her by name (20:16). Jesus tells her not to cling to the way she knew him before, as an earthly human being, but to go to the gathered community of disciples, and it is there and in them that he can now be encountered (20:17).[108] Mary faithfully fulfills Jesus' directive. She goes and announces to the disciples: "I have seen the Lord" (20:18). This is a standard formulation from the early kerygma as is seen from the identical report of the disciples to Thomas, "We have seen the Lord" (20:25).

As the tradition has been handed on to us, there has been a mighty struggle over the authority of Mary's prophetic witness. There are two strands of tradition in the canonical New Testament. The Gospels of Matthew and John tell of the risen Christ appearing directly to Mary Magdalene and commissioning her to announce the good news to the other disciples. She faithfully fulfills this command, and her testimony is favorably received by the others. By contrast, in the Gospels of Mark and

Luke, Mary and the other women encounter only divine messengers, not Jesus himself. In Mark, they fail to complete the command; in Luke, they are not believed. In another very early piece of the tradition, Paul completely omits mention of Mary Magdalene in his list of those who saw the risen Christ (1 Cor 15:3-5). The treatment of Mary Magdalene is replicated in the experience of many female prophets in the church yet today. Whereas some are at times recognized and heeded, more often, women's prophetic words and deeds are dismissed as "nonsense" (Luke 24:11). But

"When I lived in the selva, I was always silent when I saw injustices; now I have changed. I have become strong. If I see something that is wrong, I speak out the truth about it. Like Mary Magdalene, who turns around when she experienced the risen Christ, so I have turned around. It's not easy to change and leave behind what was before."

—Gloria, Surco, Lima, Peru
10 April, 2003

there is no squelching the prophetic spirit who continues to blow where she will.[109]

A Prophetic Widow (Luke 18:1-8)

One character in Luke's Gospel that can be seen as a prophetic woman appears in a parable unique to this Gospel. The original core of the parable of Jesus is found in verses 2-5. Luke has added the last verses (vv. 6-8), which append various secondary applications to the parable. He has also added the first verse, interpreting the parable as one that concerns "the need to pray always and not lose heart" (18:1).[110] The effect of Luke's introduction is to mute the provocative image of a woman who steps over cultural boundaries into the male world of adjudication and, in doing so, actually bests a corrupt judge. She is not at all the stereotypical widow, who is usually linked with vulnerable members of society, such as orphans and foreigners, for whom care needs to be provided (see Deut 27:19; Isa 10:2). Rather, she is more like Ruth and Tamar, widows who take bold steps for their own wellbeing and who advance God's plan for good for the whole of the people.[111] We are not told the nature of the injustice done to her nor why it is that her nearest male relative is not pleading her case, as would be his role. Perhaps it is he who is bilking her of her rightful property—a doubly ironic possibility! Whatever the case, this widow confronts the judge day after day after day, insisting on justice. She has neither bribe money, which may help grease the skids, nor any powerful friends to get her a favorable hearing. She has only her persistent voice, which she raises over and over saying, "Grant me justice" (Luke 18:3).[112]

This prophetic widow gives hope and courage to all who confront unjust systems and to those who keep them in place, such as the corrupt judge in the parable. Her only weapon is her persistent voice, which finally causes the judge to cave in. In a comical twist, he fears that she will resort to physical violence and give him a black eye (v. 5).[113] And so, he grants her petition. She has not transformed the whole system; the judge is still dishonorable (v. 4). Yet she has achieved one small victory for justice, which gives her energy for her next confrontation.

In her persistent pursuit of justice and her unflagging denunciation of injustice, the widow is the icon of godliness. Like the prophet Jesus in the Gospel, she fearlessly faces opposition, single-heartedly devoted to what will set relations aright. Most commentaries think that the parable uses an argument *a minori ad maius*, "from the lesser to the greater," to say that, if an unjust judge would give in to the relentless pleas of a widow, how much more would God, who is just, answer the prayers of the poor? This interpretation comes from patriarchal mindsets, wherein images of God as a powerful male prevail and which overlook the ability of a female to be the icon of God. Moreover, such an interpretation creates an abhorrent theology of prayer: if you badger God long enough, you can get what you desire. In addition, it flatly contradicts texts such as Luke 11:9-13 and Sirach 35:14-19, which speak of God as eager to give good things to those who ask.

This prophetic widow can help animate those who bemoan the fact that the systems of injustice are too big to take on. Persistent confrontation can eventually break down even the most impermeable obstacles to justice. In particular, this widow can give courage to women who have been socialized not to put themselves forward and who are inclined to simply wait patiently, in hope, praying for change. This widow urges women forward to take bold, public steps toward the pursuit of justice.[114] As one of the mothers of the Plaza de Mayo said of their prophetic witness, "We show that it is possible to fight in a nonviolent way against the evil of the dictators, gaining small victories every day. The struggle for freedom, justice, and life is over and above ideology, religion, race. In time, truth will overcome."[115]

FOLLOWERS OF A REJECTED PROPHET

Christians who follow a prophetic martyr live with the same inner freedom as Jesus, dwell in intimate relationship with God, and articulate for their world, both in word and deed, God's alternate vision of a reign of justice and peace for all. They expect suffering and death as a result of their prophetic life and ministry. But when they experience suffering as a result of injustice, they take whatever steps they can to alleviate it, rather than simply accepting it as their "cross." Communities of believers as a body are to live in this mode, while some individuals are called to live the prophetic charism more intensely. Prophetic Christians who are not poor make a deliberate choice to stand in solidarity with the crucified peoples of their world. They are realistic about the consequences for speaking and acting with and for those who are oppressed, knowing that it can cost their comfort, career advancement, economic security, and social standing, if not their very lives. Prophetic Christians who are among the crucified peoples of the world not by choice have less to lose and much more to gain by their persistent demand for justice. The crucified and risen Christ is one with them in their sufferings and engenders tenacious hope for fullness of life, a foretaste of which is to be attained in righteous living in the present.

This type of prophetic risk-taking requires a surrender to suffering. This is a very different stance from that which regards suffering as redemptive. Suffering is the expected consequence when one chooses to stand in resistance to all that traps people in cycles of violence. Careful discernment is also part of the prophetic life. The wise prophet learns "strategic risk-taking,"[116] neither plunging forward recklessly to an untimely demise nor holding back when the proper moment arrives to take the step that could even cost one's life. It is a kind of "dance with death." As Pedro Casaldáliga says, "When you dance with death, you must dance well. There is no other way. You try to keep in step and not to lose the rhythm, to be correct, don't you?"[117]

Prophets take such risks with fearlessness, for as one friend in Lima put it, "When one loves, one is not afraid." They move with unshakeable hope and with the assurance that God's power to transform death itself into new life is operative in them even now and even if there is no sign of earthly success. Prophetic resistance is not valuable only if it persuades an unjust judge to give a persistent widow her due. As Dorothee Soelle observes, "The ultimate criterion for taking part in actions of resistance and solidarity cannot be success because that would mean to go on dancing to the tunes of the bosses of this world."[118]

For women, there is not only the example of Jesus, but also a whole host of female prophets who formed him, ministered with him, and have continued his legacy. Miriam; Hannah; Huldah; Deborah; Judith; Elizabeth; Mary, the mother of Jesus; Anna; the Samaritan woman; Mary Magdalene and the other Galilean women; the widow who denounced an unjust judge; the Corinthian women prophets; and Philip's daughters all give strength and courage to women who are called to proclaim the Word and to act in prophetic ways. The dauntlessness of biblical women who face opposition and endure suffering in the exercise of their prophetic ministry emboldens contemporary women in their struggles. Some, like Huldah, Noadiah, and Anna, find themselves called to speak truth right at the heart of the institutions of religious power.

To find one's voice when it has been long silenced is not an easy process. In the Diocese of San Cristóbal de las Casas, the process has been long and arduous.[119] At the first gatherings of women, most of them said not a word. When they finally broke the silence, they spoke about concerns regarding their children, of worries about lack of money, and, as the trust level grew, of their relationships with their spouses. They discovered how much they had in common and, slowly, their isolation dissolved as they grew in sisterhood. With the prompting of the leaders, they grew in self-esteem and in solidarity, learning to speak and to listen to one another. They began to understand that, by their baptism, God called them to learn about the Word of God and wants them to participate in spreading the Word. "We taught one another how to unite our voices, so that we could become one voice together," one woman observed.[120] Another describes how, in one large gathering, she was given a microphone to speak. She was so afraid and so ashamed because she put it in her ear to hear! Now she can speak, with or without a microphone, to a group of three or four hundred persons without shame—still with a little fear, but without shame.[121] "We will no more stay quiet!" exclaims another.[122] In a gathering of women at *Nuestra Casa* in San Cristóbal de las Casas in January 2005, the leader of our group of visitors tried to wrap up the discussion before all twelve of the women hosting us had spoken. Those who had not yet addressed the group firmly insisted that each of them must speak her word, *dar su palabra,* and the rich testimony continued until all had shared.

CONCLUSION

The opposition that many women face in trying to speak their word is great. In the diocese of San Cristóbal de las Casas, despite the great strides forward, efforts to silence women are still strong.[123] In some places, men try to prevent women from meeting at all. And when women do succeed in meeting, the men intrude on the gathering. They want to hear what the women are saying. If men are present in the women's gatherings, the women are not free to speak as they would if they were by themselves. In mixed groups, men do not let the women speak. In some places, the women have succeeded in their insistence on meeting alone, and men have finally stopped intruding. The women use the example of Mary Magdalene, who went about with Jesus and the disciples (Luke 8:1-3), to justify their right to leave the house to learn and to engage in their work of proclaiming the gospel. They also look to the example of Mary, who left home to go to Elizabeth because she needed her.[124]

In some communities, men recognize the valor and faithfulness of the women but still resist giving space to their prophetic

> "We have good ideas, but most of us are too timid to speak. We are afraid we will not say it well. We need education and encouragement to express ourselves. We have to speak our word and not wait to be invited to say something."
>
> —Berta, Centro Pachamama, El Alto, Bolivia 25 March, 2003

gifts. At a gathering in Takiu'cum in the mountains in the Tzotzil region of the diocese, all were invited to "speak their word" (*dar su palabra*) after a teaching about women in the New Testament.[125] One man commented on how the men, when they are together, like to drink and brag about how strong they are. But when they are under threat of attack by paramilitary groups, the men are the first to want to flee further into the mountains. The women, he noted, respond that they do not want their children to suffer in the mountains. They insist on staying where they are and standing their ground. Even as this man marveled at the strength of the women and the truth of their words and deeds, Lucía, the wife of the leader of the meeting, who is herself a catechist, spoke out. "Many of us women would like to preach but the men never invite us to do so." Some women have looked to the story of Jesus' affirmation of the woman who anointed him in the face of other people's objections (Mark 14:3-9) to justify their own participation in ecclesial ministries, despite the protests of those who would curtail them.[126]

The very struggle to exercise their prophetic gifts is often part of the cross women disciples throughout the church bear. Yet, like the prophet Jeremiah, who found that the word could not be shut up within but was like fire in the belly burning to be released (Jer 20:9), the words and acts of prophetic women vivified by the Spirit today cannot be contained. Just as the early church invoked the memory of Miriam, Deborah, Anna, and Huldah in the ordination prayer for deaconesses (*Apostolic Constitutions* 20.8), we continue to rely on their spirit to be manifest in the church through the prophetic ministry of contemporary women and men who are willing to take up the cross of the prophet daily.

The words of Pedro Casaldáliga give poetic articulation to what we have attempted to say in this chapter:

I shall die erect, like the trees.
(They will kill me standing upright.)
The sun, as the sole witness, shall put its seal
on my doubly anointed body,
and the rivers and the sea

will become the paths of all my wishes
while the primordial forest joyfully shakes its treetops
    over me.
I shall say about my words:
I did not lie when I cried out.
And God shall say to my friends:
"I attest that he lived among you waiting for this day."
In the twinkling of an eye in death
my life will become truth.
Finally, I shall have loved![127]

In the next chapter, we look at how Jesus brings healing, reconciliation, and forgiveness, not only through his death, but also from the whole pattern of his life. We will see how women such as Simon's mother-in-law, Mary Magdalene, and Tabitha not only were recipients of healing, but ministered from that experience of wellbeing to bring the same to others.

"Everything that we experience is in the Bible. We are just like the women in the Bible, and we are able to speak about that. Too many priests manipulate the Bible in their homilies. Why can't we women preach and consecrate and officiate at Mass so that we can communicate God's love to others?"

—Carla, Torreón
9 November, 2002

CHAPTER FOUR

Healer, Reconciler, Forgiving Victim

As we have seen, in the minds of most Christians, Jesus' death effects the forgiveness of our sins. Yet in the New Testament, only a few texts explicitly connect Jesus' death with forgiveness and reconciliation. In his second letter to the Corinthians, Paul speaks of how "Christ God was reconciling the world to himself, not counting their trespasses against them" (2 Cor 5:19). To the Romans, he writes, "We were reconciled to God through the death of his Son" (Rom 5:10). The author of Ephesians, drawing on cultic imagery, says, "In him we have redemption (*apolytrōsin*) through his blood, the forgiveness of our trespasses, according to the riches of his grace" (Eph 1:7).[2] The author of 1 Peter, in the context of an exhortation to slaves to follow Jesus as a model of one who endured pain that was inflicted unjustly, affirms, "He himself bore our sins in his body on the cross, so that, free from sins, we might live for righteousness; by his wounds you have been healed" (1 Pet 2:24). We will explore some of these texts in more detail. While these speak of forgiveness, healing, and reconciliation that come to the believer through Jesus' death, there are also two powerful moments in the crucifixion scene in the Gospel of

> "As a Catholic, I felt I had a moral responsibility and obligation to forgive Joe for his violence at the moment he was about to murder me. I believed I had to imitate Jesus' final act of love during his crucifixion. I worried that rather than feeling forgiveness, I might feel hatred in my heart and that my last words would be to condemn Joe to hell for all eternity. I feared that if I failed to forgive him completely before I died, then I might end up in hell myself."
>
> —Peggy, Chicago[1]

Luke when Jesus is portrayed as extending forgiveness. The first is when he prays, "Father, forgive them; for they do not know what they are doing" (Luke 23:34). He then assures one of the others crucified with him, "Truly, I tell you, today you will be with me in Paradise" (23:43).

In this chapter, we will look at New Testament texts that concern forgiveness, healing, salvation, and reconciliation. What the gospel accounts reveal and what contemporary work in this area shows is that forgiveness, healing, and reconciliation come about through lengthy and arduous processes. The biblical witness also supports the notion that the forgiveness and reconciliation that Jesus brings is not something instantaneous, accomplished solely at the moment of his death. Nor is it something that Jesus does for us without our participation. We will look at not only how these dynamics are related to Jesus but also the ways in which several New Testament figures who, themselves having experienced healing and reconciliation, extend that to others. Several contemporary examples conclude the chapter.

DRINKING THE CUP

In chapter one, we explored how the four evangelists portrayed Jesus' own understanding of his death through his words and actions at the Last Supper. Only in the Gospel of Matthew does Jesus explicitly speak of forgiveness in connection with his death. His words over the cup at the Last Supper are, "this is my blood of the covenant which is poured out for many for the forgiveness of sins" (26:28). This saying is not to be read in isolation from the rest of the gospel. Throughout the whole of Matthew's Gospel, the emphasis on forgiveness and reconciliation is particularly strong. Jesus repeatedly speaks about forgiveness and shows his disciples how to initiate processes of reconciliation. In this final moment, when Jesus invites his disciples to drink from the cup, he is inviting them to seal their participation with him in a way of life that opens up a way out of the cycles of violence. Two powerful symbols converge: blood and cup.[3]

The metaphor of cup connotes suffering.[4] By accepting Jesus' invitation to drink from the cup, his disciples accept the suffering that befalls them as a consequence of following him and living the gospel. The significance of cup is the same as cross in Matthew

16:24, "If any want to become my followers, let them deny themselves and take up their cross and follow me." Cross and cup refer to the kind of suffering that a disciple is willing to endure as a consequence of following Jesus and living the gospel.

Blood signifies the life-force (Gen 9:4; Deut 12:23; Lev 17:14) over which only God has power. Partaking of the blood connotes acceptance of the life-force of God, which empowers disciples to endure and overcome suffering and evil. In Matthew 26:28, this power is explicitly linked with forgiveness. Jesus has lived and taught forgiveness as a means of breaking cycles of violence and effecting reconciliation. He has accepted the cup of opposition that such a life has engendered, which will culminate in his death. His own blood seals again God's covenant with God's people, just as Moses did with blood sprinkled on the people (Exod 24:8).[5] This pouring out of Jesus' blood is an act that encompasses all.[6] The phrase, "for the forgiveness of sins," not only interprets Jesus' death as effecting forgiveness for all, but also signifies an invitation to disciples *into*[7] a life of forgiveness that releases all from the bondage of violence.

In Matthew's Gospel, "blood" also refers to bloodshed. This motif is more heightened in the First Gospel than in any of the others.[8] The theme is introduced in Jesus' denunciation of the Pharisees as descendants of those who shed the blood of the prophets. He takes them to task for wrongly thinking that, had they lived in the days of their ancestors, they "would not have taken part with them in shedding the of blood of the prophets" (Matt 23:30). He warns that upon them will come "all the righteous blood shed on earth" (23:35). Judas declares that he has sinned by handing over innocent blood (27:4), and the chief priests use the blood money to buy the "Field of Blood" (27:6, 8). When handing Jesus over to be crucified, Pilate declares, "I am innocent of this man's blood" (27:24), which evokes the response from the people, "His blood be on us and on our children" (27:25).

In each of these successive moments, Matthew touches on questions surrounding involvement in bloodshed and its consequences. He faults the Pharisees for being judgmental and for falsely thinking that they are incapable of shedding the blood of a prophet. The irony is great, as they have been conspiring how to destroy Jesus since he healed on the Sabbath a man with a withered hand (Matt 12:14). Jesus asserts that they are, indeed, implicated in the bloodshed of prophets; they themselves claim their descent from the murderers of prophets (23:31), and they have inherited their evil ways. In an ironic command, Jesus urges them to go ahead and "fill up" what their ancestors measured out (23:32). Pilate, likewise, despite his wife's plea not to have anything to do with "that innocent man" (27:19), washes his hands and declares himself innocent of the bloodshed in which he is intimately involved (27:24; see Deut 21:1-9; Pss 26:6; 73:13). Matthew depicts both Pilate and the religious leaders in denial as to their own involvement in bloodshed and its consequences.

By contrast, the crowd responds to Pilate's declaration of dissociation with a recognition that the effects of Jesus' execution will continue to redound not only upon them but also upon their children (Matt 27:25). Their statement is most often read as an acceptance of responsibility or guilt for the death of Jesus: "His death be upon us and upon our children!"[9] However, there is no verb in the expression *to haima autou eph' hēmas kai epi ta tekna hēmōn*, making it possible to read the exclamation, instead, as a statement, "His death is upon us and upon our children," a recognition that the effects of violence committed by leaders reverberate onto the people as a whole[10] and continue to affect future generations.[11] At the same time, this verse asserts that the forgiving effects of the shedding of Jesus' blood also redound to them.[12]

Another contrast to the stance of Pilate and the religious leaders is that of Judas, who does recognize his involvement in handing over Jesus, and he repents of it (Matt 27:3-4).[13] In his desperate attempt to stop what he has helped set in motion, Judas goes to the religious authorities. But as Matthew has painted them, they are closed to any recognition of wrongdoing. Judas' ending is tragic. Although he has drunk from the cup that Jesus offered him at the Last Supper, he is not able to seek or accept the forgiveness it signifies from the one he has handed over.

FORGIVENESS AND JESUS' EARTHLY MINISTRY

The theme of forgiveness is a strong one in the First Gospel, and the cup saying (Matt 26:28) brings it to its culmination. Matthew, like the other evangelists, portrays Jesus as exercising this power to forgive sins during his ministry.[14] It is not something accomplished only by his death. In many gospel episodes, faith leads to forgiveness, as when Jesus heals and forgives the sins of a man who was paralyzed (Matt 9:2-8 // Mark 2:12 // Luke 5:17-26). Seeing the persistent faith of the man's friends who bring him to Jesus despite many obstacles, Jesus declares, "Take heart, son; your sins are forgiven" (Matt 9:2).[15]

Not only does Jesus himself forgive, but he also schools his disciples in this way of forgiveness. He teaches them to pray: "forgive us our debts as we also have forgiven our debtors . . . for if you forgive others their trespasses, your heavenly Father will also forgive you; but if you do not forgive others, neither will your Father forgive your trespasses" (6:12, 14-15).[16] The prayer underscores the reciprocal nature of forgiveness: one's capacity to receive forgiveness is intimately linked to the ability to offer it to others. The parable in Matthew 18:23-35 illustrates this reciprocity in narrative form. It comes on the heels of Jesus' response to Peter that he must extend forgiveness "seventy-seven times" to a brother or sister who sins against him.[17] Jesus tells of a king who decided to settle accounts with his servants. When one who owed him a huge amount of money begged for patience, the king forgave the whole amount. But when this servant demanded repayment from a fellow servant who owed him a much smaller amount, he fell deaf to his pleas for patience and had him imprisoned. The other servants, disturbed by this, report it to the master. Enraged, the master hands the first servant over to the torturers, declaring, "You wicked slave! I forgave you all that debt because you pleaded with me. Should you not have had mercy on your fellow slave, as I had mercy on you?" (18:32-33). Jesus concludes, "So my heavenly Father will also do to every one of you, if you do not forgive your brother or sister from your heart" (18:35).[18]

The meaning of this parable becomes more clear when read in the context of the whole gospel. It is God who initiates forgiveness, first with the gift of Jesus incarnate. Anticipating the birth of Jesus, the angel in Matthew's Gospel tells Joseph that "he will save his people from their sins" (Matt 1:21). In his earthly ministry, Jesus embodies the divine offer of forgiveness as he releases people from sin (Matt 9:2-8). What the Lord's Prayer and the parable about aborted forgiveness emphasize is that, when a person has received forgiveness and boundless mercy from God, the only response is to let that graciousness break open one's heart, transforming desires for revenge and repayment into willingness to forgive others. The consequences are dire if one refuses to replicate God's way of extending forgiveness. The metaphor of "torture" captures the pain that ensues when one is trapped in cycles of unforgiveness (18:35). The more one practices forgiveness, the greater the capacity to receive divine forgiveness and, in turn, to continue to extend it to others. So, too, the converse: the more one refuses to forgive others, the more one closes oneself from the wellsprings of divine compassion and the ability to be transformed by God's loving embrace.

> "Forgiveness is the key to bringing reconciliation, love, and peace. It disarms the other when you don't respond to violence with violence. It's like a karate movement that deflects the rancor by your own self-mastery and conviction to dialogue toward peace. Jesus even forgave from the cross. Each of us is the living Christ who continues to forgive. And you have to do it seventy-seven times seven."
>
> —Nina, Surco, Lima, Peru
> 10 April, 2003

ENDLESS FORGIVENESS AND CYCLES OF VIOLENCE

The New Testament texts that urge disciples to forgive endless numbers of times can have a deadly effect when abused persons understand them as a call to forgive a tormentor over and over without the perpetrator repenting of wrongdoing. In cycles of domestic violence, for example, what typically happens is that there is a buildup of aggressive acts that eventually explodes in a violent episode. Following that, the batterer is remorseful, begs for forgiveness, professes his love, and promises that it will not happen again but does nothing to seek the help needed to be able to understand what is happening and to stop the deadly cycle.[20] The victim, most frequently the wife or girlfriend, desperately

> "Forgiveness—it's always the woman who asks for it; men never do."
>
> —Marta, Lima, Perú
> 16 April, 2003[19]

wants to believe him, offers forgiveness, and feels hopeful that this time it will be as he promises. She may interpret her suffering as something that she has to endure in order to bring about her partner's "redemption," much as 1 Peter asserts of the crucified Jesus: "by his wounds you have been healed" (1 Peter 2:24). But the sad fact is that, when forgiveness is repeatedly offered by an abused person, it only feeds cycles of violence and victimization. It often costs the victim her very life and does not bring the longed-for healing and reconciliation. There is no gospel, no "good news" in such a scenario.

CYCLE OF DOMESTIC VIOLENCE

Her response
Attempts to calm him, "nurturing"
Stays away from family & friends
General feelings of walking on eggshells
Cooks his favorite dinner
Silent/talkative
Keeps kids quiet
Tries to reason
Withdraws
Agrees

Her response
Protects herself any way she can
Police called by her, her children or neighbor
Tries to reason with him
Tries to calm him
Fights back
Leaves

TENSION BUILDING

His actions:
Yelling
Withdraws affection
Moody
Drinking, drugs
Crazy-making
Put-down
Isolates her
Threatens
Criticizes
Destroys property
Sullen

His actions:
Choking
Hitting
Rape
Humiliation
Imprisonment
Hitting
Beating
Verbal abuse
Use of weapons
Kicking
Hair pulling

ACUTE EXPLOSION

DENIAL

His actions:
Declares love
"I'm sorry"
Promises to get counseling/go to church/A.A.
"I'll never do it again."
Cries
Enlists family support
Begs forgiveness
Sends flowers

HONEYMOON PHASE

Her response
Agrees to stay, return, or take him back
Sets up counseling appointments for him
Attempts to stop legal process
Feels happy & hopeful

DENIAL WORKS IN EACH STAGE TO KEEP THE CYCLE GOING

1. Tension Building
She denies it's happening; excuses it as some outside stress (work, etc.), blames self for his behavior, denies that the abuse will worsen. He denies by blaming the tension on her, work, the traffic, anything; by getting drunk denies his responsibility for his actions.

2. Explosion
She denies her injuries, only minor ("I bruise easily"); did not require police or medical help; blames it on drinking ("He didn't know what he was doing"), does not label it rape because it was her husband. He blames it on her or stress.

3. Honeymoon
She minimizes injuries ("It could have been worse"). Believes this is the way it will stay, the man of her dreams; believes his promises. He also believes it won't happen again.

Adapted from the Family Crisis Center. http://www.familycrisiscenter.info/cycle.html.

FORGIVENESS AND REPENTANCE

A necessary partner with forgiveness is repentance. Most processes of reconciliation begin with forgiveness offered by the victim. But in order for there to be reconciliation, there must be a cessation of violence and a removal of the causes of the violence, accompanied by true repentance on the part of the perpetrator. A number of New Testament texts connect repentance with forgiveness. In the opening scene of the Gospel of Mark, Jesus' mentor, John the Baptist,[21] proclaimed a baptism of repentance for the forgiveness of sins (Mark 1:4 // Luke 3:3). When Jesus takes up John's mantle, he announces the nearness of God's reign and, in his preaching, invites people to "repent and believe the good news" (Mark 1:15; similarly Matt 4:17). In the Gospel of Luke, Jesus uses the words of the prophet Isaiah to introduce his mission. He brings "good news to the poor" and "release (*aphesin*) to the captives" (Luke 4:18, quoting Isa 61:1-2). The word *aphesis*, "release," is the same word that denotes "forgiveness," that is, release from sin. At the conclusion of Luke's Gospel, the risen Jesus charges his disciples to continue his mission: "repentance and forgiveness of sins is to be proclaimed in his name to all nations, beginning from Jerusalem" (Luke 24:47). In the Acts of the Apostles, the link between repentance and forgiveness continues. To those who ask Peter after his speech at Pentecost what they must do, he responds, "Repent and be baptized every one of you in the name of Jesus Christ so that your sins may be forgiven; and you will receive the gift of the Holy Spirit" (Acts 2:38). To the council in Jerusalem that insists that Peter and his companions cease teaching in Jesus' name, Peter declares, "God exalted him at his right hand as Leader and Savior that he might give repentance to Israel and forgiveness of sins" (Acts

> "There is another dynamic, that now more women than men are able to get work or sell things to make money. Men feel frustrated not to be able to fulfill their traditional role as provider. They take out their frustration on their wives and children. What we need is to reform our ideas about roles and relations between men and women."
>
> —Amparo, Centro Bartolomé de las Casas, Lima, Peru 10 April, 2003

5:31). In a similar vein, the author of 1 John asserts, "If we confess our sins, he who is faithful and just will forgive us our sins and cleanse us from all unrighteousness" (1 John 1:9).

God's free offer of forgiveness, when accepted, breaks open the heart of the believer, transforming her and empowering her to respond to this gift by making such an offer to another who has hurt her. Repentance follows upon the gift of forgiveness; one does not earn forgiveness by deeds of repentance. Rather, freely offered forgiveness prompts a change of heart. If this offer is accepted and responded to with genuine repentance, then there is a possibility to build together a new relationship. When this is not the case, then action must be taken to ensure the safety of the victim and to eliminate the opportunity for further abuse.

RECONCILIATION[22]

In an ideal forgiveness exchange, forgiveness offered and accepted results in repentance and the building of a new reconciled relationship. Reconciliation does not mean returning to what was before; that cannot happen, because the rupture has irrevocably changed the relationship. However, the injured party and the perpetrator can, under certain circumstances, commit themselves to building a new future together.

In a number of Pauline texts, the apostle speaks about Jesus' death as effecting reconciliation between God and humankind.[23] *Reconciliation* means "the reestablishment of an interrupted or broken relationship."[24] To reconcile is to "exchange . . . hostility for a friendly relationship."[25] Paul says to the Romans, "For if while we were enemies, we were reconciled (*katēllagēmen*) to God through the death of his Son, much more surely, having been reconciled (*katallegentes*), we will be saved (*sōthēsometha*)[26] by his life. But more than that, we even boast in God, through our Lord Jesus Christ, through whom we have now received reconciliation (*katallagēn*)" (Rom 5:10-11). In this text, Paul speaks of enmity between God and humanity that is now repaired through Jesus' death. He emphasizes that the action of reconciling is done by God through Jesus; human beings receive this as gift. It is not accomplished by human initiative. It is something that we receive.[27] Later, in the same letter, Paul struggles with the question of why the majority of the Jews have not believed in Jesus, while the Gentiles have, "for their rejection is the reconciliation (*katallagē*) of the world" (Rom 11:15). "Their rejection" refers to rejection of Jesus by other Jews, which results in the rest of the world becoming reconciled with God. Paul thinks that the effect of this will be that the reconciliation experienced by Gentiles will make his own people jealous and lead some to be saved (Rom 11:14).

In his second letter to the Corinthians, Paul speaks about the new creation that comes as a result of the death of Jesus (2 Cor 5:17). He then asserts, "All this is from God, who reconciled (*katallaxantos*) us to himself through Christ, and has given us the ministry of reconciliation (*katallagēs*); that is, in Christ God was reconciling (*katallasōn*) the world to himself, not counting their trespasses against them, and entrusting the message of reconciliation (*katallagēs*) to us. So we are ambassadors for Christ, since God is making his appeal through us; we entreat you on behalf of Christ, be reconciled (*katallagēte*) to God" (5:18-20). Once again, Paul underscores that reconciliation is a gift from God. God it is who does the reconciling, through Christ. The passive voice of the verb *katallagēte*, "be reconciled," in verse 20, is a theological passive, expressing the notion that the action is performed by God, not humanity. Paul also elaborates that believers are not only recipients of this gift of reconciliation, but they also minister from it and participate in Christ's reconciling work. He considers believers to be "ambassadors" for Christ, that is, envoys who represent his person and work.

It is notable that Paul speaks of the reconciliation not only of humanity with God but also that of "the world" (*kosmos*, 2 Cor 5:19).[28] The cosmological dimension is also in view in the letter to the Colossians, "Through him God was pleased to reconcile (*apokatallaxai*) to himself all things, whether on earth or in heaven, by making peace (*eirēnopoiēsas*)[29] through the blood of his cross" (Col 1:20). The author of Colossians[30] continues, "And you who were once estranged, and hostile in mind, doing evil deeds, he has now reconciled (*apokatēllaxen*) in his fleshly body, through death, so as to present you holy and blameless and irreproachable before him" (Col 1:21-22). Here, the metaphor of reconciliation is blended with a sacrificial image. Paul uses the same verb, *paristēmi*, "to present," when he urges the Romans,

"Present your bodies as a living sacrifice, holy and acceptable to God, which is your spiritual worship" (Rom 12:1).

The one other instance of the verb *apokatallasō*, "reconcile," in the New Testament is in the letter to the Ephesians, where the author[31] says that Christ "has broken down the dividing wall, that is the hostility between us. He has abolished the law with its commandments and ordinances, that he might create in himself one new humanity in place of the two, thus making peace, and might reconcile (*apokatallaxē*) both groups to God in one body through the cross, thus putting to death that hostility through it" (Eph 2:14-16). In this text, the reconciliation effected by Christ's death not only repairs the relationship between God and humankind, but also breaks down the hostility between Gentiles and Jews.

It is important to note that Paul does not speak of the reconciliation accomplished by Christ's death as something that occurs in an isolated moment. Rather, it is something that occurs through a process that includes his healing works during his earthly ministry and that continues on in the ministry of reconciliation embraced by his followers. In 2 Corinthians 5:19, the verb *ēn katallasōn*, "was reconciling," a periphrastic imperfect, indicates an ongoing action in the past. Paul presents this paradox: while God, through Christ, has already healed the breach with humanity, the ministry of reconciliation continues to be effected through our participation in it.[32]

SALVATION, DELIVERANCE

Another way of speaking about the restoration of people to sound relationship with God is *sōtēria*, "salvation." This word denotes "the deliverance of human beings from evil: physical, moral, political, or cataclysmic. It connotes a victory, a rescue of them from a state of negation and a restoration to wholeness or integrity."[33] When used in relation to Jesus, it connotes his rescue of human beings from whatever stands in the way to reconciled relationship with God. The title, *sōtēr*, "Savior," occurs relatively infrequently in the New Testament. Its background is both Greco-Roman and Jewish. In the Greco-Roman world, the title *sōtēr* was applied to gods, philosophers, physicians, statesmen, kings, and emperors. Julius Caesar, for example, was called "god manifest and common savior of human life."[34] In the Old Testament as well, individuals whom God raises up to deliver the people are called "savior" (*môšîa'* in Hebrew, *sōtēr* in LXX),[35] such as Othniel (Judg 3:9) and Ehud (3:15). In most instances, however, it is God who is *sōtēr*.[36] In the New Testament, "Savior" and "salvation" occur primarily in Pauline writings and in the later letters,[37] while the verb *sōzō*, which means both "to save" and "to heal," occurs numerous times in the Gospels.[38]

In the majority of instances in which Paul uses *sōtēria*, he speaks of salvation as a future, eschatological event.[39] In 1 Thessalonians 5:8, he speaks of "the hope of salvation." To the Philippians, he speaks of salvation as something still in progress and something in which they participate; as he says, "Work out your own salvation with fear and trembling, for it is God who is at work in you" (Phil 2:12-13). He also speaks to them of the Savior as one who is still expected: "But our citizenship is in heaven, and it is from there that we are expecting a Savior (*sōtēr*), the Lord Jesus Christ" (Phil 3:20). In Romans 13:11, Paul talks about salvation as still approaching: "salvation is nearer to us now than when we became believers." The author of 1 Peter similarly exhorts Christians to "grow into salvation" (2:2). The author of Hebrews refers to salvation as something to be inherited (1:14). He also envisions it as brought to completion at the *parousia*, "so Christ, having been offered once to bear the sins of many, will appear a second time, not to deal with sin, but to save those who are eagerly waiting for him" (Heb 9:28).

By contrast, in the Gospels and Acts, salvation is spoken about as something that is already accomplished. In the Gospels, salvation (with the verb *sōzō*, which means both "heal" and "save") is often expressed as deliverance from evils such as sickness, disability, or sin.[40] The results of this saving action of Jesus are immediately evident in the lives of those whom he heals and forgives. The very presence of Jesus signals salvation already manifest, as in Jesus' declaration to Zacchaeus, "Today salvation has come to this house" (Luke 19:9). Jesus expresses his mission in terms of coming to "seek out and save the lost" (19:10). In many instances, both in the gospels and in the epistles, salvation is connected with faith.[41] To the woman healed of hemorrhages, for example, Jesus says, "Your faith has saved you" (Mark 5:34).[42]

In the Fourth Gospel, the one instance of *sōtēr* occurs in the passage where a town in Samaria is brought to faith on the basis of the testimony of the woman with whom Jesus dialogued at the well. After having encountered Jesus themselves, they "believed because of his word" (John 4:41) and say, "We know that this is truly the Savior of the world" (John 4:42).[43]

In a number of instances, salvation is connected with Jesus' birth, as in the Lucan annunciation to the shepherds, "To you is born this day in the city of David a Savior, who is the Messiah, the Lord" (Luke 2:11). Matthew, likewise, connects salvation with the birth of Jesus, as the angel tells Joseph, "She will bear a son, and you are to name him Jesus, for he will save his people from their sins" (Matt 1:21). The Fourth Evangelist speaks similarly about the Incarnation, "God did not send the Son into the world to condemn the world, but in order that the world might be saved through him" (John 3:17; so also John 12:47). It is notable that, in this last text, it is not only humanity that is saved but the whole of the cosmos.[44] In Acts of the Apostles, *sōtēr* is used in the context of Jesus' resurrection and exaltation (Acts 5:31). Luke relates this title to Old Testament promises of salvation, as is clear in Acts 13:23: "God has brought to Israel a Savior, Jesus, as he promised."[45] Similarly, the Johannine Jesus says to the Samaritan woman, "Salvation is from the Jews" (John 4:22).

In only a very few instances in the New Testament is a link made between Jesus' death and salvation. In his first letter to the Thessalonians, Paul asserts, "For God has destined us not for wrath but for obtaining salvation through our Lord Jesus Christ, who died for us, so that whether we are awake or asleep we may live with him" (1 Thess 5:8-9). The author of Hebrews speaks of salvation in relation to Jesus' suffering: "Although he was a Son, he learned obedience through what he suffered; and having been made perfect, he became the source of eternal salvation for all who obey him" (Heb 5:8-9). None of the evangelists makes an explicit link between salvation of humankind and Jesus' death. In a paradoxical twist, the synoptic Gospels all have repeated taunts to the crucified Jesus to save himself. Bystanders deride him, saying, "Save yourself and come down from the cross" (Mark 15:30 // Matt 27:40). The chief priests and scribes mock him among themselves, "He saved others; he cannot save himself" (Mark 15:31 // Matt 27:42 // Luke 23:35). In Luke, the soldiers join in (Luke 23:37), as well as one of the criminals crucified alongside Jesus, who derides Jesus, "Save yourself and us!" (Luke 23:39). Some of the bystanders want to "see whether Elijah will come to save him" (Matt 27:49). In the Fourth Gospel, as Jesus speaks of the hour of his glorification, he says, "Now my soul is troubled. And what should I say— 'Father, save me from this hour?' No, it is for this reason that I have come to this hour" (John 12:27). In the crucifixion scene, it becomes clear that salvation does not entail God rescuing the Beloved Son—nor any of God's beloved children—from danger, torture, or death. Jesus has previously told his disciples that salvation is not equated with self-preservation: "Those who want to save their life will lose it, and those who lose their life for my sake, and for the sake of the gospel, will save it" (Mark 8:35; similarly Matt 16:25; Luke 9:24).

Aside from the Gospel episodes in which Jesus is said to save people from sickness, disability, or demon possession, few texts specify from what it is we are saved. In most New Testament references, salvation is spoken of abstractly as the comprehensive effect of Jesus' life, death, resurrection, and exaltation. Only a few texts name the nature of deliverance. Zechariah sings of the Savior that will fulfill God's promise "that we would be saved from our enemies and from the hand of all who hate us" (Luke 1:71). In 2 Timothy 1:10, the Savior frees us from death, "but it [God's grace] has now been revealed through the appearing of our Savior Christ Jesus, who abolished death and brought life and immortality to light through the gospel." In a few instances, salvation is linked with forgiveness of sin. The angel who appears to Joseph in a dream announces to him, "You are to name him Jesus, for he will save his people from their sins" (Matt 1:21). Zechariah speaks of the child who will "give knowledge of salvation" to God's people "by the forgiveness of their sins" (Luke 1:77). In the episode of the woman who lavishes love on Jesus after having been forgiven, Jesus tells her, "Your faith has saved you, go in peace" (7:50). In Acts of the Apostles, Peter testifies before the council, "God exalted him at his right hand as Leader and Savior that he might give repentance to Israel and forgiveness of sins" (Acts 5:31).[46] While salvation is almost always spoken of as something that God accomplishes through Jesus, Paul speaks to the Corinthians about their part in experiencing godly grief that "produces a repentance that leads to salvation" (2 Cor 7:10). The Fourth Evangelist also has in view the part that believers play in effecting salvation when Jesus says, "I am the gate. Whoever enters by me will be saved" (John 10:9). In a few instances, endurance on the part of believers is saving. Speaking of the end times, Jesus tells his disciples, "The one who endures to the end will be saved" (Mark 13:13; similarly Matt 10:22; 24:13).[47]

STUMBLING BLOCKS TO RECONCILIATION

Having investigated the meaning and function of forgiveness, reconciliation, and salvation in the New Testament, we turn now to examine some of the obstacles to such processes. In the previous sections, we signaled the danger posed by endless offers of forgiveness that can feed cycles of violence. A number of other stumbling blocks or misconceptions about the dynamics in reconciliation processes can keep victimized or abused persons from moving toward healing and wholeness.

The Difficulty of Forgiveness

One stumbling block is that forgiveness, reconciliation, and healing are usually lengthy processes; they are rarely accomplished instantaneously. One image of the crucified Christ that seems to counter this assertion is that of the Lucan Jesus who, even in the midst of excruciating pain on the cross, already forgives his executioners, praying: "Father, forgive them, for they do not know what they are doing" (Luke 23:34). For victims of violence who are struggling to forgive and who want to follow Jesus' command to forgive but cannot yet bring themselves to do so, this is an image that only increases their pain and guilt. It may be far more helpful to see in this scene not a Jesus who is able to offer forgiveness instantaneously, but rather one who turns to God in prayer, asking for the God-given ability to forgive. Knowing that forgiveness is a gift from God and is not solely dependent on human ability to achieve it, he prays that God will grant it to him once again. He has shown and taught his disciples that it takes practice to do what is counterintuitive; that is, consciously to choose not to return insult for injury but to turn instead toward mending the breach with acts of forgiveness.

This kind of approach is not doormat spirituality—an attitude of resignation that accepts insult and injury and letting others walk all over you—but quite the contrary. In the Sermon on the Mount, when Jesus instructs his disciples to "turn the other cheek" (Matt 5:39), he is teaching them a way to confront an aggressor with a nonviolent response that aims to disarm the perpetrator by not retaliating in kind.[48] Jesus' admonition in verse 39 is often mistaken to mean that disciples are to ignore or walk away from abuse. Translations such as, "Do not resist (*mē antistēnai*) an evildoer" (*NRSV*), or, "Offer no resistance to one who is evil" (*NAB*), are misleading. The verb *anthistēmi* in verse 39 means, "to set oneself against, oppose, resist, withstand."[49] A command not to resist evil or an evildoer makes little sense on the lips of Jesus when the whole Gospel shows him doing just the opposite.[50] Christian tradition is replete with admonitions to oppose or withstand evil. The issue is *how* the disciple is to confront evil.[51] From this context, the sense of *mē antistēnai* is, "do not retaliate in kind."[52]

Jesus then gives a series of concrete examples of how, in situations of unequal power and status, injured persons can break the cycle of violence by actively confronting the perpetrator of the injustice with a positive and provocative nonviolent act. One who is humiliated with a backhanded slap (a blow to the right cheek, in a right-handed culture, Matt 5:39) is expected to cower in submission. Instead, turning the other cheek signals to the aggressor that, if he is to strike again, it will be an open-handed slap, a move that would recognize the victim as having equal status. Such a move destabilizes the situation and opens up a new space for the possibility of repentance and reconciliation. Or one who is brought before the court by a creditor who demands the very cloak off his back should give his underwear as well (Luke 6:29). To view another's nakedness is a shameful thing (see Gen 9:20-29). Stripping naked in front of all puts the onus on those looking on another's nakedness. It exposes the injustice of a system that would so strip the poorest of the poor and possibly shock those who participate in this system into moving toward dismantling it. Offering to carry the pack of a soldier from the occupying army one more mile when there were strictures against such action places the soldier in the ridiculous position of begging for his pack to be returned (Matt 5:41). Again, the unexpected act on the part of the victim is a way of confronting the abuse of an aggressor without retaliating with the aggressor's violent tactics. In this way, victims retrieve their own honor and open the possibility for new kinds of exchanges that move toward achieving right relation. The examples Jesus gives are meant to spark the imagination of disciples to find creative ways to stop cycles of violence by taking action to stop the abuse, while refusing to respond in kind with more violence.

The episode of the healing of a man who was paralyzed (Matt 9:2-8) brings to the fore the question of how difficult it is to forgive. Jesus' query, "Which is easier to say, 'Your sins are forgiven,' or to say 'Stand up and walk'?" (v. 5), points out that neither is easy and that the ability to walk freely is intimately tied to the ability to receive and offer forgiveness. Ironically, it is often much easier to cling to hurts inflicted by others than to enter into a process of forgiveness and reconciliation.

Truthtelling and Remembering

There is a popular maxim "forgive and forget." This is far from a gospel approach to forgiveness. Forgiveness does not obliterate the harm done, nor does it make light of its effects on the victim. What forgiveness and reconciliation processes do is to help the victim move toward a healing of memory so that the trauma does not keep them trapped in the pain. It is a matter of remembering, but remembering in a different way. In the Last Supper account in Luke's Gospel, Jesus stresses the need to remember, as he offers his disciples the bread, "This is my body, which is given for you. Do this in remembrance of me" (Luke 22:19). So, also, after the crucifixion, the disciples are not told to forget what happened to Jesus and to move on with their lives. In the Gospel of Luke, the two angelic figures tell the women at the tomb to remember what Jesus told them, and they do (Luke 24:6-8).

The Truth and Reconciliation Commission that investigated the atrocities committed in Peru from 1980 to 2000 has used as a slogan, "A country that forgets its history is condemned to repeat it."[53] One of the powerful tools they have developed for truthtelling and the healing of memories is a photo exhibit that shows the beginning of the violence in 1980–82, its gradual growth until 1989, and then the offensive launched in Lima in 1989 by the guerillas of the *Sendero Luminoso* ("Shining Path"). For many indigenous people, knowledge is first obtained visually. An exhibition of two hundred photographs entitled "Yuynapac: To Remember" took place in Lima from August 9 until December 9, 2003. Similar exhibitions were held in Ayacucho, Huánuco, Abancay, and Cuzco. Recovering the memory is a key part of the process of healing toward reconciliation and constructing a new future.[54]

Closely related to the notion of remembering and healing of memory is the importance of telling the truth about trauma. This is an essential ingredient in the work of Truth and Reconciliation Commissions in nations that have been torn apart by strife or in international situations of conflict. It is important that what happened and who was responsible be told truthfully and publicly. Oftentimes, women are reluctant to speak the truth of their own pain and they testify more easily to the suffering of others. The Truth and Reconciliation Commission in Peru[55] that investigated the atrocities of the 1980s and 1990s reported in March 2003 that, of the 15,220 persons who had testified, 75 percent of them were women. However, only 20 percent of the atrocities they detailed were of women victims. The women tended to recount, instead, what had happened to the rest of the family—to their husbands, sons, and brothers—but not the violations they themselves had suffered. Rape and sexual abuse of women was a constant but was never the prime story the women told. It was more the background music to the other crimes the women reported. Direct reporting of incidents of rape of women makes up only 3 percent of the denunciations.[56] There is a deeper truth that needs to be unmasked even in the work of a commission dedicated to uncovering the truth.

Another discovery of the Truth and Reconciliation Commission in Peru was that, when women would visit their imprisoned husbands or sons, they would often be subjected to manhandling and derision from the guards. The guards would taunt the women with accusations of blame: all the problems that their husbands and sons were experiencing, they were told, were their fault. If their husbands or sons were incarcerated or missing, it was the women's fault for having neglected their duties as good wives and mothers toward the men of their household. One woman tells how, after she had been detained and raped while looking for her missing husband, she took her children and fled for her life through the jungle, knowing they would be killed if they stayed in their village. During their flight, she had nothing with which to feed her

children. After all the trauma she had experienced, she arrived in a city, where she took her children to a hospital. The doctor there scolded her for being a "bad mother" because her children were suffering from malnutrition.[57] The truth of who was responsible for the suffering of this woman and her family was masked by deeply ingrained sexism and by the prevalent attitude that women must bear the blame for everything that befalls them and their families. Arriving at the truth is an arduous process but, as the Johannine Jesus asserts, it is the truth that frees (John 8:32).

In breaking cycles of domestic violence, it is also important to separate myth from fact. One of the prevalent myths is that batterers lose control and that they cannot help but behave violently. The truth is that abusers choose to use calculated tactics to control their partners to get what they want. Moreover, battering is a learned behavior that batterers can change, but they will not change unless they are held accountable. Another common myth is that women provoke their partners to use violence. The truth is that women do not cause the abuse. The batterer is the one who is responsible for his abusive behavior.[58] Many of the myths that allow domestic abuse to continue are also reinforced by cultural stereotypes that support male domination. Truth telling aimed at ending domestic violence includes education about the cycles of violence as well as about equality and dignity for women.

In the Fourth Gospel, when the risen Christ appears to Thomas, he insists that he look at and even touch his wounds. Resurrection does not obliterate the facts of the violence done to

Jesus, just as reconciliation does not mean that the harm inflicted no longer matters. The wounded Jesus continues to invite believers to confront the truth about any way in which they are complicit in any unjust systems and cycles of victimization. Jesus' insistence during his interrogation by Pilate on telling the truth (John 19:37) and Pilate's ironic utterance, "What is truth?" (John 19:38), underscore both the necessity and the difficulty in speaking truth. In Jesus, we have a model for truthful speaking, with his oft-repeated phrase, "Truly I tell you."[59]

Utopian Dream

Many consider the ideals depicted in the gospels about nonviolent confrontation, forgiveness, and reconciliation processes to be a "utopian dream harbored by the unrealistic."[60] Yet, countless contemporary examples of conflict transformation prove otherwise. Forgiveness processes are applicable not only in interpersonal conflicts, but they are also key to bringing about true reconciliation and peace within fractured communities and between nations. In postapartheid South Africa, for example, it is widely recognized that when blacks, under the leadership of Nelson Mandela, decided not to do unto whites what had been done unto them, a bloodbath was averted. As Desmond Tutu explained in his book *No Future without Forgiveness*, if black leaders had chosen to bring white abusers to trial rather than enter into a process of truth telling, forgiveness, and reconciliation, they could only have had justice and a South Africa "lying in ashes—a truly Phyrrhic victory if there ever was one."[61]

There is no one model to follow. As R. Scott Appleby has observed, "What is needed in each and every case, rather, is local cultural analysis wedded to political insight."[62] But there are common elements key to processes of forgiveness that lead to conflict transformation. In addition to truth telling, to which we have already referred, there must also be empathy, forbearance, and the commitment to repair fractured relationships.[63]

Empathy, not to be confused with sympathy, is grounded on the recognition that the victim and the perpetrator share a common humanity and that the enemy is more than just the enemy.[64] In the fourth year of the U.S.-led war in Iraq, Cardinal Francis George of Chicago observed that the world distrusts the United

States because "we are deaf and blind, because too often we don't understand and make no effort to understand; because we know what is best."[65] This proclivity, he said, must be surrendered, "or we will never be part of God's kingdom." Likewise, Jesus frequently exhorts his disciples to listen,[66] as does the heavenly voice at the Transfiguration (Matt 17:5 and pars.). Jesus laments the hardness of heart on the part of those who refuse to hear (13:13-15) and underscores the necessity of listening in the work of reconciliation within communities (18:17).

Forbearance, the willingness to forego responding to violence with more violence, is crucial to reconciliation processes. In the passion narratives, it is exemplified by Jesus at Gethsemane when he stops his disciples from striking the arresting party with a sword. In Matthew's Gospel, Jesus admonishes, "All who take the sword will perish by the sword" (26:52). This is not an isolated statement, but it is the climax to Jesus' consistent message from the Sermon on the Mount forward not to retaliate in kind to an evildoer.

Finally, for genuine peace, there must be a commitment to work toward repair of the fractured relationship. This means moving away from a desire to eliminate the enemy, or even icy tolerance or uneasy coexistence, toward real engagement with the other. The Matthean Jesus not only teaches his followers to avoid insulting one another and becoming angry with one another, but he also insists on face-to-face reconciliation when they have grievances (Matt 5:21-24; 18:15-20). Moreover, when there is litigation, he would have his disciples not simply resolve it and go their separate ways but "make friends" with or "think kindly" of their accuser (5:25). Jesus' practice of eating with alienated people[67] symbolizes the necessity of sharing life together in reconciled relationship.

HEALED HEALERS

The gospels are replete with stories of Jesus healing, exorcising, forgiving, and bringing wounded people to wholeness.[68] In the synoptic Gospels, Jesus commissions his disciples to heal the sick, cure diseases, cast out unclean spirits, and raise the dead (Matt 10:8; Mark 6:7; Luke 9:1-6; 10:9), as he himself does. There are no detailed narratives of them doing so, only the brief notice,

"So they went out and proclaimed that all should repent. They cast out many demons, and anointed with oil many who were sick and cured them" (Mark 6:12-13; similarly Luke 9:6; 10:17). There is also the episode in which they were unable to cast out a demon from a boy with epilepsy (Matt 17:14-20 // Mark 9:14-29 // Luke 9:37-43). There are no stories in the New Testament in which women disciples are expressly said to be agents of healing, forgiveness, and reconciliation. In Acts of the Apostles, it is primarily Peter and Paul who are shown emulating Jesus' healing deeds. Peter and John heal a man crippled from birth (Acts 3:1-10), as does Paul (14:8-10). Peter and the apostles cure all those from the towns around Jerusalem who were sick and tormented by demons (Acts 5:12-16). Philip cures many who had unclean spirits or were paralyzed or lame in Samaria (Acts 8:7). In Joppa, Peter heals Aeneas, who had suffered from paralysis for eight years (Acts 9:32-35). In Philippi, Paul casts out an oracular spirit from a slave girl (Acts 16:18). In Ephesus, handkerchiefs that touched Paul's skin were able to heal the sick and those with evil spirits (Acts 19:12). In Malta, Paul cured the father of Publius, who lay sick in bed with fever and dysentery (Acts 28:8). Afterward, the rest of the people on the island who had diseases came, and Paul cured them as well (Acts 28:9).

In the Gospel of Luke, Jesus' final commission to the disciples is to proclaim repentance for forgiveness of sins in his name to all nations, beginning from Jerusalem (24:47). Only Peter and Paul are depicted as doing such in the Acts of the Apostles. In his Pentecost speech, Peter invites people to repentance and forgiveness (Acts 2:38). He does the same in Samaria with Simon the magician (8:22). In his speeches to the Sanhedrin (5:31) and to Cornelius (10:43), Peter speaks of the forgiveness of sins through Jesus. Similarly, Paul preaches forgiveness of sins in his address in the synagogue at Antioch in Pisidia (13:38) and in his speech to King Agrippa (26:18).

While no women in the New Testament are explicitly said to be agents of healing and forgiveness, we can surmise that they were, indeed, among those who carried on Jesus' mission to bring wholeness and wellbeing to others. A number of women in the Gospels are said to have been healed by Jesus, and then responded by ministering (*diakonein*).[69] While the specifics of their ministries are not usually spelled out, it is not hard to imagine that, having experienced forgiveness and/or healing, they become agents of healing for others. In many traditional cultures yet today, it is the women who are particularly skilled in the healing arts. In Chiapas, for example, indigenous women are working collectively to recover their knowledge of local herbs and to reclaim their role and art as healers, which they have exercised in their communities for tens of thousands of years.[70] During the conflicts between the Zapatistas and the Mexican government, many women refused to flee their homes and convinced their husbands to remain, partly because the women knew all the medicinal qualities of the local plants and herbs. What would they do in a strange land without these?[71]

Simon's Mother-in-Law (Matt 8:14-15)

The story of Jesus' healing of Simon's mother-in-law is recounted in all three synoptic Gospels, with slight variations.[72] In each of the accounts, the primary focus of the evangelist is the power of Jesus. Luke, in particular, puts the spotlight on Jesus as healer by intensifying the seriousness of the fever and the immediacy of the cure. Simon's mother-in-law remains a shadowy figure. We do not know her name. We do not hear her voice. She does not speak for herself about her suffering; the others tell Jesus of her plight. Likely, she is a widow, as she resides in the home of her son-in-law.[73]

There is an additional clue to the identity of Simon's mother-in-law as a disciple in Matthew's account, where there are discernible traces of a call story.[74] Matthew's version (8:14-15) is briefer than the other two and is missing some of the standard elements of a healing miracle. When compared to the call of Matthew (Matt 9:9), we find the same elements. In both stories, Jesus takes the initiative; he sees (*eiden*) the one to be called (8:14; 9:9). Then there is a description of the person: Matthew is sitting at the tax booth (9:9); Simon's mother-in-law is lying in bed with a fever (8:14). This is followed by a word or action by Jesus: "Follow me," (9:9); "he touched her hand" (8:15). The story concludes with the response of the one called: "he got up (*anastas*) and followed him (*autō*)" (9:9); "she got up (*ēgerthē*) and began to serve (*diēkonei*) him (*autō*)" (8:15). In the Gospel of Matthew, the story has the form of a call story with a healing motif; Mark and Matthew convert it to a healing story. It is most probable that the tradition that preserves the call of Simon's mother-in-law to discipleship was conserved in circles of women disciples.

It is significant that, in Matthew's version, the response of Simon's mother-in-law is directed to Jesus himself (*autō,* "him," is singular), in contrast to Mark and Luke, where her response is to "them" (*autois,* Mark 1:31; Luke 4:39). The first response to a call to discipleship is to Jesus himself; this response is then manifest in service toward others. As we explored earlier, the verb *diakonein* connotes many different kinds of ministry. As her response to a call to discipleship, Simon's mother-in-law's "serving" should be understood in ministerial terms, not as domestic table service. Did she preach, teach, or evangelize in a *diakonia* of the word? Did she oversee the *diakonia* of the table when the community gathered for Eucharist in her and Peter's home? Did she, like Mary Magdalene, Joanna, and Susanna, have monetary resources from which she exercised her *diakonia*? Answers to these questions are not available to us from the scant evidence we have of her. But whatever her ministry entailed, we might also remember her as one whose call was accompanied by healing and envision her as ministering from that healing in ways that lifted burdens and brought wellbeing to others in the community. Like Jesus, her resurrection[75] brings wholeness and peace to others.[76]

Mary Magdalene (Luke 8:1-3)

All four Gospels agree that Mary Magdalene witnessed Jesus' crucifixion and was the first to find the tomb empty. Only Luke introduces Mary earlier in the narrative, although the other evangelists indicate that she and the other women[77] had been following and ministering all along (Mark 15:41; Matt 27:55). The verb *akoloutheō,* "to follow," is the response of disciples when called by Jesus, as in the case of Simon, Andrew, James, John (Mark 1:160-20 // Matt 4:18-22 // Luke 5:1-11), and Levi (Mark 2:13-14 // Luke 5:27-32) or Matthew (Matt 9:9-13). The verb is in the imperfect tense, indicating customary action beginning in the past.

Luke recounts that, in the midst of the Galilean ministry, as Jesus is proclaiming the good news through cities and villages along with the Twelve, there were also "women who had been cured of evil spirits and infirmities" who accompanied him (Luke 8:2). Luke gives their names and a few other details: "Mary, called Magdalene, from whom seven demons had gone out, and Joanna, the wife of Herod's steward, Chuza, and Susanna, and many others, who provided for them out of their resources" (8:2-3). Much is left to the imagination about these women. Were others besides Joanna married? Were they widows? Did they have children? Did they go about with Jesus for days on end, or were they day trips that allowed them to return home at night? Were others scandalized by this?[78] From where did their money come? The text does not say.

Mary Magdalene is always named first in the lists of Galilean women disciples, indicating her prominence in the early Christian communities. She is identified by the place from which she comes, nor as the wife, daughter, or mother of a significant male, as is often the case with biblical women. Magdala was an important fishing village. Its name derives from *migdal*, the Hebrew word for "tower." In the Talmud, the town is referred to as *Migdal Nunya*, "Tower of Fish." Josephus calls it by its Greek name, *Tarichaea*, meaning "place where the fish are salted." In Roman times, the city was known for its export of salted fish. Perhaps Mary's money came from her work in this industry. It is not only in modern times that women worked at a trade. We have the example of Lydia, who was a dealer in purple goods (Acts 16:14), and of Prisca, who worked alongside her husband, Aquila, in tent making and leather working (Acts 18:3). Or, if she had no brothers, Mary might have inherited money and property from her father (Num 27:8). It may be that, just as Jesus called male disciples who were fisherfolk, so too, he encountered Mary in that trade when he invited her to follow him.

Although all the synoptic evangelists note that Mary and the other women had been "ministering" or "providing for" Jesus (*diēkonoun*, Mark 15:41; *diakonousai*, Matt 27:55), only Luke specifies that the ministry they exercised was financial. They were not doing domestic chores, as some imagine,[79] but "provided for them out of their resources (*hyparchontōn autais*)." In Luke and Acts, *hyparchontōn* always refers to monetary resources, possessions, property, or goods.[80] The money belongs to the women, as the feminine plural possessive pronoun *autais*, "their," indicates. The women are not simply administering the common purse, as Judas is said to do in John 12:6. Since Jesus does not seem to work any longer at his trade once he begins his itinerant ministry and since his family does not seem to support him (Mark 3:21, 31-33), it would be crucial to gain patrons who would bankroll the mission.[81]

Another detail that Luke supplies about Mary Magdalene is that she and other women had been cured of evil spirits and infirmities. Mary's case was particularly severe: "seven demons had gone out of her" (8:2), seven being symbolic for a full number.[82] It is not specified who did the exorcising, but from their response directed toward Jesus and his companions, we can surmise that it was Jesus who freed the women from their infirmities. On the one hand, this detail serves to highlight the power of Jesus, as when Luke increases the severity of the fever of Simon's mother-in-law. But the claim that Mary had been possessed by demons may also reflect the way she was labeled by those who wanted to undermine her authority in the early church.[83] Just as Jesus' opponents tried to subvert his credibility by charging that he was demon-possessed (Mark 3:22; John 7:20; 8:48; 10:20), so Mary Magdalene's influence did not go unchallenged.

Another way to undermine Mary's authority is to imagine the nature of her demon-possession as sexual. Many Christians still think that Mary Magdalene was a prostitute, although there is not a shred of evidence for this in the New Testament. She is nowhere said to be even a sinner. She is popularly confused with the nameless woman caught in adultery (John 7:53—8:11); the nameless woman who had been forgiven her sins who anoints Jesus' feet (Luke 7:36-50); Mary of Bethany, who anoints Jesus for burial (John 12:1-12); or Mary of Egypt, whose story is not from the New Testament but from seventh-century legends.[84] The confusion was fueled by an Easter homily by Pope Gregory the Great in 597 C.E., when he conflated the biblical Marys and identified them all as Mary Magdalene.

We have also seen that Mary would have exercised power through her financial backing for Jesus and his movement. In chapter three, we explored Mary's prophetic ministry of proclamation and evangelizing. We can also imagine that Mary

Magdalene and the other women who were healed became agents of healing to others who were sick or in pain. From what they themselves had suffered, they would have been sensitive to others who were in pain and would have been intent on bringing them release from anything that held them bound. When we encounter these women at the foot of the cross (Mark 15:40-41; Matt 27:55; Luke 23:49; John 19:25-27), they not only are watching so as to give testimony concerning Jesus' death, but they also stand in solidarity with Jesus the victim in his agony, bringing a healing and loving presence. Powerless to stop the execution, they nonetheless refuse to abandon their friend, soothing him with the healing balm of their love and God's, even as they do not know how God will accomplish wellbeing and wholeness through this torturous death. When they go to the tomb to anoint his body with spices (Mark 16:1; Luke 24:1), their intention is to continue their healing ministrations toward him. The healing circle is completed when the risen Christ mends their broken hearts with the peace and joy of their experience of him alive (Luke 24:36, 41; John 20:19, 21, 26) and his commission to them to continue extending that *shalôm* to all (Matt 28:19-20; Mark 16:15-18; Luke 24:47-49; John 20:21-23; 21:15-19).

Tabitha: Resurrected Life-Giver (Acts 9:36-43)

Each of the gospels has stories of Jesus restoring a dead person to life. The most extended narrative is the raising of Lazarus in John 11:1-44. Luke tells of the resuscitation of the widow's son at Nain (Luke 7:11-17). The synoptic evangelists preserve an account of Jesus raising the daughter of Jairus (Matt 9:18-19, 23-26; Mark 5:21-24, 35-43; Luke 8:41-42, 49-56). In the Acts of the Apostles, Peter restores Tabitha to life (9:39-41), as does Paul, for a young man named Eutychus who fell from an upper-story window after falling asleep during Paul's lengthy preaching (Acts 20:9-12). There are no narratives of women disciples raising others from the dead. However, the story of Tabitha makes

"There is a lot of machismo in the church. The sermons of the priests are so dry. Why couldn't women be priests, even Pope? Then women could transform the whole world with their love."

—Sara, El Alto, Bolivia
24 March, 2003

it clear that she not only was a recipient of restored life, but she also raised up others through her vivifying ministry.[85]

Tabitha is introduced in Acts 9:36 as a "disciple," *mathētria*, the only time in the New Testament that this title is attached to a single individual. *Disciple* literally means "one taught," "pupil."[86] That the term is given to her indicates that the community recognizes that she is schooled in the ways of Jesus. From what Jesus says of disciples, we can surmise that she is "like the teacher" (Luke 6:40), is willing to place the demands of the mission over family relationships (14:26), and accepts the suffering that accompanies discipleship (14:27). She is willing to place her possessions at the service of the community (14:33) and is schooled in ways of forgiveness (17:3). The description of her in Acts 9:37 confirms this: "She was devoted to good works (*plērēs ergōn agathōn*) and acts of charity (*eleēmosynōn hōn epoiei*)."

Tabitha is depicted as a woman who, like Mary Magdalene and the Galilean women (Luke 8:2-3), uses her financial resources to advance the mission.[87] Tabitha opens her home to house widows devoted to ministry.[88] The widows are not professional mourners but are Tabitha's companions in weaving cloth and sewing garments.[89] Whether this clothing was given away to those in need or sold to sustain the work of the community, the text does not say. Like Lydia, who also worked with textiles (Acts 16), Tabitha is depicted as a leader of a house church.[90] The urgency with which the disciples plead for Peter to come to Lydda from Joppa when Tabitha falls ill and dies indicates her importance to the whole community. That Tabitha's resuscitation takes place in an upper room in a house recalls that the community in Jerusalem also was gathered in an upper room when they were resuscitated from their grief and fear by the life-giving Spirit at Pentecost (Acts 1:13). It is also the place where disciples were gathered in Troas when the youngster Eutychus fell out of the window and was brought back to life by Paul (20:8). The

> "To struggle for the liberation of women is to struggle for the liberation of the whole people. Women work not only for their own liberation, but for that of her children, her people, her world."
>
> —Adelaida, Centro Bartolomé de las Casas, Lima, Peru 10 April, 2003

community of believers, gathering as house churches, are finding God's healing, restorative, and life-giving gifts manifest therein.[91]

Tabitha's ministry is described first as "good works," an expression that occurs frequently in the New Testament.[92] This is a "comprehensive concept within which all acts of love and mercy are subsumed."[93] Similarly, the "acts of charity" (*eleēmosynōn*) refer to a wide range of loving deeds. The term *eleēmosynē* is sometimes translated as "almsgiving" (see *NAB*). The term, however, does not connote handing out leftover crumbs or giving out of one's abundance, but rather giving all of whatever one has for the restoration of right relation. Disciples who exercise goodness and mercy (*eleos*), as does Tabitha, mirror and make present God's very self, as these are two of the most frequently highlighted attributes of God (Luke 6:35-36).

We can also surmise that Tabitha's ministry has a healing dimension. In the account of the man with a withered hand whom Jesus healed on a Sabbath, the phrase "to do good" (*agathon poiēsai*) refers to Jesus' healing work. Jesus confronts his accusers: "Is it lawful to do good (*agathon poiēsai*) or to harm on the sabbath, to save life or to kill?" (Mark 3:4; Luke 6:9). The good that Tabitha does may well have included such healing. In addition, the term *eleēmosynē* can also imply healing. In the story of the man who was crippled and begging at the Beautiful Gate (Acts 3:1-10), what he asks of Peter and John is *eleēmosynē* (3:3). He then fixes his eyes on them, "expecting to receive something from them" (3:4). When Peter responds that he has no silver or gold to give him and then raises him up (*ēgeiren*) with healing power, it is not that he has substituted a healing for the desired money. Rather, *eleēmosynē* encompasses all deeds, including healing, that manifest God's gracious, merciful love. In like manner, when Peter raises up Tabitha, he restores her to the healing, vivifying ministries by which she has been known and through which God continues to bring all to life and wholeness.

CONTEMPORARY RECONCILERS

Las Abejas

In addition to the witness of the biblical women, there are numerous contemporary examples of women whose ministries bring healing, forgiveness, and wholeness to their communities and beyond. One such community is that of Las Abejas, in the town of Acteal, Chiapas. They name themselves "the bees" to indicate that all are equal, as worker bees, with the reign of God as their queen bee.[94] They are a community of women and men who agree with the aims of the Zapatista movement, but they do not agree in taking up arms to achieve the desired goals. On December 22, 1997, members of Las Abejas were in their third day of praying and fasting for peace. They were gathered in their little wooden chapel, when forty-five of them, mostly women and children, were murdered by paramilitaries. When our group met with the governing council of Las Abejas on January 16, 2005, one companion asked, "Weren't you tempted to give up your commitment to nonviolence after the massacre of your beloved mothers and daughters and fathers and brothers?" The leader, Sebastian, a handsome young lawyer, responded honestly that, indeed, some had parted ways with them after the massacre, but most had stayed. He said, "There is no other way; Jesus told us we have to love our enemies and pray for them, and so we continue to do."[95] And indeed, they do continue the difficult work of nonviolent action toward dismantling the structures of injustice that bind their lives.

"I Have No Enemies"

Such an attitude was fostered by Don Samuel Ruiz, bishop of San Cristóbal de las Casas from 1960 until 2000. He tells of how he was converted by the indigenous peoples, the majority of whom are poor and make up 80 percent of the diocese.[96] They led him to commit himself and all those who ministered in the diocese to give preferential treatment to the poor. In the process of defending the rights of the poor and in trying to mediate the conflict between the Zapatistas and the Mexican government, he received many death threats. In an interview on January 9, 2005, I asked him how he had come to live so clearly the command to love our enemies when he had so many of them. He looked at me, puzzled, and said, "I don't have any enemies." Now it was my turn to be puzzled, for he had arrived at our meeting in a bulletproof van with three beefy, armed bodyguards supplied by the Mexican government, which does not want another martyred bishop on its hands! He continued, "There are those who want to make themselves enemy to me, but I have no enemies." "Love your enemies" (Matt 5:44) takes on a whole new meaning when one considers how to act with love and integrity in ways that dismantle any attempt of others to make themselves enemy to you.

Rosario and María

It was in the middle of the night on January 18, 1988, when five military men broke into the house of María Pisco Pizango, who was sleeping uneasily with her mother- and father-in-law and her three youngest daughters, Anilsa (age 8), Rosario (age 6), and María (age 4). María was not surprised. For some ten days, she had been searching for her husband, Pablo, who had been missing, and now they had come for her. They tortured, raped, and killed María, while her in-laws were tied and gagged and the young girls cowered beside them in terror. The three girls were separated after that. Rosario stayed with her maternal grandparents; Anilsa and little María went to live with her paternal grandparents. Eventually, little María was sent to Lima, because of an outbreak of poliomyelitis. Her godmother eventually took her to live in Emmanuel House. After fourteen years of separation, it was thanks to the testimony that Rosario gave to the Truth and Reconciliation Commission that the girls were reunited. María, the youngest, had no recollection of the murder of her parents and thought she had been abandoned by them. Nor did she have any memory of her sister Rosario; she thought she had only one sister, Anilsa, and that she had died. Only after knowing the truth were they able to begin the journey toward healing and reconstruction of their lives.[97]

> "The major preoccupation here is the dehumanizing poverty that limits and impedes the advancement of women. Everything falls on the woman, who suffers double oppression for being poor and a woman."
>
> —Adelaida, Centro Bartolomé de las Casas, Lima Peru
> 10 April, 2003

CONCLUSION

In this chapter, we have examined some of the texts that associate healing, salvation, forgiveness, and reconciliation with the death of Jesus. We have elaborated how this wellbeing comes, not only, nor even primarily, from the death of Jesus, but rather from the whole of Jesus' life and mission, which was permeated with his offer of *shālôm*. Forgiveness, healing, and reconciliation are complex, difficult, and often very lengthy processes. These are ultimately not achieved by human effort but are gifts from God. New Testament stories of women, such as Simon's mother-in-law, Mary Magdalene, and Tabitha, who were healed and restored to life and who then minister to others from their wellbeing, give hope and courage to contemporary believers. Movements toward peace building, such as the Truth and Reconciliation Commission in Peru, aid in the healing of a fractured nation. Leaders such as Don Samuel Ruiz in San Cristóbal de las Casas and Las Abejas in Acteal continue to give witness that such a way of life is not just a utopian ideal, but is possible to taste, even now.

In the next chapter, we take up the image of Jesus' death as a birth to new life. We will focus primarily on the Fourth Gospel, which is particularly rich with this symbol. Experiences of contemporary women will be woven together with images of the mother of Jesus and Jesus as mother.

CHAPTER FIVE

Birthing New Life

As ONE DEEPENS IN THE spiritual life, one's images of God and Jesus change, reflecting inner transformation and outward expression in self-gift toward others. Many women find that traditional images of God, Jesus, and Mary are no longer adequate and that many are, in fact, dangerous in the ways that they serve patriarchal interests. There is a particularly rich lode of images and symbols in the Fourth Gospel. Prominent are language and imagery of birthing and mothering, which we explore in this chapter, particularly in relation to the mother of Jesus and divine mothering expressed in Jesus.

In the Gospel of John, unique details in the scene of Jesus' crucifixion open up a distinct image of his death as a portal to new life. Only in the Gospel of John is there the detail of a soldier who pierces with a spear the side of the dead Jesus. From Jesus' opened side flow blood and water (19:34), the same liquids that flow from an open womb and accompany the birth of a child. Distinctive to this Gospel is also the presence of Jesus' own mother at the foot of the cross (19:25). The one who gave him physical birth and who was midwife for the birth of his public ministry (2:1-11) now witnesses his death as the culmination of his life-giving earthly ministry and the birth canal toward life eternal for all. Birthing imagery does not appear for the first time in the crucifixion scene but is

> "Twenty-two years ago when I first gave birth, I had a caesarian section. My arms were strapped to boards that went straight out to stabilize the IV's and made me immediately aware of being in the 'crucifix' position. When the cut was made, much water and blood poured out and because of how it lowered my blood pressure, I lost consciousness. When I revived the words came in my head, 'My body given up for you.' It was a mystical and powerful experience."
> —Marcia, Grand Rapids, Michigan[1]

woven throughout the whole of the Fourth Gospel, beginning with the prologue.[2] We will examine key passages that prepare for the climactic scene that depicts Jesus as birthing a renewed people of God through his death.

THE BIRTHING OF CREATION AND OF CHILDREN OF GOD (JOHN 1:3-4, 12-13)

From the opening lines of the Gospel of John, it is stressed that Jesus' purpose is to birth life for all. The prologue says of the *Logos* that "all things came into being through him" and "what has come into being in him was life, and the life was the light of all people" (1:3-4). In these verses, the verb *ginomai* is used to express that life and all things "come into being." By contrast, a distinctly maternal verb is used in verse 13: "To all who received him, who believed in his name, he gave power to become children of God, who were born (*egennēthēsan*) not of blood or of the will of the flesh, or of the will of man,[3] but of God" (1:12-13). These verses focus attention on the birthing of God's children through their faith in the *Logos*, using the verb *gennaō*, "to give birth, to beget." This verb is used both of women giving birth (John 16:21) and of male begetting (Matt 1:2-20),[4] but in the Fourth Gospel it evokes primarily the female imagery of birthing[5] and is a distinctive way this evangelist expresses the relationship between God and God's children.[6]

What John 1:13 emphasizes is that the birthing of God's children comes about through divine action. The evangelist contrasts this manner of birthing with that of human procreation, which comes about through mixing of woman's "blood" with man's seed, through carnal desire and man's initiative. "Not of blood" in 1:13 likely refers to the belief in antiquity that conception occurs through the mingling of woman's blood with male seed.[7] The "will of the flesh" refers to human desire. "Flesh," *sarx*, does not connote here a wicked principle opposed to God but simply the earthly, carnal aspect of existence.[8] This is clear when, in the next verse, the hymn reaches its high point,

> "Jesus is present in everything that has life."
>
> —Marina, El Alto, Bolivia
> 27 March, 2003

asserting that the *Logos* became *sarx:* "the Word became flesh and lived among us" (1:14). The third phrase in 1:13, "the will of man," refers to the notion in antiquity that the male was the primary agent in human procreation. Sexual activity was by his initiative, and woman was thought to be only the vessel for the embryo. Birthing by God is by a different means. One of the curious details in John 1:13 is that "blood," *haimatōn*, is plural. In Hebrew, the plural *dāmîm* means "bloodshed." Taken in this sense, there is a link created between 1:13 and 19:34, where the blood shed at the death of Jesus is a new act of divine birthing.

THE BIRTH OF JESUS' PUBLIC MINISTRY (JOHN 2:1-11)

Another frame that encapsulates the metaphor of birthing arches from the wedding at Cana (2:1-12) to the crucifixion (19:25-34). These two scenes involve Jesus' mother—the only two scenes in which she in John appears—and are unique to the Fourth Gospel. She remains nameless, as does the Beloved Disciple. Just as the anonymity of the Beloved Disciple functions to allow any disciple to insert herself or himself into the role of the one who loves and is most loved by Jesus, so, too, the namelessness of Jesus' mother allows every disciple to enter into the task of birthing Christ in the world.[9] The Fourth Gospel focuses not on the unique role of Jesus' mother in giving him physical birth, but on the way in which she is midwife to the birthing of his public ministry and is witness to the birthing of new life through his death.

The verbal and thematic links between the Cana story and the crucifixion are often noted. Jesus addresses his mother as "Woman," *gynai*, in both scenes (John 2:4; 19:26).[10] In both episodes, water plays a symbolic role: the water in the jars that becomes wine (2:6-7), and the water that flows from the side of Jesus (19:34).[11] There is reference in both scenes to the "hour," *hōra* (2:4; 19:27). The first occurrence of this theologically charged word is at Cana, where Jesus says to his mother, "My hour has not yet come" (2:4). This response is enigmatic and remains so until 19:25-27, when what is begun to be birthed at Cana is completed at the crucifixion.[12] Birth and death are juxtaposed, as *hōra* signifies the hour that comes for a woman to give birth (16:21), as well as the hour of Jesus' death. In 12:23, Jesus tells his disciples, "The hour has come for the Son of Man to be glorified." He explains further, using the metaphor of a grain of wheat that must fall to the ground and die in order to bear fruit (12:24). A few verses later, the evangelist asserts that "Jesus knew that his hour had come to depart from this world and go to the Father" (13:1). In two other instances, Jesus' "hour had not yet come" (7:30; 8:20), and so attempts to seize him fail. The "hour" is also the time for glorification, as Jesus prays, "Father, the hour has come; glorify your Son so that the Son may glorify you" (17:1). The Cana scene makes a connection with the hour of glory, as the concluding verse notes, "Jesus did this, the first of his signs in Cana of Galilee, and revealed his glory, and his disciples believed in him" (2:11). Belief features also in the crucifixion scene, where the evangelist tells that the one who saw the blood and water flow from Jesus' side "testifies so that you also may believe" (19:35). While Cana is the first instance in which faith is birthed in disciples (2:11), the crucified Jesus completes the birthing of the community of disciples. With his words to his mother, "Here is your son" (19:26), and to the disciple whom he loved, "Here is your mother" (19:27), Jesus entrusts his mother and the community of disciples (symbolized in the Beloved Disciple)[13] to one another. Jesus not only gives the community of faith the "power to become children of God" (1:12), but they also share now the same relationship to his mother as Jesus had during his earthly life.[14] Reference to the "hour" concludes the scene and links it to Cana: "And from that hour the disciple took her into his own home" (19:27).[15]

One final way in which the Cana episode points ahead to the end of the Gospel is that it begins with the phrase "on the third day" (2:1). Although the Fourth Evangelist does not preserve the Synoptic sayings about Jesus rising on the third day,[16] this was a well-known part of the early Christian kerygma (for example, 1 Cor 15:4) and can easily be understood as a symbolic reference to Jesus' resurrection.[17]

BORN AGAIN/FROM ABOVE (JOHN 3:1-21)

The theme of birthing is most explicit in Jesus' dialogue with Nicodemus in John 3. The scene is rife with double entendre, misunderstanding, and irony. Jesus tells Nicodemus, "No one can see the kingdom of God without being born from above (*gennēthē anōthen*)" (3:3), to which Nicodemus replies, "How can one be born (*gennēthēnai*) after having grown old? Can one enter a second time into the mother's womb and be born (*gennēthēnai*)?" (3:4). Jesus counters with, "Very truly I tell you, no one can enter the kingdom of God without being born (*gennēthē*) of water and the Spirit . . . Do not be astonished that I said to you, 'you must be born from above (*gennēthē anōthen*)'" (3:5, 7). There is a play on words, as *anōthen* denotes both "again" and "from above." As Nicodemus understands Jesus to say "born again," Jesus explains that being born "from above" means birth in water and the Spirit.[18]

The meaning of birth in water and Spirit comes clearer at the crucifixion scene.[19] At Jesus' death, water flows from his pierced side (John 19:34), and as Jesus breathes his last, he hands over the Spirit (19:30).[20] This latter is an ambiguous phrase, connoting both Jesus' expiration as well as the giving of the promised Spirit to his disciples. The birthing process of the community of believers comes to fullness at Jesus' death, signaled by flowing water and the gift of the Spirit. Toward the end of the exchange between Jesus and Nicodemus, one more image is evocative of birthing. Jesus tells Nicodemus, "Just as Moses lifted up the serpent in the wilderness, so must the Son of Man be lifted up" (3:14). This is the first of three instances in which the phrase "lifted up" is used to speak of Jesus' death (8:28; 12:32-34).[21] But at the same time, the mind's eye is drawn to the image of the jubilant lifting up of a newborn by its parents as it is presented to family, friends, and community, a practice still used in many churches. There is a stacking of images superimposed on one another, at the center of which is crucifixion as birth, giving intelligibility to all the metaphors.[22]

LIVING WATER FROM THE WOMB (JOHN 4:4-42; 7:37-39)

Jesus' encounter with the woman of Samaria (John 4:4-42) also advances the theme of birthing, as he offers to her of the gift of "living water" (4:10). Like the scene with Nicodemus, there is double entendre, misunderstanding, and irony, as Jesus and the woman reveal themselves to one another and the meaning of the metaphor unfolds. A "well of living water" can carry sexual overtones (Prov 5:15-18; Song 4:12, 15).[23] In addition, Old Testament writers and others of the period used *water* to refer to the processes of human reproduction and particularly to the actual coming forth from the womb after the breaking of the mother's water.[24] The water promised to the Samaritan woman also foreshadows the water of birth at the cross (19:34), when Jesus promises, "Those who drink of the water I give them will never be thirsty. The water that I will give will become in them a spring of water gushing up to eternal life" (4:14).[25]

This metaphor is further extended in John 7:37-39, where, during the Feast of Dedication,[26] Jesus "cried out, 'Let anyone who is thirsty come to me, and let the one who believes in me drink. As the Scripture has said, "Out of the believer's heart (*koilia*) shall flow rivers of living water."' Now he said this about the Spirit, which believers in him were to receive; for as yet there was no Spirit, because Jesus was not yet glorified." In verse 38, the word *koilia*, often translated in this passage as "heart," is actually the word for "womb, uterus,"[27] clearly evoking a birthing image and pointing ahead to the water that flows from the pierced side of Jesus in 19:34. There is ambiguity in 7:38 as to whose womb it is from which the rivers of living water flow.[28] In the Greek text, *koilias autou*, "his womb," could refer either to the believer or to Jesus. Both referents are in view, when read in light of 19:34. The mission birthed by Jesus of bringing forth life is carried forward by believers, who are not mere receptacles for living water but themselves become conduits of it.[29]

> "For a woman, bringing into being theology is like bringing into being a life, a new creature. It means carrying it in her womb, giving birth to it after many months, feeding it, and protecting it with her body, defending it, and watching it grow. It means thinking about it, pondering on, and talking about the revealed word with power and courage, but also with patience—doing, building, and talking, but also being silent, waiting, hoping, and celebrating."
>
> —María Clara Bingemer[30]

LABOR PANGS IN BIRTHING A RENEWED PEOPLE OF GOD (JOHN 16:21)

In the Farewell Discourse, Jesus explicitly uses the metaphor of birthing to speak to his disciples about his impending passion: "Very truly, I tell you, you will weep and mourn, but the world will rejoice; you will have pain, but your pain will turn into joy. When a woman is in labor, she has pain, because her hour has come. But when her child is born, she no longer remembers the anguish because of the joy of having brought a human being into the world. So you have pain now; but I will see you again, and your hearts will rejoice, and no one can take your joy from you" (16:20-22). The metaphor is similar to that found in Isaiah 26:17-18, where Israel's anguish over a longed-for peace and restoration is like childbirth: "Like a woman with child, who writhes and cries out in her pangs when she is near her time, so were we because of you, O LORD; we were with child, we writhed, but we gave birth only to wind. We have won no victories on earth, and no one is born to inhabit the world." Despite the apparent failure to give birth in this text, the next verse gives an assurance that the Johannine author may have seen in relation to the resurrection of Jesus, "Your dead shall live, their corpses shall rise. O dwellers in the dust, awake and sing for joy!" (Isa 26:19). A similar image is found in Isaiah 66:7-8, but there the emphasis for a despairing nation is on the speed and effortlessness of Zion's birthing of a renewed people: "Before she was in labor she gave birth; before her pain came upon her she delivered a son. Who has heard of such a thing? Who has seen such things? Shall a land be born in one day? Shall a nation be delivered in one moment? Yet as soon as Zion was in labor she delivered her children."[31] The Fourth Evangelist calls on the image of Daughter of Zion as the paradigmatic suffering one, rather than the Servant of Isaiah 52–53.[32] The travail that accompanies the birthing of a renewed people of God is expressed with the image of Zion's travail at the time of exile and the pangs of Jesus' disciples at the time of his passion. The parable in John 16:21 both explains Jesus' death as linked to biblical history and gives hope and meaning to the Johannine community as they undergo duress.[33]

> "I have endured so much suffering unjustly imposed, the same as Jesus. But I have been reborn. I have died to my former life and I have been reborn."
>
> —Griselda, Torreón
> 9 November, 2002

Not only does this parable apply to the anguish of the disciples, but it also can be seen as a metaphor for Jesus' own birth pangs in his passion. The phrase "hour has come" is a distinct echo of the Cana scene in which Jesus tells his mother his "hour has not yet come" (John 2:4) and the footwashing scene, introduced with the notation, "Jesus knew that his hour had come" (13:1). The coming hour is a constant refrain throughout the Gospel, signifying the death and glorification of Jesus.[34] The verb *erchomai*, "come," with the phrase *eis ton kosmon*, "into the world," in verse 21 evokes Jesus' prophetic messianic mission.[35]

Jesus' birthing of a renewed people through his death recalls the birth pangs of God in bringing forth Israel. Isaiah speaks thus: "For a long time I have held my peace, I have kept still and restrained myself; now I will cry out like a woman in labor, I will gasp and pant" (Isa 42:14). The Deuteronomist also portrays God as a birthing mother: "You were unmindful of the Rock that bore you; you forgot the God who gave you birth" (Deut 32:18), as does the Psalmist: "You are my son; today I have begotten you" (Ps 2:7). In Isaiah 49:15 are juxtaposed images of God as nursing mother and birth mother: "Can a woman forget her nursing child, or show no compassion for the child of her womb? Even these may forget, yet I will not forget you." Isaiah also portrays God as a comforting mother: "You shall nurse and be carried on her arm, and dandled on her knees. As a mother comforts her child, so I will comfort you; you shall be comforted in Jerusalem" (Isa 66:12-13).

In Psalm 22, there is an image of God, not as the mother, but as midwife: "Yet it was you who took me from the womb; you kept me safe on my mother's breast. On you I was cast from my birth, and since my mother bore me you have been my God" (Ps 22:9-10).[36] Similarly, in Isaiah 66:9, "Shall I open the womb and not deliver? says the LORD; shall I, the one who delivers, shut the womb? says your God." In one of the hymns from Qumran, there is an image of God as a midwife assisting the community through its afflictions. What is notable is that the moment of birth, with its agony, is seen as identical with death:

> "What does God do all day long? God lies on a maternity bed giving birth all day long."
>
> —Meister Eckhart

And I was in distress,
As a woman in travail brings forth her first child;
For her birth pangs wrench,
And sharp pain, upon her birth canal
(or, with her birth throes),
To cause writhing in the crucible of the pregnant one.
For sons have come to the deathly birth canal,
And she who is pregnant with a man is distressed by her pains;
For through deathly contractions she brings forth a male child,
And through infernal pains, there burst forth from the crucible of the pregnant one,
A Wonderful Counselor with his might,
And a man is delivered from the birth canal by the pregnant one. (1QH 3:7-18)[37]

In Psalm 131, the image is that of God as a mother with her weaned child on her lap: "I have calmed and quieted my soul, like a weaned child with its mother; my soul is like the weaned child that is with me" (Ps 131:2). Job juxtaposes images of a begetting father and a birthing mother when speaking of God's creative work: "Has the rain a father, or who has begotten the drops of dew? From whose womb did the ice come forth, and who has given birth to the hoarfrost of heaven?" (Job 38:28-29). It is notable that images of birthing occur in two of the most crucial and painful times in Israel's history: the slavery in Egypt and the exile in Babylon.[38] Like Jesus' crucifixion, these death experiences open the way for new life.

The Fourth Evangelist draws on this familiar metaphor of God as a woman giving birth and as a midwife drawing forth new life to interpret the suffering of Jesus and his followers as a death that is at the same time a birth. The weeping of which Jesus speaks (John 16:20) is embodied in Mary Magdalene, who stands weeping outside the tomb (20:11) and who twice is

> "Every time the women come together, you can see that, despite all the hardships, their joy increases more and more."
>
> —María del Rosario, San Cristóbal de las Casas[39]
> 12 November, 2002

asked, "Woman, why are you weeping?" (20:13, 15). The evangelist notes her turning (20:16) away from grief, but does not explicitly tell of her joy. In the subsequent scene, when Jesus appears to the disciples, presumably with Mary present, they rejoice at the sight of him (20:20).

Many commentators see in John 16:21 an allusion to Genesis 3:16, in which God says to the woman, "'I will greatly increase your pangs in childbearing; in pain (LXX: *lypais*) you shall bring forth children." Both passages speak of a "woman"[40] who experiences *lypē*, "pain," in childbearing. The term *lypē* does not elsewhere occur in relation to birth pangs;[41] it usually refers to mental anguish, as in John 16:6, where talk of Jesus' departure causes "sorrow," *lypē*, to fill the disciples' hearts.[42] Another link is that, at the birth of Cain, Eve declares not that she has brought a child into the world but, "I have produced a man ('*îsh* in Hebrew; *anthrōpon* in LXX) with the help of the LORD" (Gen 4:1). Similarly, the woman in John 16:21 is said to rejoice "at having brought a human being (*anthrōpos*) into the world."[43] A traditional interpretation of Gen 3:16 is that it details the consequences of the fall of humanity, brought on by human sinfulness. From this perspective, the recollection of the so-called fall, when talking about the death of Jesus, serves to underscore his atonement for and reversal of the consequences of sin by his death. But such an interpretation does not accord with Johannine theology. In the Fourth Gospel, Jesus' death is not portrayed as a means of expiation for sin. An alternative approach to Genesis 3:16 is to see it as part of a myth of human maturation rather than a sin/fall story.[44] The myth depicts woman and man in a struggle for survival, with their roles delineated as "life-producing wife/mother/parent and worker" (3.16) and as "life-sustaining farmer and father/parent" (3.17-19).[45] Both have "pain," *lypē* (3:16, 17). Both share in the tasks of survival, though in different ways. Both experience unrelenting difficulty that accompanies their toil. Reflecting the societal conditions of the Iron Age settlement period of Palestinian hill country, Genesis 3:16-17 speaks of the increase in human toil that was required. A multiplication of women's contributions was needed in the areas of subsistence living and childbearing and of men's agricultural toil.[46] This was a world in which generations of abundant progeny symbolizes salvation.[47]

In a similar fashion, salvation is depicted in the Johannine Jesus' birthing of an abundant number of disciples as children of God.

BIRTH FROM THE SIDE OF JESUS (19:34)

The pervasiveness of images of birth in the Fourth Gospel climaxes in the crucifixion scene. After Jesus has died, instead of breaking his legs, "one of the soldiers pierced his side with a spear, and at once blood and water came out" (John 19:34).[49] The birthing of a renewed people of God is symbolized by the breaking of the amniotic fluid, accompanied by uterine blood.[50] The "power to become children of God" that was assured in the prologue (1:12) is accomplished. The presence of Jesus' mother (19:25), who gave physical birth to Jesus and who mediated the

> "We work in a constant process of breaking away, as though in an ongoing childbirth, in which we seek to release ourselves from old frameworks, and from categories imposed by the patriarchal system in order to give birth to something closer to life, something more densely packed with meaning for us."[48]

birth of his public ministry, now witnesses the fulfillment of his earthly life and mission and his birthing of the people who will continue to bring life to the full for all. Nicodemus, who struggled to understand what "born again/from above" could mean in 3:1-21, returns with Joseph of Arimathea with one hundred pounds of myrrh and aloe with which to embalm Jesus' body (19:39). As they wrap Jesus' body with the spices in linen cloths (19:40), images of death and birth meld, as they swaddle him with bands of cloth, as with a newborn (Luke 2:7).[51] The presence of Nicodemus also recalls Jesus' words to him about being born by water and the Spirit (3:5), which is now accomplished.[52] Jesus' offer of "living water" (4:10) and his promise that from his womb and that of the believer would flow "rivers of living water" (7:38) are brought to fulfillment as he hands over the Spirit (19:30). Jesus' final declaration, "It is finished" (19:30), can be understood as a cry of victory like that of a mother who cries out in joy when the birthpangs are over, and her child is born.[53]

To see Jesus' passion as labor in childbirth is an ancient tradition.[54] Clement of Alexandria said, "The Lord Himself brought forth in throes of flesh, which the Lord Himself swathed in his precious blood" (*The Instructor* 1.6). Ambrose refers to Christ as the "Virgin who bare us" (*On Virgins* 1:5). In Syriac tradition, there is a comparison made between Adam's side that gave birth to Eve and the pierced side of Jesus that gave birth to the church. Jacob of Serugh wrote in the sixth century:

> For from the beginning God knew and depicted
> Adam and Eve in the likeness of the image of his Only-
> begotten;
> He slept on the cross as Adam had slept his deep sleep,
> his side was pierced and from it there came forth the Daughter
> of Light,
> water and blood as an image of divine children
> to be heirs to the Father who loves his Only-begotten. . . .
>
> Adam's side gave birth to a woman who gives birth to
> immortals.
> In the crucifixion he completed the types that had been
> depicted,
> and the hidden mystery that had been covered revealed
> itself.

And in another place, Jacob writes,

> His side was pierced in his sleep,
> he gave birth to the Bride, as happened with Eve . . .
> And from him came forth the Mother who gives birth to all
> spiritual beings:
> . . . water and blood for the fashioning of spiritual babes
> flowed from the side of that Living One who died, in order to
> bring life to Adam.

In the Middle Ages, maternal images of Jesus were most prevalent.[55] For example, Carthusian prioress Marguerite Oingt, who died in 1310, speaks of mother Jesus, "Ah, my sweet and lovely Lord, with what love you labored for me and bore me through your whole life. . . . when the hour of your delivery came you were placed on the hard bed of the cross . . . and your nerves and all your veins were broken. And truly it is no surprise that your veins burst when in one day you gave birth to the whole world."[56] Julian of Norwich, who lived during the middle of the fourteenth century, says that Jesus "our savior is our true Mother in whom we are endlessly born and out of whom—we shall come."[57] And further, "all the lovely works, all the sweet and loving offices of beloved motherhood are appropriated to the second person for in him we have this godly will, whole and safe forever, both in nature and grace, from his own goodness proper to him."[58]

INSUFFLATION WITH THE BREATH OF LIFE (John 20:19-23)

One final image associated with birth is found in the scene in which the risen Christ appears to his disciples, gifts them with peace, entrusts to them his mission, and breathes on them saying, "Receive the holy Spirit" (John 20:21-22). Just as the midwife attending the birth of a child may blow breath into its nostrils to help it breathe on its own, so Jesus breathes the breath of the Spirit on his disciples, enabling them to go out on their own, extending his life-giving mission.[59] The beginning of the episode also recalls the parable of the woman who experiences joy after her child is born (16:21), for at the sight of Jesus, the disciples rejoiced (19:20). Jesus' breathing on the disciples also evokes God's creation of the first human being into whose nostrils God breathed "the breath of life," and the human became a "living being" (Gen 2:7). There is also an echo of the resuscitation of Israel, when God commanded the prophet Ezekiel to prophesy to a valley of dry bones saying, "I will cause breath to enter you and you shall live" (Ezek 37:5). Wisdom 15:11 also speaks of the failure of God's people who "failed to know the one who formed them and inspired them with active souls and breathed a living spirit into them."

GODLY BEING IN FEMALE FORM

The image of Jesus' death as birth offers rich theological and pastoral possibilities not found in other metaphors. With this image, gender boundaries are blurred and transcended in the person of Jesus.[60] This opens the way for women disciples to identify themselves with Christ in a profound way. In addition, this metaphor gives dignity to the bodily experience of women and sees it as a locus for the holy.[61] Furthermore, since Jesus is one with the Father (John 10:30) and Jesus'

presence continues in the Spirit (Jesus asks the Father to give the disciples "another Advocate," John 14:16), female metaphors for the other persons of the Trinity are also in order.[62] When the prologue speaks of believers who are "born (*egennēthēsan*) of God" (1:13), it is a female image of

> "We can identify with Jesus when we see his feminine aspects: how kind, patient, and loving he was. Like the women who stayed at the foot of the cross, he stays with us in our sufferings"
>
> —Rosalinda, La Paz, Bolivia 24 March, 2003

birthing that is evoked, reprised at the death of Jesus with the blood and water that flow from his side (19:34), and completing the invitation to Nicodemus to be born again/from above in water and Spirit. Creator, Christ, and Spirit all give birth to God's renewed people. It is not that one of the members of the Trinity is the female face of God. The whole of the divine being and divine activity is expressed in the female form and action. Not only in the Gospel of John, but also in several of Jesus' parables preserved in the synoptic Gospels are divine being and activity portrayed in female form. Jesus likens God's relentless search for the lost to that of a woman who goes to extraordinary lengths to find a lost coin (Luke 15:8-10). He speaks of godly agitation for transformation as the action of a woman who hides leaven in three measures of flour (Matt 13:33; Luke 13:20-21). He tells how the divine pursuit of justice is akin to the persistent protests of a powerful widow in the face of a corrupt judge (Luke 18:1-8).[63] Jesus also speaks of himself as embodying the maternal desire to gather under his wings the rebellious chicks of Jerusalem (Matt 23:37 // Luke 13:34).

From such an image of God's action in Jesus and the Spirit come liberation and empowerment. As María Clara Bingemer describes:

> The poor who are discovering themselves as active makers of history and are organizing for liberation are experiencing God as the God of life, as embodying the very fullness of life,

as the only source from which it is possible to derive hope and promise in the situation of death they live every day. God's female entrails—maternal *rahamin*, fertile, in labor and compassionate—enable this liberation to come about with force and firmness, but also with creativity and gentleness, without violence. Once God is experienced, not only as Father, Lord, strong warrior, but also as Mother, protection, greater love, struggle is tempered with festivity and celebration of life, permanent and gentle firmness ensures the ability "to be tough without losing tenderness," and uncompromising resistance can be carried on with joy, without excessive tension and sterile strain. God's compassion, flowing from female and maternal entrails, takes on itself the hurts and wounds of all the oppressed, and a woman who does theology is called to bear witness to this God with her body, her actions, her life.[64]

Such female imagery of God also opens up new possibilities for women who have survived incest or sexual abuse by a male relative. For many such survivors, relating to a male image of God is impossible. As Shirley Gillett observes, "Depictions of God as a loving Father wanting a close relationship with his children may be comforting to those who have had loving earthly fathers, but for women whose fathers approached them looking for close relationships that involved pain and humiliation, these depictions are both terrifying and distancing."[65]

Julia Esquivel articulates what will be the effect when women and men are equally recognized as the image and likeness of God. The impossible will become possible, and there will be "equality in difference, flourishing in a creative, fruitful harmony, in the couple and in the relationships of all peoples and societies."[66] She correlates the prophecy of Isaiah, "On every lofty mountain and on every hill there will be brooks running with water . . . the light of the moon will be like the light of the sun . . . on the day when the LORD binds up the injuries of his people" (Isa 30:25-26), to Mayan cosmology. Mayans, as do many indigenous

> "My mother talked to me about God the Father, but I felt that if God is a man, then he can't understand me at all. I couldn't pray the "Our Father"; it scared me."
>
> —Ángeles, Torreón
> 9 November, 2002

peoples, understand the sun to correspond to the male and the moon to the female. Accordingly, Isaiah's prophecy speaks of the time when men and women achieve equal brightness, and then all the wounds of the people will be healed and the land will flourish. "Equality of access to true development will make both the male aspect and the female aspect shine, and will enrich both, without detriment to either. This maturing will mark the *kairos* for the rising again of true life on the earth as the home of all."[67]

The metaphor of birth can help move us in this direction. Unlike the kinds of economic transactions between God and humanity implied in sacrificial and ransom metaphors, the birthing image evokes an exchange of love that is mutual and self-replicating. The image of Jesus' death as birth emphasizes bodily-ness, underscoring the incarnational reality of God-with-us in our all humanness, in pain and joy. This metaphor does not see suffering as deserved[68] or desirable. It gives value to travail as part of a natural process and recognizes that pain is not an end in itself. Suffering can be endured when one knows that the birth pangs herald new life. The resultant joy all but obliterates the memory of the travail.

With the emphasis in the Fourth Gospel on death as birth, the question of forgiveness of sin in relation to Jesus' death plays out in a different mode. Jesus' death is not an atoning sacrifice.[69] As "the Lamb of God who takes away the sin of the world" (John 1:29), he dies at the moment that the Passover lambs are being slaughtered in the Temple, and his legs are not broken (19:33), just as no bone may be broken of the Passover lamb (Exod 12:46). The Passover lamb is a sign of liberation, not of sacrificial atonement. Jesus, as Lamb of God, frees the children of God from whatever holds them bound.

When forgiveness is spoken of explicitly, it is a power given to the disciples by the risen Christ to continue his mission when he says to them, "Receive the Holy Spirit. If you forgive (*aphēte*) the sins of any, they are forgiven them; if you retain (*kratēte*) the sins of any they are retained" (John 20:22-23). This verse is often read in light of the words of Jesus to Peter, which are repeated to all the disciples in the Gospel of Matthew, "Whatever you bind (*deō*) on earth will be bound in heaven, and whatever you loose (*luō*) on earth will be loosed in heaven" (Matt 16:19; 18:18). However, John 20:23 should be read within the theology of the Fourth Evangelist, who has emphasized that Jesus' mission is to lose nothing of what has been given him (6:39) and who "will never drive away" anyone who comes to him (6:37). Nor will he allow anyone to snatch away any who have been given to Jesus by the Father (10:27-29). In his final prayer, Jesus asserts that he has protected and guarded all whom God has given him, "and not one of them was lost" (17:12), an affirmation he repeats at his arrest (18:9). Just so, Jesus is commissioning his disciples to continue his mission of holding on to anyone whom the Father gives them in the community of believers. It is notable that the verb *krateō* does not mean "retain," but "hold fast," "grasp," as in Matthew 28:9, where the Galilean women hold on to the feet of the risen Jesus. Nor is the word *sins* found in the Greek text in the second half of 20:23. Literally, the verse says, "Of whomever you forgive the sins, they are forgiven to them; whomever you hold are held fast." The Johannine Jesus says nothing about "retaining" sins, only the forgiveness of sins and the retention of all community members.[70] The task of Jesus' disciples is not to exercise judgment (which was not a task done by Jesus either, 12:47) but to birth life to the full for all (10:10).

Another way of understanding the mission of holding fast, or "binding," entrusted to the disciples in John 20:23 is by way of allusion to Ezekiel 34.[71] The prophet chastises the shepherds of Israel for failing to bind up the injured (Ezek 34:4). So God declares, "I myself will be shepherd of my sheep . . . and I will bind up the injured" (Ezek 34:15-16). Although there is a difference in the verbs used in the two texts (*krateō* in John 20:23; and *katadeō*, "to bind up," in Ezek 34:4, 16, LXX), the two are in the same semantic range. In addition to "hold fast," the verb *krateō* can also mean "to repair" (2 Kgs 12:6, LXX), and the cognate *kratēma* can be used "of a bandage."[72] The mission of Jesus' disciples is to emulate Jesus, the Good Shepherd (John 10), by "binding" up whatever is wounded and "loosing" whatever inhibits the breath of the Spirit.

DANGEROUS DIRECTIONS

As empowering as is the image of Jesus' death as birth, there are also dangerous aspects. Birthing and motherhood are easily romanticized.[73] The reality that not all children are conceived in love, that some are unwanted and that some are the product of rape,[74] can become obscured in a romantic aura painted around motherhood. Not all birth pangs give way to joy. As Kathleen Rushton points out, "Particularly for young women, childbirth may be the result of lack of information and choice, poverty, exploitation, sexual and cultural violence. Hazards arise from fertility control, or lack of it, and the low priority given to diseases affecting women."[75] There can be increased anxiety about the ability to economically support more children and the impact of pregnancy and childrearing on one's ability to work.[76] In addition, childbirth can result in death for the mother, the child, or both. In antiquity, approximately one in three women died in childbirth.[77] Today in the developing world, 61 percent of women receive no prenatal care, 50 percent of women give birth without professional medical assistance, and one in forty-eight women die in childbirth.[78] Or consider the anguish of a mother who endures agonizing labor only to have her child stillborn or live only a brief time. Currently in Bolivia, the poorest country in Latin America, 420 women per 1,000 die in childbirth; 68 of every 1,000 children born die as infants; and 93 of every 1,000 die before they reach 5 years of age.[79] There is also the danger posed by the idealized image of mothers who die to give life to their children, which can all too easily render women sacrificial victims to others' desires.

Another problematic aspect is when motherhood is seen as the epitome of woman's calling and when "mother" is the only female image offered for God. Other images than mother, such as sister, midwife, friend, are needed to speak of the ways that single women, vowed celibate women, childless married women, and widows, incarnate divine

> "When I was a schoolgirl I pictured God as tall, with green eyes, like a foreigner. But God isn't like that. God has to be just like us."
>
> —Cecilia, El Alto, Bolivia
> 28 March, 2003

being.[80] There is a danger, too, in parental metaphors for God, both mother and father, in that it narrows our ways of relating to the divinity and keeps us in perpetual childhood. As Sallie McFague remarks, "At a time when we need desperately to be 'adults,' to take responsibility for our world and its well-being, we cannot support a model that suggests that the 'great mother' or 'great father' will take care of our crises of poverty, discrimination, damage to the ecosystem, and so forth."[81]

One other problematic aspect is that this image, particular to women, has been co-opted by men to give voice to their experience, thus obliterating specifically female embodiment of the divine. Whereas the transcendence of gender boundaries in the depiction of a male Jesus who gives birth can help work toward dissolving hierarchies and inequities based on gender differences,[82] it can also obscure the ability of women to fully image the divine. From as early as the apostle Paul, male spiritual writers have appropriated to themselves the images of birthing and mothering. Paul writes to the Galatians, "My little children, for whom I am again in the pain of childbirth until Christ is formed in you" (Gal 4:19). Using the image of a nursing mother, he says to the Thessalonians, "We were gentle among you like a nurse tenderly caring for her own children" (1 Thess 2:7). A challenge today is for female bodies and experience in themselves to be seen as fully expressive of divine being and action. In some cultures, this will take a considerable stretch of the imagination and will call for radically different patterns of relating between women and men.

> "The expressions of faith, the prayers, the architecture of the church, is all constructed by men. It is machista and vertical. It doesn't correspond to our Andean vision of the cosmos. Nonetheless we try to do what Jesus did: serve our neighbor, accompany those who carry crosses, listen, dry their tears, and struggle. And this is what unites us. As we think in terms of family, community, nation, the world, each one adds her grain of sand. All of the members of the body of Christ are necessary."
>
> —Berta, Centro Pachamama, El Alto, Bolivia 25 March, 2003

MOTHER JESUS AND THE MOTHER OF JESUS

The role that the mother of Jesus plays in the Fourth Gospel in relation to Jesus' death has much potential for opening new liberative avenues. In Latina theologies of the cross, Mary is omnipresent. Most Latinas identify primarily with the sorrowful mother who agonizes at the foot of the cross over the loss of her precious son. Women who have lost sons to gang violence or to death squads, for example, find solace in a mother who knows what they, too, are suffering.[83] Women who struggle derive comfort, strength, encouragement, and hope from a Mary who endures the same kind of hardships they do. They reason that Mary watched her son be crucified, suffer, and die. "But he rose from the dead! Therefore, things will be well, despite the torment, pain, alienation, loneliness, confusion, and suffering."[84]

In Latin American popular piety, images of the suffering Jesus going to his death are always accompanied by images of the Dolorous Mother. Statues of the two in juxtaposition are ubiquitous. In Lima, Peru, for example, in the church of Nuestra Señora de Cocharcas during the Holy Thursday liturgy, the statue of the grieving mother stands alongside that of the crucified Christ, equal in size and veneration. The closing hymn at the Holy Thursday liturgy when I visited there in 2003 was *María la Buena Madre* ("Mary the Good Mother"). In the Good Friday procession, the image of the Dolorous Virgin is carried alongside that of the Recumbent Christ. The Basilica de la Merced in Lima celebrates *"Solemnes Cultos en Honor de Jesús Nazareno y de la Santísima Virgen de los Dolores,"* a Mass and procession in honor of both Jesus and the "Blessed Virgin of Sorrows." Such an image of Mary provides comfort, companionship, and strength to endure suffering. Women who feel helpless to protect their children from dangers see Mary as one like them, who could do nothing to stop her son's passion.[85] Nevertheless, their daily rituals of nurturing and caring for others achieve a sacredness when identified with similar actions imagined of Mary.[86]

Contemporary reenactments of the *Via Crucis*, the "Way of the Cross," such as the one that takes place through the streets of the Pilsen neighborhood of Chicago each Good Friday, function to give voice to injustices and struggles, and serve as a vehicle of grace. By setting the stations of the cross at modern-day sites of struggle, the message is conveyed that the sufferings of Jesus did not only happen long ago; they are happening right now.[87]

Breaking the silence that surrounds and maintains architectures of domination is central to the *Via Crucis,* and this kind of prayer in the street has a visible effect on the neighborhood.[88] What it does not help to change, however, are the patriarchal structures at the root of much of women's suffering.[89] Instead of liberating women, the traditional images of Mary have "confirmed and confined women in their ancient oppression."[90]

> "We always identify our sufferings with Mary's. But we dress her as a queen, one who has power. She represents our struggle as a people."
>
> —Fiorenza, Centro Bartolomé de las Casas, Lima, Peru
> 10 April, 2003

The image of the mother of Jesus in the Fourth Gospel has potential for confronting patriarchal attitudes and for opening other horizons for women. At Cana, Jesus' mother is not resigned and accepting of the plight in which the hosts and guests find themselves. She takes initiative toward resolving the distress and insists that her son alleviate the situation. Despite his protest, she recognizes that it is the correct time for him to take action. She does not back down from her expectations. On a human level, a lack of wine at a wedding is not exactly a situation of injustice that needs to be confronted. But on a theological level, the necessity for Jesus to manifest himself so as to begin the birthing process of bringing disciples to belief in him was a matter of life and death. The fortitude and perceptiveness of Jesus' mother are qualities essential for contemporary women as they recognize the opportune moments for initiating change and gather their strength to act as midwife to justice and new life. Likewise, the image of Jesus' mother at the foot of the cross (19:25-27) cannot only be seen as a dolorous mother who is helpless to stop her son's execution and who can only offer her pain up to God, but it can also be viewed as a witness to the injustice of Jesus' execution, who protests it by her presence and her testimony. She refuses to let the death-dealing of the empire have the upper hand, as she once again mediates the birth of new life, acquiring new children in the community of the Beloved Disciple and nurturing their mission, as she first did with her biological son.

Mary refuses to be defeated by the powers of domination and death, and empowered by the Spirit, she accompanies the fledgling community of disciples into their mission for life.[91]

For Mexican and Mexican American women, the image of Our Lady of Guadalupe can also be a seen along the emancipatory lines we have been sketching. Like the biblical Mary, however, she has been interpreted in ways that reinforce traditional models of motherhood: submission, sweetness, and self-sacrifice. Stereotypically, Mexican and Mexican-American women's role in a culture marked by machismo[92] and racism is to be "submissive, naive, rather childlike 'sainted mother,' whose purity is preserved by her husband's refusal to bring the world and its sins into the home."[93] Patriarchal views of the Virgin Mary feed what Rosa María Gil and Carmen Inoa Vázquez call *marianismo*. "*Marianismo*," they explain, "is about sacred duty, self-sacrifice, and chastity. About dispensing care and pleasure, not receiving them. About living in the shadows, literally and figuratively, of your men—father, boyfriend, husband, son—your kids, and your family."[94] Ten commandments of *marianismo*, according to Gil and Vázquez, are (1) Do not forget a woman's place; (2) Do not forsake tradition; (3) Do not be single, self-supporting, or independent-minded; (4) Do not put your own needs first; (5) Do not wish for more in life than being a housewife; (6) Do not forget that sex is for making babies—not for pleasure; (7) Do not be unhappy with your man or criticize him for infidelity, gambling, verbal and physical abuse, or alcohol or drug abuse; (8) Do not ask for help; (9) Do not discuss personal problems outside the home; (10) Do not change those things that make you unhappy that you can realistically change.[95]

Paradoxically, Mexican and Mexican American women perceive Guadalupe as being "both meek and strong-willed, independent and dependent, assertive and shy—all at the same time."[96] One woman put it this way: "Our Lady of Guadalupe represents to me everything we as a people should strive to be:

> "When you grow and start to live a new life, you can't leave your husband and others behind. You have to bring them into this resurrected life too."
>
> —Margarita, Torreón
> 9 November, 2002

strong yet humble, warm and compassionate, yet courageous enough to stand up for what we believe in."[97] These contradictory images may be due to women projecting onto Our Lady of Gudalupe the transitions they themselves are experiencing when traditional qualities they have been encouraged to emulate come into conflict with those valued in contemporary American culture.[98] The liberating instinct reflected in these conflicting depictions of Guadalupe can be heightened when women know the whole story of Guadalupe, tell it in emancipatory ways,[99] and connect it with the biblical Mary. In this way, Guadalupe can serve as a powerful icon for liberation from all types of oppression, including from sexist stereotypes.

> "We women are always the ones who suffer most, at home, at work, everywhere. And still this does not satisfy our husbands. That is why I wouldn't want to have any more girl children. For what? So that they suffer like I have? It's not worth it, my dear sister. In spite of suffering, one has to keep working, for my children's sake. What else can you do?"
>
> —Mariá Victoria González[100]

Guadalupe presents a strong symbol of God's solidarity with and care for the poorest and the least powerful. Appearing as an Indian, with dark skin and adorned with symbols of Aztec divinity, she embodies God's presence with and predilection for the conquered native peoples. Like Jesus, who became one with humanity by taking on flesh (John 1:14), so Guadalupe takes on the appearance of an indigenous woman, incarnating God's presence with those who suffer most. And like Jesus, she is not simply present with people who suffer, but she embodies God's power to alleviate suffering through her embrace of tender motherly love and through transformation of unjust structures. When Guadalupe appears to Juan Diego, she births in him the courage to confront the Spanish archbishop Zumárraga with her liberating message. By wrapping Juan Diego in her tenacious motherly protection and treating him with dignity and respect, Guadalupe emboldens him to move from his dejection and submission as a conquered person to one who takes action for the restoration and dignity of his people. Like Jesus whose death is a birth to new life, Guadalupe appears as pregnant, heralding hope of new life for a victimized people. She opens the way to envision and take action toward a different world.[101]

In the experience of contemporary Mexican and Mexican American women, a notable feature is the personal relationship they have with Guadalupe. They speak with her on a daily basis about their struggles and pain, sensing that, as a woman, Guadalupe understands. There is a mutuality and reciprocity in their relationship. A woman may light a candle, bring roses, and visit the church or shrine when praying to Guadalupe. From her, they receive unconditional love and acceptance, understanding, and nonjudgmentalness. For those who have no such relationship with the powerful of this world, she is accessible, approachable, and powerful. Some envision her as able to influence God, while others see her as the maternal or feminine face of God. But as Jeannette Rodríguez rightly observes, the attributes of Guadalupe—of unconditional love, self-giving, solidarity, never-failing presence, creative and transformative power, and maternal nurturance—rightly belong to God.[102] "Our Lady of Guadalupe is not God; she is a metaphor for God."[103] She represents God and affirms God's hope for the world. In a religious culture shaped by patriarchal images, it is difficult to see God as represented in female form. One woman remarked, "Some people don't like the idea or the image that portrays a woman representing a man, but that's the way it has always been. She has always been an activist representing Him."[104]

Just as the mother of Jesus in the Johannine episodes of the wedding at Cana (John 2:1-11) and at the crucifixion (19:25-27), and as Jesus himself, birthing through death (John 19:34), Guadalupe "tells us something about who we are (in the Mexican American women's case, that they are female, mother, *morena*, marginalized). And she tells us something about who God is: God is the

> "Most women identify more with Mary than with Jesus. God is not like a man, who is authoritarian and distant. Mary, by contrast, is maternal, and close by. She stood under the cross and understands all that we experience. She accompanied her son to the very end, experiencing all the pain he endured. She is strong and valiant, like us."
>
> —Marta, La Paz, Bolivia
> 24 March, 2003

source of all life, maternal, compassionate, and present, and protects the poor and marginalized."[105] Guadalupe is a powerful icon who reaffirms *mestiza* women's identity as created in God's image, builds self-esteem, and gives power to endure the birth pangs of new creation with hope. Although she is grounded in Mexican history, she can function as a symbol of God's love for all people. Her felt presence has not diminished since her appearance to Juan Diego in 1531, just as God continues to remain powerfully present with us even after Jesus' earthly sojourn ended. In the Gospel of Matthew, this is expressed in the name "Emmanuel, God-with-us" (Matt 1:23; 28:20); in John (19:30; 20:23) and Acts of the Apostles (1:14), it is the Spirit who embodies God's ongoing presence. So, too, Guadalupe. One indigenous woman, when asked at the shrine of Our Lady of Guadalupe in Mexico City, "What makes her so different from the other Marys that have appeared around the world?" responded with a twinkle in her eye, "Se quedó"—"She stayed."[106]

CONCLUSION

Both Latina popular piety and biblical depictions of Jesus and his mother provide potent images of God's power to birth new life out of death. Such portrayals give us an antidote to images that make God's wrath or human sinfulness the focus. God's love, freely given, life-giving, and productive, evokes a response in kind, transforming even the most hopeless of situations. The Jesus who entered into a lengthy process of leading Nicodemus to the light so that he could be born again/from above continues to do so as women still *dar luz*, "give birth," (literally, "give light") to godly hope. As Ivone Gebara says,

> To be birthed anew is "to return to our roots, to re-enter the maternal uterus, in the bosom of the earth," and so . . . "rediscover who we are. . . . The image of a Father God, who exists independently from its child, who causes all to submit to himself—this is not our true origin. This image is . . . not capable of uniting humanity, respecting differences in expression. We have to return to the matrix, earth, suck primal energy from her. . . . This entails a spiritual-ethical-political movement, which does not accept that we can just contemplate pas-

sively the mystery of life. It enters constantly into the work of birthing, so that women and men passionate for life and for a unifying anthropological vision, can overcome deadly dualisms."[107]

Images such as those of Jesus who births through his death, Mary who is midwife for the new life, and Guadalupe pregnant with hope can empower and sustain all those wise women who birth hope in others daily. Such women have a "close connection with life's realities," which "enables them to listen to, feel for, advise and help those (of both sexes) who come to them. They are those who without title, belonging to no officially recognized institution, 'widen their tents' in order to provide their share of love for the process of building life. . . . These women—widows, married, single parents, with few or numerous dependents—exercise a 'spiritual motherhood' among the people without giving their daily gift of life, their begetting of the Spirit, this or any other name."[108] In the end, we can say that what impels women to enter into the birthing process, with all its attendant suffering, is not the assurance that new life always results but rather, the idea that "one embraces travail because one is in the embrace of God."[109]

Conclusion

"It's not possible to explain the violence and inhumanity involved in the death of Jesus. I have to look at it from the perspective of resurrection, because otherwise, I wouldn't be able to stand thinking about how cruel, inhuman, and dehumanizing was his violent death."

—Rayo, Chicago, Illinois
26 October, 2002

"We never lose faith and hope. As women united, we can struggle together to continue moving ahead."

—Anita, El Alto, Bolivia
28 March, 2003

"Knowledge of the Word of God makes you stronger. It awakens you to be able to see differently, and that another way is possible."

—Marta, Surco, Lima, Peru
10 April, 2003

"After all the abuse and self-abnegation I've been through, I could feel like I would never come down off my cross. But no. I am resurrected. I am here!"

—Ángeles, Torreón
9 November, 2002

AFTER TWO MILLENNIA OF CHRISTIAN efforts to make meaning of the cross of Jesus and what it signifies for his followers to take up the cross, words and images fail. No one image or metaphor captures it all; each contributes a significant tessera to the mosaic of meaning. We have looked at metaphors and images of sacrifice and self-gift, obedience, prophetic witness, healing, forgiveness, reconciliation, and birthing. We have investigated the ways in which these images and metaphors are developed in the New Testament, attending to the worlds behind the texts, the world of the text, and the world in front of the text. We have looked for the liberating possibilities each hold, as well as the deadly directions in which they can take us. We have been particularly concerned with the experience of women in Latin and North America, attentive to the ways in which "carrying the cross" keeps women crucified, rather than experiencing its freeing love. We have explored female imagery in the Scriptures that has been overlooked or submerged in the effort to validate women's experience and to find there a locus for divine revelation and encounter.

> "What has always impressed me about Jesus' passion is that all his friends left him, and the women were the ones who stayed close to him and sustained him with their presence. And it was to these women that he first appeared when he rose."
> —Ana, Torreón
> 9 November, 2002

While the focus of this study has been the cross, our reflection has come from the perspective of resurrection faith and the assuredness that the resurrection of Jesus reveals God's unrelenting desire to draw all into fullness of life and love and that a taste of that life and love is already present in this life. Insisting that God does not desire the suffering or death of any, we have sought to make meaning of the cross in ways that will bring flourishing for all. It is vitally important how we tell the story of the cross. What we say of Jesus' passion reflects how we understand God's involvement in our own suffering. Any way of telling the story that does not take us more deeply into the freeing and empowering love of God and impel us to radiate that to others is not an adequate version of

> "Despite all the suffering, we always believe that a new day will dawn—a kind of resurrection."
> —Rosa, El Alto, Bolivia
> 28 March, 2003

the story. Nor is it an adequate version if it ignores, trivializes, or increases the sufferings of real women and men, particularly those who suffer most in our world. It is particularly incumbent on preachers, teachers, and ministers to tell the story well and to help deconstruct and replace versions that are especially abusive toward women.

Taking up the cross with resurrection faith means that we journey in relationship with the One whose love is not extinguished even by death. Emulating Christ, our freely chosen acts of self-gift to others out of love are the fruit of lifelong obedience that draws us into listening and discerning intimacy with the Beloved. Communities of believers continue Jesus' prophetic witness, denouncing violence and injustice and announcing God's way of life to the full for all. Willingness to bear the suffering this entails includes working through arduous processes of healing and reconciliation, and even giving up one's life in witness, that is, martyrdom. God's labor pangs and joy are embodied in us yet as we continue what God birthed in Jesus.

> "Our devotion to the cross is not only to the bloody images of the suffering Christ. We also adorn the cross with bright colors and flowers, giving it another sense—it is the tree of life. Our people have a strong sense of affirmation of life."
>
> —Amparo, Centro Bartolomé de las Casas, Lima, Peru
> 10 April, 2003

I am no longer afraid of death,

I know well

its dark and cold corridors

leading to life.

I am afraid rather of that life

which does not come out of death

which cramps our hands

and retards our march.

I am afraid of my fear
and even more of the fear of others,
who do not know where they are going,
who continue clinging
to what they consider to be life
which we know to be death!

I live each day to kill death;
I die each day to beget life,
and in this dying unto death,
I die a thousand times and
am reborn another thousand
through that love
from my People,
which nourishes hope![1]

"Each one contributes her grain of sand."

—María, El Alto, Bolivia
27 March, 2003

Abbreviations

AARAS	American Academy of Religion Academy Series
ABD	Anchor Bible Dictionary
ABRL	Anchor Bible Reference Library
ANEP	*The Ancient Near East in Pictures Relating to the Old Testament.* Edited by James B. Pritchard. Princeton: Princeton University Press, 1954
AThR	*Anglican Theological Review*
BAR	*Biblical Archaeology Review*
BBB	Bonner biblische Beiträge
BDAG	Bauer, W., F. W. Danker, W. F. Arndt, and F. W. Gingrich. *Greek-English Lexicon of the New Testament and Other Early Christian Literature.* 3d ed. Chicago, 1999
BETL	Bibliotheca Ephemeridum Theologicarum Lovaniensium
Bib	*Biblica*
BR	*Biblical Research*
BRev	*Bible Review*
BSac	*Bibliotheca sacra*
BTB	*Biblical Theology Bulletin*
CahRB	Cahiers de la Revue biblique
CBQ	*Catholic Biblical Quarterly*
CBQMS	Catholic Biblical Quarterly Monograph Series
C.E.	Common Era
CEDIMSE	Centro de Desarrollo Integral de la Mujer, Santa Escolástica
CODIMUJ	Coordinación Diocesana de Mujeres
CrossCur	*Cross Currents*
CTQ	*Concordia Theological Quarterly*
CurTM	*Currents in Theology and Mission*
DRev	*Downside Review*
ExpTim	*Expository Times*
FCB	Feminist Companion to the Bible

FCNT	Feminist Companion to the New Testament and Early Christian Writings
GCT	Gender, Culture, Theory
HDR	Harvard Dissertations in Religion
HTI	Hispanic Theological Initiative
HTR	*Harvard Theological Review*
HTS	Harvard Theological Studies
ICC	International Critical Commentary
Int	*Interpretation*
JBL	*Journal of Biblical Literature*
JFSR	*Journal of Feminist Studies in Religion*
JHTL	*Journal of Hispanic/Latino Theology*
JR	*Journal of Religion*
JSNTSup	Journal for the Study of the New Testament: Supplement Series
KJV	*King James Version*
NAB	*New American Bible*
NIV	*New International Version*
NJB	*New Jerusalem Bible*
NovT	*Novum Testamentum*
NovTSup	Novum Testamentum Supplements
NRSV	*New Revised Standard Version*
NSBT	New Studies in Biblical Theology
NTOA	Novum Testamentum et Orbis Antiquus
NTR	*New Theology Review*
NTS	*New Testament Studies*
OBT	Overtures to Biblical Theology
RB	*Revue Biblique*
Rel & Int Life	*Religion and Intellectual Life*
RIBLA	*Revista de interpretación bíblica latino-americana*
SAC	Studies in Antiquity and Christianity
SacPag	Sacra Pagina
SBL	Society of Biblical Literature
SBLDS	Society of Biblical Literature Dissertation Series
SBLMS	Society of Biblical Literature Monograph Series
SBLSymS	Society of Biblical Literature Symposium Series
SNTSMS	Society of New Testament Studies Monograph Series

ST	*Studia Theologica*
Str-B	Strack, H. L. and P. Billerbeck. *Kommentar zum Neuen Testament aus Talmud un Midrasch*. 6 vols. Munich: Beck, 1922-1961
TBT	*The Bible Today*
TDNT	*Theological Dictionary of the New Testament*. Edited by G. Kittel and G. Friedrich. Translated by G. W. Bromiley. 10 vols. Grand Rapids, 1964-1976
ThTo	*Theology Today*
TJT	*Toronto Journal of Theology*
TS	*Theological Studies*
USCCB	United States Conference of Catholic Bishops
USQR	*Union Seminary Quarterly Review*
ZNW	*Zeitschrift für die Neutestamentliche Wissenschaft und die Kunde der älteren Kirche*

Notes

Introduction Notes

1. All quotations of Scripture are from the *New Revised Standard Version* (*NRSV*), 1989.

2. See Gerald A. Arbuckle, *Violence, Society, and the Church: A Cultural Approach* (Collegeville, Minn.: Liturgical Press, 2004), 4–32, for analysis of how symbols and myths operate in cultures and how they relate to expressions of violence and power. See also Joseph Campbell, *The Power of Myth, with Bill Moyers*, ed. Betty Sue Flowers (New York: Doubleday, 1988).

3. See Alan Kirk, "Social and Cultural Memory," in *Memory, Tradition, and Text: Uses of the Past in Early Christianity*, edited by Alan Kirk and Tom Thatcher (*SBL Semeia* 52; Atlanta, 2005), 1–24, for analysis of how memory shapes identity, culture, and politics. In the same volume, Arthur J. Dewey, "The Locus for Death: Social Memory and the Passion Narratives," 119–28, observes that "ancient memory was heuristic, not simply mimetic" (126) and shows how the social memory was operative in the pattern of the "tale of the Persecution and Vindication of the Innocent One" (122) that emerges in the gospel passion narratives. Elizabeth A. Castelli, *Martyrdom and Memory: Early Christian Culture Making* (New York, N.Y.: Columbia University Press, 2004) shows how it is not so much the historical event but the stories that are later told about martyrs that are important. These stories serve specific theological, cultural, and political ends.

4. As Kenan B. Osborne observes in *The Resurrection of Jesus: New Considerations for Its Theological Interpretation* (New York: Paulist, 1997), there has never been a defined official statement on the meaning of the death of Jesus. "There are, of course, statements in the various creeds, which indicate that Jesus suffered under Pontius Pilate, was crucified, died, and was buried. But these creedal statements simply repeat the brief passages of the New Testament itself. . . . From earliest Christian times down to today, the theological investigation of the meaning of the death of Jesus has taken many paths. No one path is the standard, official, defined church doctrine, Protestant or Roman Catholic, as regards the meaning of the arrest, trial, and death of Jesus" (161–62). See also Francis Schüssler Fiorenza, "Redemption," in *The New Dictionary of Theology*, edited by J. Komonchak, M. Collins, and D. Lane (Wilmington, Del.: Michael Glazier, 1987), 836–51.

5. Renita Weems, *Battered Love: Marriage, Sex, and Violence in the Hebrew Prophets* (Minneapolis, Minn.: Fortress Press, 1995), 115.

6. Wendy M. Wright, "'A Wide and Fleshly Love': Images, Imagination, and the Study of Christian Spirituality," *Journal for the Society for the Study of*

Christian Spirituality 7, no. 1 (1999): 6. See also Richard Viladesau, *The Beauty of the Cross: The Passion of Christ in Theology and the Arts—From the Catacombs to the Eve of the Renaissance* (Oxford: Oxford University Press, 2006), for an analysis of how art and symbolism of the cross function as an alternative strand of theological expression.

7. There is a longstanding debate about what term to use to describe Spanish-speaking peoples who come to the United States from diverse realities and cultures in Latin America. Many use the term *Hispanic*; others prefer *Latino/a*. For a time, *chicano/a* held sway among Mexicans. Some prefer not to be identified by such a generic designation, but rather with their specific country of origin, e.g. Cuban-American, *puertoriqueña*, etc. Although women in Latin America would not ordinarily use the term *Latina* of themselves, for purposes of expediency, in this study, I will use the term *Latina* to speak both of women in Latin America and of women of Latin American ancestry living in the United States, realizing that they have vastly different situations and experiences.

8. This has become a popular expression among Latin American theologians. See, for example, Jon Sobrino, *The Principle of Mercy: Taking the Crucified People from the Cross* (Maryknoll, N.Y.: Orbis, 1994), especially 49–57.

9. Sobrino, *The Principle of Mercy*, 51–57.

10. Carmen Nanko-Fernández, "We Are Not Your Diversity. We Are the Church! Ecclesiological Reflections from the Marginalized Many," *Perspectivas. Hispanic Theological Initiative. Occasional Papers 10* (Fall, 2006), 96.

11. Elisabeth Schüssler Fiorenza, "'Waiting at Table': A Critical Feminist Theological Reflection on Diakonia," in *Concilium 198. Diakonia: Church for the Others*, ed. N. Greinacher and N. Mette (Edinburgh: T. & T. Clark, 1988), 84–94. Christine Smith, *Risking the Terror: Resurrection in This Life* (Cleveland, Ohio: Pilgrim, 2001), 19, speaks of the danger in preaching of appropriating another's voice as if it were one's own.

12. Susan Thistlethwaite, *Sex, Race, and God: Christian Feminism in Black and White* (New York: Crossroad, 1989), 89, warns of this sin: "As a member of the white women's movement, I have not confronted the terror of difference. I have sought to obliterate it in connections."

13. I understand feminism as "a commitment to the humanity, dignity, and equality of all to such an extent that one will work for changes in structures and in relationship patterns so that these occur to the equal good of all." Joan Chittister, "Yesterday's Dangerous Vision: Christian Feminism in the Catholic Church," *Sojourners* (July 1987), 18.

14. Elisabeth Schüssler Fiorenza, *Wisdom Ways: Introducing Feminist Biblical Interpretation* (Maryknoll, N.Y.: Orbis, 2001).

15. The term *hermeneutics* derives from the Greek word, *hermeneuō*, which means "to interpret." Hence, hermeneutical methods are methods of interpretation.

16. Schüssler Fiorenza, *Wisdom's Ways*, especially chap. 6, "Wisdom's Dance: Hermeneutical Moves and Turns," 165–91.

17. The term *kyriarchy* ("rule of the lord") is used by Schüssler Fiorenza to name interlocking structures of domination by elite males over women and disadvantaged men. This is in contrast to *patriarchy* ("rule of the father"), which is limited to the sex/gender system.

18. *Androcentricism*, derived from the Greek word *anēr*, "male," means "male-centeredness." It is a perspective that considers males to be normative humans and females as derivative and subordinate. See Mary E. Hunt, "Androcentrism," in *Dictionary of Feminist Theologies*, ed. Letty M. Russell and J. Shannon Clarkson (Louisville, Ky.: Westminster John Knox, 1996), 7.

19. Schüssler Fiorenza, *Wisdom's Ways*, 175.

20. Schüssler Fiorenza, *Wisdom's Ways*, 178.

21. Schüssler Fiorenza, *Wisdom's Ways*, 179. In her article, "Los ecos de la amistad: perspectivas del placer desde Honduras" (*Conspirando* 46 [2004]: 14–19), Mónica Maher describes the program "Misericordia Tejedoras de Sueños" ("Mercy Weavers of Dreams") in San Pedro Sula, Honduras, a program dedicated to helping women realize their dreams. Maher recounts how daily life is so hard, with so much poverty and violence that many women do not even know how to dream; they cannot imagine other possibilities. The objective of the program is to help women know they have a right to happiness and to encourage them to dream of other ways of being.

22. Schüssler Fiorenza, *Wisdom's Ways*, 185.

23. See Phyllis Trible, *Texts of Terror: Literary-Feminist Readings of Biblical Narratives* (Philadelphia: Fortress Press, 1984), who analyzes the stories of Hagar (Gen 16:1-16; 21:9-21), Tamar (2 Sam 13:1-22), the concubine from Bethlehem (Judg 19:1-30), and the daughter of Jephthah (Judg 11:29-40) from this perspective.

24. The term *mujerista*, from *mujer*, the Spanish word for "woman," is used by some Latinas to express the fact that their realities and modes of struggle differ from white North American and European women who call themselves feminists. See especially, Ada María Isasi-Díaz, *En La Lucha. In the Struggle: Elaborating a Mujerista Theology* (Minneapolis: Fortress Press, 1993); Isasi-Díaz, *Mujerista Theology* (Maryknoll, N.Y.: Orbis, 1996); and Isasi-Díaz, *La Lucha Continues: Mujerista Theology* (Maryknoll, N.Y.: Orbis, 2004). Others, like María Pilar Aquino ("Latina Feminist Theology: Central Features," in *A Reader in Latina Feminist Theology*, ed. María Pilar Aquino, Daisy L. Machado, and Jeannette Rodríguez [Austin: University of Texas Press, 2002], 133–60, especially 138–39), prefer the term *Latina feminists*. Many Latinas do not identify themselves with the liberation agendas of either *mujeristas* or Latina feminists.

25. Insights here are drawn from Ivone Gebara's nine steps toward a feminist biblical hermeneutics in *Teología a ritmo de mujer* (México, D.F.: Ediciones Dabar, 1995), 34–43; Pilar Aquino, "Latina Feminist Theology," 133–60; *Our Cry for Life: Feminist Theology from Latin America* (Maryknoll, N.Y.: Orbis, 1993), 121–31; Maricarmen Bracamontes, *Jesús de Nazaret y las Mujeres de su Tiempo*, 3ra ed. (Mexico, D.F.: Ediciones Schola, 2005); Isasi-Díaz, *Mujerista Theology*; and Elsa Támez, "Mujer y Biblia: Lectura de la Biblia desde la perspectiva femenina," in *Aportes para una Teología desde la Mujer*, ed. María Pilar Aquino (Madrid: Editorial Biblia y Fe, 1988), 70–79.

26. Pilar Aquino, "Latina Feminist Theology," 139; and Schüssler Fiorenza, *Wisdom's Ways*, 1–2.

27. Isasi-Díaz, "*Lo Cotidiano:* A Key Element of *Mujerista* Theology," *JHLT* 10, no. 1 (2002): 5–17; Isasi-Díaz, *Mujerista Theology*, 66–73; Isasi-Díaz, *La Lucha Continues*, 92–106; and Aquino, *Our Cry for Life*, 38–41.

28. For current United Nations statistics on poverty, illiteracy, pay gap, and violence toward women, see http://unstats.un.org/unsd/default.htm (accessed February 14, 2005). The UN Commission on the Status of Women estimates that women perform two-thirds of the world's work hours, for which they earn one-tenth of the world's income and own only one one-hundredth of the world's property. For the UN Millenium Development Goals, one of which is to promote gender equality and empowerment of women, see http://www.un.org/millenniumgoals/ (accessed February 27, 2007). For Amnesty International's Campaign to Stop Violence against Women, see http://www.amnestyusa.org/women/index.do (accessed February 27, 2007).

29. Támez, "Mujer y Biblia," 77–78. Aquino ("Latina Feminist Theology," 140) identifies the four most prominent characteristics of the global reality at the end of the twentieth century as poverty, inequality, social exclusion, and social insecurity.

30. "*Mestizaje* refers to the mixture of white people and native people living in what is now Latin America and the Caribbean. *Mulatez* refers to the mixtures of black people and white people" (Isasi-Díaz, *Mujerista Theology*, 64). See also Virgilio Elizondo, "*Mestizaje* as a Locus of Theological Reflection," in *Frontiers of Hispanic Theology in the United States*, ed. Allan Figueroa Deck (Maryknoll, N.Y.: Orbis, 1992), 104–23. Gloria Inés Loya, "Pathways to a *Mestiza* Feminist Theology," in Aquino, *Reader*, 217–40, explores the experience of Latinas living in the United States in light of the paradigmatic figures of Guadalupe and Malinalli Tenepal, or Malintzin, commonly called "La Malinche," the Indian woman who was taken by Hernán Cortéz to be his interpreter.

31. Isasi-Díaz, *Mujerista Theology*, 64–66; and Isasi-Díaz, *La Lucha Continues*, 69–91.

32. See Ivone Gebara, *Longing for Running Water: Ecofeminism and Liberation*, trans. David Molineaux (Minneapolis: Fortress Press, 1999); and Mary Judith Ross, *Ecofeminism in Latin America* (Maryknoll, N.Y.: Orbis, 2006).

33. Támez, "Mujer y Biblia," 76–77. Aquino, *Our Cry for Life*, 121–31, links the hermeneutics of suspicion with daring. See also María Clara Bingemer, "Women in the Future of the Theology of Liberation," in *The Future of Liberation Theology: Essays in Honor of Gustavo Gutiérrez*, ed. Marc H. Ellis and Otto Maduro (Maryknoll, N.Y.: Orbis, 1989), 473–90.

34. Isasi-Díaz, *Mujerista Theology*, 74–75. See also Arturo Bañuelas, "U.S. Hispanic Theology," *Missiology* 20, no. 2 (1992): 290–91.

35. Isasi-Díaz, *La Lucha Continues*, 9.

36. Isasi-Díaz, *Mujerista Theology*, 73; Isasi-Díaz, *La Lucha Continues*, 51.

37. Isasi-Díaz, *La Lucha Continues*, 4.

38. Pablo Richard, "Cinco Peqeñas Esperanzas en la Lectura Comunitaria de la Biblia," *RIBLA* 39 (2001): 7–9, outlines five ways in which communal reading of the Bible gives transformative hope. For each baptized person

who learns to read and interpret the Bible, the act fosters authority, legitimacy, security, autonomy, and liberty.

39. Bracamontes (*Jesús de Nazaret*, 52) notes that women, especially those in Latin America who are poor, speak of the Bible as the "light of our life," "Word of life that strengthens our faith," and "liberating word that brings to light the value of every human person."

40. Ada Maria Isasi-Díaz and Yolanda Tarango, *Hispanic Women Prophetic Voice in the Church* (San Francisco: Harper & Row, 1988), 66.

41. The following was recounted to me by Don Samuel in an interview in Mexico City on January 10, 2005. See also Samuel Ruiz con la colaboración de Carles Torner, *Cómo me convirtieron los Indígenas* (Santander, Spain: Sal Terrae, 2002).

42. See *Con Mirada, Mente, y Corazón de Mujer* (México, D.F.: CODIMUJ, 1999), 29–35. A description of the work of CODIMUJ is available in English at www.ciepac.org/archivo/bulletins/ingles/Ing152.html (accessed February 27, 2007).

43. Excellent tools authored by two of the Benedictine Sisters, Patricia Henry Ford and Maricarmen Bracamontes, are *Mujeres y Derechos Humanos. Aportes Sociales y Eclesiales: Perspectivas y Alternativas* (México, D.F.: Ediciones Schola, 1998), *Jesús y las Mujeres; Ensayo de Una Espiritualidad Para el Nuevo Milenio* (Mexico, D.F.: Ediciones Schola, 1999), and the third revised edition by Maricarmen Bracamontes, *Jesús de Nazaret y las Mujeres de su Tiempo* (Mexico, D.F.: Ediciones Schola, 2005). See their website at www.avantel.net/~cedimse/main.php (accessed February 27, 2007).

44. A handbook and materials entitled "Construyendo Hogares Sin Violencia" has been developed by Hna. Patricia A. Dieringer, CSC, with Hna. Alicia Rojas, A.S. Martha Salvatierra Ponce, Dra. Carmen Cuadros Salas, Hna. Noyli Rios, and A.S. Nelly Meza Jaimes (Caritas Chosica, 2001).

45. This was shared with me in conversation with Sister Patricia, Marta, and Mari in Ate, Peru, on April 16, 2003.

46. *Pachamama* ("Mother Earth," from Aymara *pacha*, "earth," and *mama*, "mother") is the benevolent fertility goddess in ancient Inca mythology, who presides over planting and harvesting.

47. Catherine Williams, quoted by Joseph Fedora in "Of One Heart," *Maryknoll* 97, no. 8 (2003): 27.

48. These dynamics are described in Isasi-Díaz and Tarango, *Hispanic Women*, 98. I have been privileged to see these in action in each of the communities described.

49. Amparo, at a gathering of women leaders and educators at Centro Bartolomé de las Casas, Lima, Peru, on April 10, 2003. In many cases in this study, I will use only first names, sometimes fictitious, because many of the women with whom I spoke preferred not to be identified. In most instances, quotations represent similar articulations by many other women.

50. Elizabeth A. Johnson, *She Who Is: The Mystery of God in Feminist Theological Discourse* (New York: Crossroad, 1992), 6.

51. Johnson, *She Who Is*, 6.

52. María José F. Rosado Nunes, "Women's Voices in Latin American Theology," in *The Power of Naming: A Concilium Reader in Feminist Liberation Theology*, ed. Elisabeth Schüssler Fiorenza (Maryknoll, N.Y.: Orbis, 1996), 14–26.

53. Rosado Nunes, "Women's Voices in Latin American Theology," 19.

54. Rosado Nunes, "Women's Voices in Latin American Theology," 20.

55. Rosado Nunes, "Women's Voices in Latin American Theology," 20.

56. Mary Daly, *Beyond God the Father* (Boston: Beacon Press, 1973), 77.

57. Rita Nakashima Brock, *Journeys by Heart: A Christology of Erotic Power* (New York: Crossroad, 1988); Rita Nakashima Brock and Rebecca Ann Parker, *Proverbs of Ashes: Violence, Redemptive Suffering, and the Search for What Saves Us* (Boston: Beacon, 2001); Jacqueline Grant, *White Women's Christ and Black Women's Jesus: Feminist Christology and Womanist Response* (Atlanta: Scholars Press, 1989); Mary Grey, *Redeeming the Dream: Feminism, Redemption and Christian Tradition* (London: SPCK, 1989); Grey, *Feminism, Redemption and the Christian Tradition* (Mystic, Conn.: Twenty-Third Publications, 1990); Carter Heyward, *Saving Jesus from Those Who Are Right* (Philadelphia: Fortress Press, 1999); Heyward, *The Redemption of God: A Theology of Mutual Relation* (Lanham, Md.: University Press of America, 1982); Johnson, *She Who Is*; Chung Hyun Kyung, *Struggle To Be the Sun Again: Introducing Asian Women's Theology* (London: SCM Press, 1990); Hyun Kyung, "Han-Pu-Ri: Doing Theology from a Korean Woman's Perspective," in *We Dare to Dream*, ed. Virginia Fabella and Sun Ai Lee Park (Hong Kong: AWCCT, 1989); Kwok Pui-Lan, "God Weeps with Our Pain," in *East Asia Journal of Theology* 2, no. 2 (1984): 220–32; Elisabeth Moltmann-Wendel, *A Land Flowing with Milk and Honey* (London: SCM, 1986); Moltmann-Wendel, "Gibt es eine feministische Kreuzestheologie," in *Das Kreuz mit dem Kreuz Hofgeismarer Protokolle*, ed. Eveline Valtink (Hofgeismar, Ger.: Evangelische Akademie, 1990); Luise Schottroff, *Let the Oppressed Go Free: Feminist Perspectives on the New Testament* (Louisville, Ky.: Westminster/John Knox, 1993); Elisabeth Schüssler Fiorenza, *Jesus: Miriam's Son, Sophia's Prophet* (New York: Continuum, 1994); Dorothee Sölle, *Theology for Sceptics: Reflections on God* (Philadelphia: Fortress Press, 1995); Regula Strobel, "Feministische Kritik an traditionellen Kreuzestheologien," in *Vom Verlangen nach Heilwerden Christologie in feministisch-theologischer Sicht*, ed. Doris Strahm and Regula Strobel (Fribourg, Switzerland: Exodus, 1991), 52–64; Strobel, "New Ways of Speaking about the Cross: A New Basis for Christian Identity," in *Toward a New Heaven and a New Earth: Essays in Honor of Elisabeth Schüssler Fiorenza*, ed. Fernando F. Segovia (Maryknoll, N.Y.: Orbis, 2003), 351–67; and Delores Williams, *Sisters in the Wilderness: The Challenge of Womanist God-Talk* (Maryknoll, N.Y.: Orbis, 1993).

58. Joanne Carlson Brown and Rebecca Parker, "For God So Loved the World?" in *Christianity, Patriarchy, and Abuse*, ed. Joanne Carlson Brown and Carole R. Bohn (New York: Pilgrim Press, 1989), 2.

59. Rita Nakashima Brock, *Journeys by Heart: A Christology of Erotic Power* (New York: Crossroad, 1988).

60. Anna María Santiago, "Women, Why Do You Weep? Reassessing the Meaning of Suffering in the Pastoral Care of Victims of Domestic Violence," unpublished paper, 1999. Used with permission.

61. Delores Williams, "A Womanist Perspective on Sin," in *A Troubling in My Soul: Womanist Perspectives on Evil*, ed. Emilie Townes (Maryknoll, N.Y.: Orbis, 1993), 130–49.

62. Schüssler Fiorenza, *Jesus: Miriam's Child, Sophia's Prophet*, 102.

63. Moltmann-Wendel, "Gibt es eine feministische Kreuzestheologie," 92; and Grey, *Feminism, Redemption, and the Christian Tradition*, 186.

64. Julia Esquivel, *Threatened with Resurrection: Prayers and Poems from an Exiled Guatemalan* (Elgin, Ill.: Brethren Press, 1982) 59–63.

Chapter 1 Notes

1. This and the next three quotations are from women in the diocese of San Cristóbal de las Casas, Chiapas, whose reflections are recorded in CODIMUJ, *Con mirada, mente y corazón de mujer* (Mexico, D.F.: Author, 1999), 17–22.

2. Of late, many scholars, in addition to those listed in chap. 1 n. 55, have critiqued objectionable aspects of the doctrine of atonement. For a brief overview, see the introduction in Stephen Finlan, *Problems with Atonement: The Origins of, and Controversy about, the Atonement Doctrine* (Collegeville, Minn.: Liturgical Press, 2005), 1–3. See also Anthony W. Bartlett, *Cross Purposes: The Violent Grammar of Christian Atonement* (Harrisburg, Pa.: Trinity, 2001); Hans Boersma, *Violence, Hospitality, and the Cross: Reappropriating the Atonement Tradition* (Grand Rapids, Mich.: Baker, 2004); Colleen Carpenter Cullinan, *Redeeming the Story: Women, Suffering and Christ* (New York: Continuum, 2004); S. Mark Heim, *Saved from Sacrifice: A Theology of the Cross* (Grand Rapids, Mich.: Eerdmans, 2006); Stephen J. Patterson, *Beyond the Passion: Rethinking the Death and Life of Jesus* (Minneapolis: Fortress Press, 2004); Peter Schmiechen, *Saving Power: Theories of Atonement and Forms of the Church* (Grand Rapids, Mich.: Eerdmans, 2005); Mark W. Thomsen, *Christ Crucified: A 21st-Century Missiology of the Cross* (Minneapolis: Lutheran University Press, 2004); Deanna A. Thompson, *Crossing the Divide: Luther, Feminism, and the Cross* (Minneapolis: Fortress Press, 2004); and Marit Trelstad, ed., *Cross Examinations: Readings on the Meaning of the Cross Today* (Minneapolis: Augsburg Fortress, 2006).

3. Women from five different indigenous ethnicities participate in CODIMUJ in Chiapas: Ch'oles, Tojolobales, Tzeltales, Tzotziles, and Zoques. I was privileged to meet with groups of women who were Tzeltal and Tzotzil.

4. Vicenta Mamani Bernabé, *Identidad y espiritualidad de la mujer Aymara* (La Paz, Bolivia: Misión de Basilea-Suiza, 2000), 88.

5. An observation made by a woman student in the School of Social Work at Universidad San Andrés, La Paz, Bolivia, on March 25, 2003. See also Mamani, *Identidad y espiritualidad de la mujer Aymara*, 89, for similar remarks.

6. An observation by Amparo, a pastoral worker, during a conversation with women leaders who work on gender issues at Instituto Bartolomé de las Casas in Lima on April 10, 2003. These are professional women with theological education, who had been meeting for seven years at the time of our meeting. The center was founded by Gustavo Gutiérrez and houses

his library. See their webpage at http://www.bcasas.org.pe/ (accessed Febraury 28, 2007). See CODIMUJ, *Con mirada, mente y corazón de mujer*, 37, for a similar observation on the internalization of guilt by women in Chiapas.

7. Martin Hengel, *The Atonement: The Origins of the Doctrine in the New Testament*, trans. John Bowden (Philadelphia: Fortress Press, 1981), 34–39, categorizes the Pauline soteriological statements in two forms: (1) statements that express the "giving up" of Jesus, using the verb *didōmi* ("give") and its compound *paradidōmi* ("hand over"), and (2) those expressed in terms of "dying for." In almost all instances, Paul formulates it as Christ's action; in Romans 4:25 (expressed with a theological passive) and Romans 8:32, it is God who gives up the Son.

8. For an analysis of various metaphors for redemption in Pauline texts in dialogue with contemporary questions concerning violent deaths of innocent persons in Peru, see Leif E. Vaage, "Redención y Violencia: El Sentido de la Muerte de Cristo en Pablo. Apuntes hacia una relectura," *RIBLA* 18 (1994): 133–53. David Balch, "Paul's Portrait of Christ Crucified (Gal 3:1) in Light of Paintings and Sculptures of Suffering and Death in Pompeiian and Roman Houses," in *Early Christian Families in Context. An Interdisciplinary Dialogue*, ed. David L. Balch and Carolyn Osiek (Grand Rapids, Mich.: Eerdmans, 2003), 84–108 shows how contemporary domestic art emphasizing pathos would have provided a meaningful cultural context, whether consciously or unconsciously assimilated, for understanding Paul's gospel of Christ's suffering and his saving death. For other studies on Paul and the cross, see Stephen A. Cummins, *Paul and the Crucified Christ in Antioch: Maccabean Martyrdom and Galatians 1 and 2* (Cambridge: Cambridge University Press, 2001); Michael J. Gorman, *Cruciformity: Paul's Narrative Spirituality of the Cross* (Grand Rapids, Mich.: Eerdmans, 2001); Jerome Murphy-O'Connor, "'Even Death on a Cross': Crucifixion in the Pauline Letters," in *The Cross in Christian Tradition: From Paul to Bonaventure*, ed. Elizabeth A. Dreyer (New York: Paulist, 2000), 21–50; Raymond Pickett, *The Cross in Corinth: The Social Significance of the Death of Jesus* (Sheffield: Sheffield Academic Press, 1997); and Demetrius K. Williams, *Enemies of the Cross of Christ: The Terminology of the Cross and Conflict in Philippians* (Sheffield: Sheffield Academic Press, 2002).

9. Stephen Finlan, in his scholarly study *The Background and Content of Paul's Cultic Atonement Metaphors* (Atlanta: SBL, 2004), and his more popular version, *Problems with Atonement: The Origins of, and Controversy about, the Atonement Doctrine* (Collegeville, Minn.: Liturgical Press, 2005), analyzes the origin and meanings of these metaphors in Paul. I follow Finlan in much of what follows in this section.

10. See Gary A. Anderson, "Sacrifice," ABD, 5.870-86, for a description and history of the various kinds of sacrifices described in the Old Testament. Jacob Milgrom, *Leviticus 1-16* (New York: Doubleday, 1991), 440, lists four possible purposes that scholars of comparative religions have identified behind the institution of sacrifice: (1) to provide food for the god; (2) to assimilate the life force of the sacrificial animal; (3) to effect union with the deity; and (4) to induce the aid of the deity by means of a gift. Bruce Malina, "Mediterranean Sacrifice: Dimensions of Domestic and Political

Religion," *BTB* 26 (1996): 26–44, examines Greek, Roman, and Israelite sacrifice and defines it as "a ritual in which a deity or deities is/are offered some form of inducement, rendered humanly irretrievable, with a view to some life-effect for the offerer(s)" (37). Sacrifice is concerned with either "maintenance of life, the restoration of life or the establishment of life" (38). Malina investigates the meaning of sacrifice in ancient Greek, Roman, and Israelite culture and the social systems in which sacrifice made sense, concluding that in modern social systems with "a configuration of social features including economics as focal institution, the demise of the cult of omnipotence, the emergence of individualism, the rise of empathy and the awareness of universal human rights, it seems sacrifice would not make sense, except as metaphor in a celebratory or fellowship context" (42). Thus, he notes a shift since Vatican II in the Roman Catholic understanding of the Mass, from an expiatory sacrifice to a community celebration and fellowship sacrifice.

11. See Hans-Josef Klauck, "Sacrifice," ABD, 5.886-91 for a comprehensive treatment of New Testament texts that speak of sacrifice.

12. Finlan, *Problems*, 20–29, outlines a six-pronged process of the transformation and eventual abandonment of sacrifice through substitution, moralizing, internalization, metaphor, rejectionism, and philosophic reflection.

13. Finlan, *Problems*, 49.

14. See NRSV, NIV. In KJV, it is rendered "propitiation"; in NJB, "a sacrifice for reconciliaton"; in NAB, "expiation"; in *Reina-Valera*, *"expiación."* The only other New Testament occurrence of *hilastērion* is in Hebrews 9:5, where the author is describing the "earthly sanctuary" of the "first covenant" (Heb 9:1). The only occurrence of the verb *hilaskomai* is in the prayer of the toll collector in the Temple, "God, be merciful (*hilasthēti*) to me, a sinner!" (Luke 18:13).

15. Finlan, *Problems*, 40. See also Dan P. Bailey, "Jesus as the Mercy Seat: The Semantics and Theology of Paul's Use of *Hilastērion* in Romans 3:25," PhD diss., Cambridge University, 1999.

16. Although Hebrews traditionally has been clustered with the Pauline letters, it is clear from the writing style and theology that it is not written by Paul. From his use of the Hebrew scriptures, it is most likely that the author is a Jewish Christian. He has a good Hellenistic education and interprets scripture in a manner of homiletic midrash, similar to Philo. Hebrews fits the genre of homily better than the genre of a letter. In his closing, the author calls it a "word of exhortation" (13:22). It was written before 95 C.E., as it is quoted extensively in 1 Clement.

17. The word *archiereus* ("high priest") occurs eighteen times: Hebrews 2:17; 3:1; 4:14, 15; 5:1, 5, 10; 6:20; 7:26, 27, 28; 8:1, 3; 9:7, 11, 25; 10:11; 13:11. Historically, Jesus was not of priestly lineage; the author uses a lengthy midrash to establish the legitimacy and surpassing nature of Jesus' high priesthood in chapters 5–7.

18. Leaven is a symbol of corruption in Exodus 12:15-20, 34; Leviticus 2:11; Mark 8:15; Luke 12:1; 1 Corinthians 5:6-7; and Galatians 5:9. See also Plutarch, *Mor.* 289 E-F.

19. For a detailed discussion, see Raymond E. Brown, *The Gospel According to John i-xii* (Garden City, N.Y.: Doubleday, 1966), 58–63.

20. Brown, *The Gospel According to John*, 63, notes, however, that more often it was a bull or a goat that was sacrificed as a sin offering.

21. The chronology of the Fourth Gospel differs from that of the synoptic Gospels. In the former, Jesus is executed on the day of preparation for Passover (John 19:14). The latter portray Jesus' Last Supper with his disciples as a Passover meal at which they partake of the lamb that has already been slaughtered.

22. Francis J. Moloney, *The Gospel of John* (Collegeville, Minn.: Liturgical Press, 1998), 59.

23. This observation is made by Raymond Brown, *The Gospel According to John*, 62. He notes, however, that "by Jesus' time the sacrificial aspect had begun to infiltrate the concept of the paschal lamb because the priests had arrogated to themselves the slaying of the lambs." Brown thinks that the Fourth Evangelist intends the reference to Jesus as both the Suffering Servant and the paschal lamb (63).

24. For other occurrences of *apolytrōsis*, see Romans 8:23; 1 Corinthians 1:30; Ephesians 1:7, 14; 4:30; Colossians 1:14; Hebrews 9:15; 11:35; Luke 21:28.

25. BDAG: Bauer, W., F. W. Danker, W. F. Arndt, and F. W. Gingrich. *Greek-English Lexicon of the New Testament and Other Early Christian Literature*. 3d ed. Chicago, 1999, 117.

26. These are the only two New Testament instances of *lytron*. In Luke's version, the reference to ransom is missing: "I am among you as one who serves" (22:27). Several other times, Luke uses words from this root but not in a way that explicitly links redemption to Jesus' death. In Luke 21:28, the Third Evangelist uses the noun *apolytrōsis*, but here it is associated with Jesus' coming again, not with his death. Luke uses the verb *lytroomai* ("to free by paying a ransom, redeem," BDAG, 606) in the resurrection appearance to Cleopas and his companion on the road to Emmaus: "We had hoped that he was the one to redeem (*lytrousthai*) Israel" (24:21). This echoes the prophecy on the lips of Zechariah that God has looked favorably on the people "and redeemed (*epoiēsen lytrōsin*) them" (Luke 1:68) and the words of the prophet Anna, who kept speaking in the Temple about the child "to all who were looking for the redemption (*lytrōsin*) of Israel" (Luke 2:38). In these latter two instances, the noun *lytrōsis* connotes the experience of being liberated from captivity and continues to carry the underlying nuance of redemption of something for a price. However, these prophecies are situated in the chapters that concern Jesus' birth and do not explicitly allude to his death. See also Finlan, *The Background*, 164–65.

27. BDAG, 605.

28. 1 Corinthians 6:20; 7:23; Galatians 3:13; 4:5; similarly 1 Peter 1:18-19; 2 Peter 2:1; Revelation 5:9. The same concept is found in Acts 20:28, but with the verb *peripoieō*, "to gain." See Finlan, *The Background*, 164–65.

29. Similarly, see Ephesians 1:7; Hebrews 9:12.

30. See further Gustaf Aulén, *Christus Victor: An Historical Study of the Three Main Types of the Idea of the Atonement* (London: Society for Promoting Christian Knowledge, 1931); J. Denny Weaver, *The Nonviolent Atonement* (Grand Rapids, Mich.: Eerdmans, 2001); and Josephine Massyngbaerde

Ford, *Redeemer, Friend, and Mother: Salvation in Antiquity and in the Gospel of John* (Minneapolis: Fortress Press, 1997), 6–22.

31. Finlan, *Problems*, 67–71.

32. Variations on this theme can be seen in Irenaeus, Origen of Alexandria, Gregory of Nyssa, Augustine, and Pope Gregory the Great. Augustine further formulates the theory of original sin, by which he sees humanity incapable of not sinning, necessitating Christ's redeeming death. Gregory the Great carries this further, insisting that human sin was so great that only a human sacrifice, and a sinless one at that, would be sufficient payment to God. See also Finlan, *Problems*, 67–71.

33. For analyses of redemption from feminist perspectives, see Gail Paterson Corrington, *Her Image of Salvation: Female Saviors and Formative Christianity* (Louisville: Westminster John Knox, 1992); Cullinan, *Redeeming the Story*; Mary Grey, *Feminism, Redemption, and the Christian Tradition* (Mystic, Conn.: Twenty-Third, 1990); Rosemary Radford Ruether, *Women and Redemption: A Theological History* (Minneapolis: Fortress Press, 1998); and Radford Ruether, *Introducing Redemption in Christian Feminism* (Cleveland: Pilgrim, 1998). See also David H. Kelsey, *Imagining Redemption* (Louisville: Westminster John Knox, 2005).

34. Israel was not alone in using expulsion rituals. For a brief description of how these were used in Hittite, Greek, and Mesopotamian societies, see Finlan, *Problems*, 6–8, 31–38. For more technical analysis, see David P. Wright, *The Disposal of Impurity: Elimination Rites in the Bible and in Hittite and Mesopotamian Literature* (Atlanta: Scholars, 1987); and Walter Burkert, *Structure and History in Greek Mythology and Ritual* (Berkeley: University of California Press, 1979). René Girard, *The Scapegoat*, trans. Yvonne Freccero (Baltimore: Johns Hopkins University Press, 1986), analyzes scapegoating mechanisms from an anthropological perspective.

35. See also Romans 6:6; 7:4; 8:3; 1 Corinthians 4:13; 5:7; 2 Corinthians 5:15; Finlan, *Problems*, 6–8, 48–52. Hengel, *The Atonement*, 24–28, describes the Greek use of scapegoating, or the *pharmakos* ritual, in which a man is driven out of the city or even killed for purification of the country. However, in this tradition, the person is not a heroic figure but one who is crippled or poor.

36. Finlan, *Problems*, 7–8. We will examine reconciliation more closely in chapter 4. The adoption metaphor is evident in texts such as Romans 8:15, 23; Galatians 4:5; Ephesians 1:5.

37. See further Barbara E. Reid, "Justification," in *Collegeville Pastoral Dictionary of Biblical Theology*, ed. Carroll Stuhlmueller (Collegeville, Minn.: Liturgical Press, 1996), 520–22.

38. Finlan, *Problems*, 9.

39. For a collection of passages on martyrdom and noble death from Greek, Hellenistic, Jewish, and early Christian sources, see Jan Willem van Henten, *Martyrdom and Noble Death* (London and New York: Routledge, 2002). See also Hengel, *The Atonement*, 6–18.

40. Aristotle, *Eth. Nic.*, 1169a.

41. Plato, *Crito*, 50B–51E, 52D.

42. Scholars disagree on the dating of the Maccabean literature. While some date 2 Maccabees as late as the middle of the first century C.E. and oth-

ers as early as mid-second-century B.C.E. most consider it pre-Christian. The narrative setting begins with the reign of Seleucus IV (187–175 B.C.E.) leading to the Maccabean revolt and concludes with Judas Maccabeus' defeat of Nicanor (161 B.C.E.). Dates between 63 B.C.E. and 120 C.E. are proposed for 4 Maccabees, with most scholars dating it to the first century C.E. While the narrative setting for the martyr traditions recounted in chapters 3–18 is Jerusalem, the actual locale of composition of the book is unknown.

43. Note this juxtaposition of several images akin to Romans 3:23-26.

44. Similarly, see 1 Thessalonians 5:10.

45. We will take up the image of martyr further in chapter 3.

46. See, for example, Romans 3:23-26; 6:6; 8:3; Galatians 3:10-13; and Finlan, *Problems*, 7, 45, 49.

47. Finlan, *Problems*, 66, 79.

48. James Alison, *On Being Liked* (New York: Crossroad, 2003), 23–24.

49. Finlan, *Problems*, 9.

50. Finlan, *Problems*, 82–83.

51. Alison, *On Being Liked*, 14.

52. Joanne Carlson Brown and Rebecca Parker, "For God So Loved the World?" in *Violence against Women and Children: A Christian Theological Sourcebook*, ed. Carol J. Adams and Marie M. Fortune (New York: Continuum, 1998), 40.

53. Brown and Parker, "For God So Loved," 40.

54. Alison, *On Being Liked*, 26.

55. Brown and Parker, "For God So Loved," 42.

56. Brown and Parker, "For God So Loved," 44–45. The opposite dynamic is often operative: women who are abused are convinced that whatever is awry in the relationship is *their* fault and it is *they* who need to change.

57. Rita Nakashima Brock and Rebecca Ann Parker, *Proverbs of Ashes: Violence, Redemptive Suffering and the Search for What Saves Us* (Boston: Beacon, 2001), 41.

58. René Girard, *The Scapegoat*, trans. Yvonne Freccero (Baltimore: Johns Hopkins University Press, 1986); Girard, *I See Satan Fall Like Lightning*, trans. James G. Williams (Maryknoll, N.Y.: Orbis, 2001). See Patricia M. McDonald, *God and Violence: Biblical Resources for Living in a Small World* (Scottdale, Pa: Herald Press, 2004), 293–305; Walter Wink, *Engaging the Powers: Discernment and Resistance in a World of Domination* (Minneapolis: Fortress Press, 1992), 144–55; and Finlan, *Problems*, 89–93, for summaries and critiques of Girard's theory.

59. For reasons why the designation "Old Testament" is preferable to "Hebrew Bible," "First Testament," or "Jewish Scriptures," see Amy-Jill Levine, *The Misunderstood Jew: The Church and the Scandal of the Jewish Jesus* (SanFrancisco: Harper, 2006), 193–99.

60. James Alison, *Faith Beyond Resentment* (New York: Crossroad, 2001), 158.

61. Wink, *Engaging the Powers*, 148, 153, 159, 163. Wink rightly criticizes Girard for not seeing that the sacrificial, expiatory death of Jesus is far more pervasive in the New Testament than Girard allows (153).

62. Finlan, *Problems*, 93; and Jack Nelson-Pallmeyer, *Jesus Against Christianity: Reclaiming the Missing Jesus* (Harrisburg: Trinity, 2001), 223. A similar criticism can be made of Robert G. Hammerton-Kelly, *Sacred Violence: Paul's Hermeneutic of the Cross* (Minneapolis: Augsburg Fortress, 1992).

63. Nelson-Pallmeyer, *Jesus Against Christianity*, 223.

64. Joanna Dewey, "Sacrifice No More," in *Distant Voices Drawing Near: Essays in Honor of Antoinette Clark Wire*, ed. Holly Hearon (Collegeville, Minn.: Liturgical Press, 2004), 159. What follows is a summary of Dewey's position.

65. Dewey, "Sacrifice No More," 170.

66. See further Stanley K. Stowers, "Greeks Who Sacrifice and Those Who Do Not: Toward an Anthropology of Greek Religion," in *The Social World of the First Christians: Essays in Honor of Wayne A. Meeks*, eds. Michael White and O. Larry Yarbrough (Minneapolis: Fortress Press, 1995), 330.

67. Cyprian, Letter 63, quoted in Nancy Jay, *Throughout Your Generations Forever: Sacrifice, Religion, and Paternity* (Chicago: University of Chicago Press, 1992), 116; and Dewey, "Sacrifice No More," 167.

68. Dewey, "Sacrifice No More," 170.

69. Alison, *Faith Beyond Resentment*, 164–65.

70. Alison, *Faith Beyond Resentment*, 161.

71. Alison, *Faith Beyond Resentment*, 161.

72. Robert J. Daly, "Sacrifice: The Way to Enter the Paschal Mystery," *America* 188, no. 16 (May 12, 2003): 14.

73. Daly, "Sacrifice," 15.

74. Daly, "Sacrifice," 16.

75. Robert J. Daly, "Sacrifice Unveiled or Sacrifice Revisited: Trinitarian and Liturgical Perspectives," *TS* 64 (2003): 41.

76. Daly, "Sacrifice," *America*, 17.

77. Elisabeth Moltmann-Wendel, *Rediscovering Friendship: Awakening to the Promise and Power of Women's Friendships* (Minneapolis: Fortress Press, 2000), 31.

78. Moltmann-Wendel, *Rediscovering Friendship*, 43.

79. Finlan, *Problems*, 112.

80. Hans-Josef Klauck, "Sacrifice," ABD, 5.887.

81. Finlan, *Problems*, 113.

82. Dewey, "Sacrifice No More," 170; Finlan, *Problems*, 114.

83. Finlan, *Problems*, 117–24 makes the case forcefully that the Incarnation is the central doctrine of Christianity, not the Atonement.

84. Luke 22:15 makes the reference to Passover most explicit.

85. See further Joachim Jeremias, *The Eucharistic Words of Jesus* (Philadelphia: Fortress Press, 1966).

86. The theme of Jesus' inclusive table practice is present in all the gospels but is particularly emphasized by Luke. See E. P. Sanders, *Jesus and Judaism* (Philadelphia: Fortress Press, 1985), 174–211, on how Jesus' eating with sinners was a sign that God would save them and the controversy this engendered because he ate with them while they were still regarded as sinners, without first requiring repentance from them.

87. Matthew adds the instruction to "eat": "Take, eat, this is my body" (26:26).

88. As Joseph A. Fitzmyer, *The Gospel According to Luke* (Garden City, N.Y.: Doubleday, 1985), 2.1399-1400, points out, the Greek word *sōma* should be understood, not only in the sense of "body," but even of "self"—a sense found also in 1 Corinthians 9:27; 13:3; Romans 12:1; Phillipians 1:20, and also in Hellenistic Greek. Moreover, flesh and blood together designate the whole person. See also Jeremias, *The Eucharistic Words of Jesus*, 198–201.

89. The Lucan wording is close to that found in 1 Corinthians 11:24, where Paul preserves the tradition of Jesus' words: "This is my body that is for you. Do this in remembrance of me."

90. See Fitzmyer, *Luke*, 1400-01. Jeremias, *Eucharistic Words of Jesus*, 237–55, explores the possible links between the Lucan remembrance formula and commemorative meals for the dead in Hellenistic Christian circles and memorial formulae in Palestinian Judaism. He understands Jesus' words at the Last Supper to mean, "'This do, that God may remember me': *God remembers the Messiah in that he causes the kingdom to break in by the parousia*" (252, italics in the original).

91. In the Gospel of Luke, there are two cups. The first (22:17) precedes the offer of the bread and does not have an interpretive word. It is framed by two declarations of Jesus' abstinence until the reign of God is fulfilled. The second cup, after the supper (22:20), has an interpretation similar to Mark and Matthew. There is a text-critical problem concerning Luke 22:19b-20. There are six different known forms. On the basis of the principle of *lectio dificilior* and because of the number of Greek manuscripts that support the longer reading that includes vv. 19b-20, it is most likely that they were original. See Fitzmyer, *Luke*, 2.1387-89. Bradly S. Billings, "The Disputed Words in the Lukan Institution Narrative (Luke 22:19b-20): A Sociological Answer to a Textual Problem," *JBL* 125, no. 3 (2006): 507–26, offers a hypothesis to explain the origin of the shorter reading.

92. Isaiah 51:17; Jeremiah 25:15, 49:12, 51:7; and Lamentations 4:21. See also *Mart. Isa.* 5:13.

93. John R. Donahue and Daniel J. Harrington, *The Gospel of Mark* (Collegeville, Minn.: Liturgical Press, 2002), 396.

94. Moses typology is particularly strong in the First Gospel. The threats to the infant Jesus' life (Matt 2:16-18) mirror those toward Moses (Exod 1:15-22). Matthew depicts Jesus as authoritative Teacher of the Law, often instructing from a mountaintop (5:1; 15:29; 17:1; 28:16). The evangelist's arrangement of five major blocks of teaching can be seen as a deliberate parallel to the five books of the Law of Moses. Explicit references to Moses occur at Matthew 8:4; 17:3-4; 19:7-8; 22:24; 23:2.

95. Paul also preserves this wording in 1 Corinthians 11:25: "This cup is the new covenant in my blood." Unlike Luke, Paul adds the same instruction as for the bread, "Do this, as often as you drink it, in remembrance of me."

96. Guy P. Coutourier, "Jeremiah," in *Jerome Biblical Commentary*, ed. Raymond E. Brown, Joseph A. Fitzmyer, and Roland E. Murphy (Englewood Cliffs, N.J.: Prentice-Hall, 1968), 327.

97. Luke Timothy Johnson, *Luke* (Collegeville, Minn.: Liturgical Press, 1991) 339. See 1 Corinthians 11:25; 2 Corinthians 3:6; Galatians 3:15; 4:24; Hebrews 7:22; 8:8-10; 9:15; 10:16; 12:24; Revelation 11:9.

98. Fitzmyer, *Luke*, 2.1403.

99. See W. D. Davies and Dale C. Allison, *The Gospel According to St. Matthew*, 3 vols. (Edinburgh: T & T Clark, 1988, 1991, 1997), 3.474. In Matthew 26:28, the preposition *peri* carries the connotation usually conveyed by *hyper*, "on account of, for." It also has a sense of encircling, encompassing, "around." See BDAG, 798; Maximilian Zerwick, *Biblical Greek* (Rome, 1963), §96. Thus, all are "encompassed" in the effects of Jesus' death. In 1 Timothy 2:6, the all-encompassing effect of Jesus' self-gift is clear: Jesus "gave himself a ransom for all (*hyper pantōn*)."

100. The same expression, "for you," *hyper hymōn*, occurs in 1 Corinthians 11:24 in connection with Jesus' offer of the bread: "This is my body that is for you." Martin Hengel, *The Atonement*, 71, sees this as a tendency on the part of the early Christians to reduce the scope of salvation from a universal gift "for all" (Mark 10:45; 14:24; 1 Tim 2:6) to that limited to one's own community.

101. Sharyn Dowd and Elizabeth Struthers Malbon, "The Significance of Jesus' Death in Mark: Narrative Context and Authorial Audience," in *The Trial and Death of Jesus: Essays on the Passion Narrative in Mark*, ed. Geert Van Oyen and Tom Shepherd (Leuven, Belgium: Peeters, 2006), 1–31. It was Morna D. Hooker, *Jesus and the Servant: The Influence of the Servant Concept of Deutero-Isaiah in the New Testament* (London: SPCK, 1959), who first developed the argument cautioning against overreading Isaiah 52–53 into New Testament texts, particularly the Gospel of Mark, thereby importing a theology of vicarious atonement.

102. The invitation is the same as in Mark 8:34 (// Matt 16:24 // Luke 9:23), "If any want to become my followers, let them deny themselves and take up their cross and follow me." Both "cross" and "cup" refer to a very specific kind of suffering: that which a disciple is willing to take upon herself or himself as a consequence of following Jesus and living the gospel.

103. Elisabeth Schüssler Fiorenza, *In Memory of Her: A Feminist Theological Reconstruction of Christian Origins* (New York: Crossroad, 1994), 130, argues that "the interpretation of Jesus' death as atonement for sins is much later than is generally assumed in New Testament scholarship. The notion of atoning sacrifice does not express the Jesus movement's understanding and experience of God but is a later interpretation of the violent death of Jesus in cultic terms. . . . The death of Jesus was not a sacrifice and was not demanded by God but brought about by the Romans." Sam K. Williams, *Jesus' Death as Saving Event: The Background and Origin of a Concept* (Missoula, Mont.: Scholars Press, 1975) advances that "the concept of Jesus' death as saving event had as its creative source a tradition of beneficial, effective human death for others." He finds no evidence for such a tradition in any Jewish writing not greatly influenced by Greek ideas, as 4 Maccabees, for example, and so concludes that "this concept originated among Christians who not only spoke Greek but were also thoroughly at home in the Greek-Hellenistic thought world" (230).

104. For example, Hengel, *The Atonement*, 53; and Jeremias, *Eucharistic Words of Jesus*, 231. Johnson, *Luke*, 339, points out that *enkynnō / enkeō*, "to pour out," is used throughout the Torah in sacrificial contexts, as in Leviticus 4:18, 25, 30, and so on. He also cites Hebrews 9:22: "without the shedding of blood there is no forgiveness of sins." However, there were actually a number of other means of effecting forgiveness: contrition of heart (Ps 51:19), fasting (Joel 2:12), and almsgiving (Sir 3:29). See further Jeremias, *Eucharistic Words of Jesus*, 229–31, who lists various means of atonement besides sacrifice.

105. See Josephine Massyngbaerde Ford, *Redeemer, Friend and Mother. Salvation in Antiquity and in the Gospel of John* (Minneapolis: Fortress Press, 1997), 139, for a list of different interpretations of the symbolism of the footwashing. Among the many variations are purification of believers, baptism for remission of sin, the Eucharist, an act of humiliation that the disciples should imitate, Jesus' submission to death, his offer to the disciples of a share in his own "personality" and his destiny, and an act of eschatological hospitality.

106. See my article, "The Cross and Cycles of Violence," *Int 58*, no. 4 (2004): 376–85, where I explore how the metaphor of friendship in the Gospel of John begins in the prologue (1:1-18), where *theos*, God, befriends humanity through the gift of the *Logos*, the Word; continues as John the Baptist takes on the role of mentoring friend (3:22-30); climaxes as Jesus risks his life for his friends Martha, Mary, and Lazarus (11:1-54); is acted out parabolically in the footwashing (13:1-20); and culminates in Jesus' creation of a community of friends, as he entrusts to one another those bound to him by blood ties and those bound to him by ties of discipleship (19:25-27), and as the risen Christ returns to his friends (20:1-18).

The metaphor of friendship has been the subject of exploration by a number of feminist scholars. See Carter Heyward, *The Redemption of God: A Theology of Mutual Relation* (Washington D.C.: University Press of America, 1982); Mary Hunt, *A Fierce Tenderness: A Feminist Theology of Friendship* (New York: Crossroad, 1991); Massyngbaerde Ford, *Redeemer, Friend and Mother*; Sallie McFague, *Models of God* (Philadelphia: Fortress Press, 1987) 157-80; Elisabeth Moltmann-Wendel, *Rediscovering Friendship* (Minneapolis: Fortress Press, 2000); Sharon Ringe, *Wisdom's Friends: Community and Christology in the Fourth Gospel* (Louisville: Westminster John Knox, 1999); Deanna Thompson, *Crossing the Divide: Luther, Feminism, and the Cross* (Minneapolis: Fortress Press, 2004). For a list of classical and contemporary studies on friendship see McFague, *Models of God*, 218 n. 22.

107. See R. A. Culpepper, "The Johannine Hypodeigma: A Reading of John 13," *Semeia* 53 (1991): 133–52.

108. This is the only occurrence of the term *apostle* in the Gospel of John.

109. This interpretation draws heavily on Sandra Schneiders, "The Footwashing (John 13:1-20): An Experiment in Hermeneutics," *CBQ* 43 (1981): 76–92.

110. John 3:14-16; 4:14; 12:50; 17:2; 20:31.

111. See also Moltmann-Wendel, *Rediscovering Friendship*, 36, who observes the same with regard to the synoptic portrayals of Jesus at table with sinners and people made marginal. Jesus "did not die for our sins but

for those women and men who had been his friends, for friendship as a passional human relationship and liberation."

112. This will be further elaborated in chapter 5.

113. Mary Hunt, *A Fierce Tenderness: A Feminist Theology of Friendship* (New York: Crossroad, 1991), has critiqued this metaphor, insisting that women would not put the death of a friend at the center of the narrative, but rather the triumph of a group of women over injustice that is achieved without losing one of them.

114. See the suggestions given by Fitzmyer, *Luke*, 2.1318, for what this expression might mean.

115. Addison G. Wright, "The Widow's Mites: Praise or Lament?—A Matter of Context," *CBQ* 44 (1982): 256–65, was the first to propose this interpretation. A lively debate has ensued among New Testament scholars. See further Elizabeth Struthers Malbon, "The Poor Widow in Mark and her Poor Rich Readers," *CBQ* 53 (1991): 589–604.

116. BDAG, 176.

117. Mark 14:3-10; Matthew 26:6-13; John 12:1-8. See chapter 3, where we will discuss the action of the woman in Mark 14:3-10 as a prophetic act.

118. Although it is not narrated who was the agent of the forgiveness, the story implies that it was Jesus. The woman's grateful actions are directed toward him, and in verse 49 the others at table murmur among themselves, "Who is this who even forgives sins?"

119. It is also important to note that the conjunction *hoti* in verse 47 should be taken in a consecutive sense, not a causal sense; see Joseph A. Fitzmyer, *The Gospel According to Luke I-IX* (Garden City, N.Y.: Doubleday, 1981), 691–92. It means "hence," or "therefore," not "because," following the logic of the parable in vv. 41-43: one who is forgiven much loves much. This also makes an important theological assertion that is consistent throughout the biblical literature: divine forgiveness is not conditioned on repentance or love. Forgiveness is prior and freely offered; the loving response follows. At the end of the episode, Jesus reaffirms to the woman, "Your sins are forgiven" (v. 48). Here again, the verb is *apheōntai*, which should be translated "have been forgiven."

120. See further Barbara E. Reid, "'Do You See This Woman?': A Liberative Look at Luke 7:36-50 and Strategies for Reading Other Lukan Stories against the Grain," in *A Feminist Companion to Luke*, ed. Amy-Jill Levine with Marianne Blickenstaff (Sheffield, U.K.: Sheffield University Press, 2002), 106–20. For a different perspective, see Teresa J. Hornsby, "The Woman Is a Sinner/The Sinner Is a Woman," in the same volume, 121–31; and Luise Schottroff, *Let the Oppressed Go Free: Feminist Perspectives on the New Testament*, trans. A. S. Kidder (Louisville: Westminster John Knox, 1993), 138–57.

121. See Leticia Guardiola Saenz, "Borderless Women and the Borderless Texts: A Cultural Reading of Matthew 15.21-28," *Semeia* 78 (1997): 69–81, who relates the situation of the woman in the story to her own condition of growing up in the borderlands of the U.S. empire.

122. Amy-Jill Levine, "Matthew," in *Women's Bible Commentary*, expanded edition with Apocrypha, ed. Carol A. Newsom and Sharon H. Ringe (Louisville: Westminster John Knox, 1998), 346.

123. See Gail O'Day, "Surprised by Faith," in *A Feminist Companion to Matthew*, ed. Amy-Jill Levine with Marianne Blickenstaff (Sheffield, U.K.: Sheffield Academic Press, 2001), 114–25, who sees the story neither as a miracle story nor an apothegm but as "a narrative embodiment of a lament psalm" (119).

124. Matthew 1:1; 9:27; 12:23; 20:30, 31; 21:9, 15; 22:42, 45.

125. Similarly, when sending his disciples on mission, the Matthean Jesus insists they go only "to the lost sheep of the house of Israel" (10:6).

126. Some commentators attempt to soften the slur to an endearing puppy or to explain it in terms of the differing customs of Jews and Gentiles with regard to keeping dogs as pets, for example, Francis Dufton, "The Syrophoenician Woman and her Dogs," *ExpT* 100 (1989): 417. This line of interpretation explains *dog* as a term for "outsider," since Jews did not keep dogs inside the house as pets as did Gentiles. But, as Sharon Ringe points out in "A Gentile Woman's Story Revisited: Rereading Mark 7.24-31," in *A Feminist Companion to Mark*, ed. Amy-Jill Levine with Marianne Blickenstaff (Sheffield, U.K.: Sheffield Academic Press, 2001), 79–100, these attempts to see Jesus' retort as less than the extreme insult it is falter in view of the sayings about "dogs" in the Old Testament that "portray them as contemptible scavengers who lick human blood," and that use the term as a metaphor for Israel's enemies (see 1 Sam 17:43; Ps 22:11; Prov 26:11; Isa 56:10-11). There is no evidence that *dogs* was a term used by Jews to refer to Gentiles in general, but rather that they used it to label groups overtly hostile to God's people or to God's law (89).

127. Matthew 6:30; 8:26; 14:31; 16:8; 17:20.

128. See further Elaine M. Wainwright, "The Gospel of Matthew," in *Searching the Scriptures*, vol 2, *A Feminist Commentary*, ed. Elisabeth Schüssler Fiorenza (New York: Crossroad, 1994), 650–59; Wainwright, *Towards a Critical Reading of the Gospel According to Matthew* (Berlin: de Gruyter, 1991), 217–47; Wainwright, *Shall We Look for Another? A Feminist Rereading of the Matthean Jesus* (Maryknoll, N.Y.: Orbis, 1998), 86–92; and Wainwright, "Not without My Daughter: Gender and Demon Possession in Matthew 15:21-28," in *A Feminist Companion to Matthew*, 126–37. In this last essay, Wainwright focuses on the character of the daughter and the significance of demon-possession.

129. See Joanna Dewey, "'Let Them Renounce Themselves and Take Up Their Cross': A Feminist Reading of Mark 8.34 in Mark's Social and Narrative World," in *A Feminist Companion to Mark*, 23–36.

130. It is at this point in the story that I wish I could report that they had found a means of confrontation without threatening to return violence for violence, but this is a true story, and I will be faithful to reporting it as it was told to me.

131. As well as oral versions told to me, this story is also recounted in CODIMUJ, *Con Mirada, Mente, y Corazón de Mujer*, 134.

132. See the chronicle of Red Científica Peruana: http://www.yachay .com.pe/especiales/moyano/INGLES.HTM (accessed February 24, 2007).

133. Ibid.

Chapter 2 Notes

1. Portions of this chapter appeared previously in "Telling Mark's Story of the Cross," *CurTM* 32, no. 6 (December 2005): 426–33, and in a paper delivered at the Society of Biblical Literature Annual Meeting on November 21, 2006, in Washington, D.C., entitled "Matthean Perspectives on Bloodshed, Obedience, and Bearing Arms." The latter is posted on the SBL website with the 2006 seminar papers for S21-15 Matthew Section at http://www.sbl-site.org/PDF/Reid_War.pdf.

2. Adapted from the voices of several women of Chiapas recorded in CODIMUJ, *Con Mirada, Mente y Corazón de Mujer* (Mexico, D. F.: Author, 1999), 17–22.

3. See further E. Elizabeth Johnson, "Colossians," in *Women's Bible Commentary*, rev. ed. (Louisville: Westminster/John Knox, 1998), 437–39; Johnson, "Ephesians," in *Women's Bible Commentary*, 428–32; Sharyn Dowd, "1 Peter," in *Women's Bible Commentary*, 462–64; Carolyn Osiek and David Balch, *Families in the New Testament World: Households and House Churches* (Louisville: Westminster John Knox, 1997), 118–23; Elisabeth Schüssler Fiorenza, *In Memory of Her: A Feminist Theological Reconstruction of Christian Origins* (New York: Crossroad, 1984), 251–84; Edgar Krentz, "Order in the 'House' of God: The Haustafel in 1 Peter 2:11–3:12," in *Common Life in the Early Church: Essays Honoring Graydon F. Snyder*, ed. Julian V. Hills (Harrisburg, Pa.: Trinity, 1998), 279–85; Carolyn Osiek, "Women in House Churches," in *Common Life in the Early Church*, 300–315; Marc Girard, "Love as Subjection, the Christian Ideal for Husbands and Wives: A Structuralist Study of Ephesians 5:21-33," in *Women Also Journeyed with Him: Feminist Perspectives on the Bible*, ed. Gérald Caron, et al. (Collegeville, Minn.: Liturgical Press, 2000), 125–52.

4. New Testament scholars are divided over whether Colossians is an authentic Pauline letter. More would place Ephesians in the corpus of Deutero-Pauline letters. 1 Peter is the work of a later Christian who writes in the name of the apostle. See further Raymond E. Brown, *An Introduction to the New Testament* (New York: Doubleday, 1997), 610–15, 626–30.

5. The parable appears also in Matthew 21:33-46 and Luke 20:9-19, but we will focus on the Marcan version.

6. Zechariah, son of Jehoiada, in 2 Chronicles 24:20-21; and Uriah, son of Shemaiah, in Jeremiah 26:20.

7. Matthew 23:31-32; Luke 13:34; Acts 7:52; Hebrews 11:36-38; 1 Thessalonians 2:15.

8. This is also so for the Lucan version. The Matthean account also warns Christians to bear good fruit at the proper time. See further Barbara E. Reid, *Parables for Preachers: Year A* (Collegeville, Minn.: Liturgical Press, 2001), 163–76; and *Parables for Preachers: Year B* (Collegeville, Minn.: Liturgical Press, 1999), 111–20.

9. There are actually two parables in Mark 12:1-12. The first (vv. 1-9) deals with the murderous tenants; the second (vv. 10-12) introduces the rejected stone. In the present arrangement, each part helps interpret the other, but many scholars question whether the two were always joined and whether or not they came from the lips of Jesus or were composed by the early church. It is important not to take the parable as an allegory of the Gentiles sup-

planting the Jews as tenants of God's vineyard. If the parable is authentically from Jesus, then he is speaking of his Jewish followers replacing the current corrupt Temple leadership. Moreover, from the perspective of the Marcan community, Christianity is still a movement within Judaism.

10. Stephen Finlan, *Problems with Atonement: The Origins of, and Controversy about, the Atonement Doctrine* (Collegeville, Minn.: Liturgical Press, 2005), 109. I am in agreement with Finlan that the killing was not what the vineyard owner intended. I would point out, however, that the parable itself does not directly report the sentiments of the vineyard owner. One might surmise, though, that the owner is angry when he comes and destroys the tenants and gives the vineyard to others (v. 9). Similar criticism can be made of interpretations of texts such as John 3:16; Galatians 4:4 and Romans 8:3 that speak of God sending the Son. The sending should be understood in terms of incarnation, not that "God sent him to die," which is a formulation not found in the New Testament.

11. Mark 14:32-42; Matthew 26:36-46; Luke 22:39-46.

12. The metaphor of "cup" was used often in the scriptures to speak of the suffering of Israel (Isa 51:17; Jer 25:15; 49:12; 51:7; Lam 4:21; *Mart. Isa.* 5:13). See above, pp. 43–45, for interpretation of the cup at the Last Supper.

13. The detail of the comforting angel is unique to Luke (22:43). The authenticity of this verse is debated. For further discussion, see Joseph Fitzmyer, *The Gospel According to Luke* (Garden City, N.Y.: Doubleday, 1985), 2.1443-44.

14. The evangelists do not answer the question of why the earthly Jesus asked to be baptized by John. That the early Christians, believing Jesus to be sinless, had difficulty with Jesus' request for John's baptism, which was for repentance and forgiveness of sin (Matt 3:1-12), is reflected in Matthew's version, where John objects, "I need to be baptized by you, and do you come to me?" (3:14). Jesus replies, "Let it be so for now; for it is proper for us in this way to fulfill all righteousness" (3:15).

15. See also Ezekiel 1:1; John 1:51; Acts 7:55-56; 10:11; Revelation 11:19; 19:11-21, for other biblical examples of the opening of the heavens.

16. In the book of Judges, the spirit of the Lord is said to come to Othniel (3:10), Gideon (6:34), Jephthah (11:29), and Samson (13:25; 14:6, 19; 15:14). Isaiah declares, "The Spirit of the Lord is upon me" (Isa 61:1, words that Jesus echoes in Luke 4:18). Ezekiel speaks of the spirit entering him (Ezek 2:2; 3:24), lifting him up (Ezek 3:12, 14; 8:3; 11:1, 24; 43:5), and falling on him (Ezek 11:5). Joel prophesies the pouring out of the spirit on all flesh (Joel 2:28-29), which is recalled in Peter's Pentecost speech in Acts 2:17-18.

17. In the Gospels of Mark and Luke, the heavenly voice is directed to Jesus alone: "You are my Son, the beloved, with you I am well pleased" (Mark 1:11; Luke 3:22). In the Gospel of Matthew (3:17), it is directed to all: "This is my Son."

18. See chapter 3 (pp. 90–91, 94–95) of this book for further exploration of the meaning of the Transfiguration.

19. Compare Mark 15:29-30, where there is also the derision about the Temple, followed by the taunt, "Save yourself, and come down from the cross," with no reference to "Son of God."

20. Matthew 13:9, 13, 15, 16, 17, 18; Mark 4:3, 9, 12, 15, 16, 18, 20, 23, 24, 33; Luke 8:8, 10, 12, 13, 14, 15, 18.

21. Among the evangelists, Luke emphasizes this theme the most, showing Jesus customarily going apart to pray (5:16). Before every important step along the way, Jesus is at prayer: at his baptism (3:21), before his choice of the Twelve (6:12), before Peter's profession of faith in him as the Messiah (9:18), at the Transfiguration (9:28-29), before his arrest on the Mount of Olives (22:39-46), and on the cross (23:46). Jesus gives voice to a spontaneous prayer of thanks to God for revealing to infants what has been hidden from the wise and intelligent (10:21-23). He assures Peter that he has prayed for him that his faith will not fail (22:32). He instructs his disciples how to pray (6:28; 10:2; 20:45-47; 21:36; 22:40, 40), sometimes in the form of a parable (11:1-13; 18:1-14). Five times, Luke's mention of prayer comes from Mark: 9:1; 20:47; 22:40, 41, 46. Three times, Luke inserts references to prayer in his redaction of Marcan material: Luke 3:21; 5:16, 33. In four instances, prayer appears in Q material (Luke 6:28; 10:2; 11:1, 2). Eight of Luke's references to prayer occur in uniquely Lucan material: 1:10, 13; 2:37; 18:1, 10, 11; 21:36; 22:32.

22. David M. Moffitt, "Righteous Bloodshed, Matthew's Passion Narrative, and the Temple's Destruction: Lamentations as a Matthean Intertext," *JBL* 125, no. 2 (2006): 299–320, argues that the allusion in 27:46 is not to Psalm 22 but to Lamentations 2:15, which serves to interpret Jesus' crucifixion "as the act of righteous bloodshed par excellence that directly results in the destruction of Jerusalem and the temple" (319). As such, Matthew engages in intra-Jewish polemic, patterning his critique of the religious leadership on the Jewish prophetic tradition.

23. Verse 54 is a unique addition by Matthew; verse 56 has a parallel in Mark 14:49.

24. Luke also emphasizes the theme of fulfillment of scripture, but in a different way from Matthew. In addition to explicit citations, Luke often alludes to the scriptures. He uses the expression *dei*, "it is necessary," eighteen times (compared to six times by Mark, eight times by Matthew), and the verb *pleroō*, "to fulfill," nine times (this is also a favorite of Matthew, who uses it sixteen times). This theme climaxes in the story of the disciples on the road to Emmaus, when the resurrected Christ says to them, "Was it not necessary (*dei*) that the Messiah should suffer these things and then enter into his glory?" (Luke 24:26).

25. The Johannine Jesus clearly spells out what is the will of God: "Everything that the Father gives me will come to me, and anyone who comes to me I will never drive away; for I have come down from heaven, not to do my own will, but the will of him who sent me. And this is the will of him who sent me, that I should lose nothing of all that he has given me, but raise it up on the last day. This is indeed the will of my Father, that all who see the Son and believe in him may have eternal life; and I will raise them up on the last day" (John 6:37-40).

26. Likewise, in the Gospel of Mark, God's will to save is expressed in the story of the woman healed of hemorrhages (Mark 5:34) and the man who was cured of blindness (Mark 10:52). Jesus tells them that their faith has "healed" and "saved" them (the verb *sōzein* conveys both meanings).

27. See chapter 4 (pp. 124–126) for further examination of the forgiveness element in the Matthean saying over the cup.

28. Gary Strauss, "'9/11' Documents a Mother's Grief," *USA Today*, June 28, 2004, www.usatoday.com/life/movies/news/2004-06-28-fahrenheit-lipscomb_x.htm (accessed October 10, 2006).

29. "Army Specialist Casey Sheehan—Someone You Should (Have) Know(n)," http://www.blackfive.net/main/2005/08/army_specialist.html (November 4, 2006).

30. As reported by Hal Bernton, "Officer at Ft. Lewis Calls Iraq War Illegal, Refuses Order to Go," *Seattle Times*, June 7, 2006, http://www.seattletimes.nwsource.com/html/localnews/2003044627_nogo7m.html (October 17, 2006).

31. Bernton, "Officer at Ft. Lewis."

32. In Romans 4:1-25 and Galatians 3:6-18, Paul uses the example of Abraham to argue for justification by faith apart from works of the Law.

33. The story of Abraham's near-sacrifice of Isaac also holds a central place for Jews and Muslims. As Carol Delaney, *Abraham on Trial: The Social Legacy of Biblical Myth* (Princeton: Princeton University Press, 1998), notes, "Jews recite Genesis 22 annually at the new year services of Rosh Hashanah; it is also included as part of the daily morning prayers of the devout. . . . And Muslims each year dramatically reenact the event on the most sacred day of the Muslim calendar—the feast of the Sacrifice—that occurs at the end of the rituals of the Hajj" (8–9). See also Jon D. Levenson, *The Death and Resurrection of the Beloved Son: The Transformation of Child Sacrifice in Judaism and Christianity* (New Haven: Yale University Press, 1991).

34. Rita Nakashima Brock, *Journeys by Heart: A Christology of Erotic Power* (New York: Crossroad, 1988). Similarly, see Joanne Carlson Brown and Rebecca Parker, "For God So Loved the World?" in *Christianity, Patriarchy, and Abuse: A Feminist Critique*, ed. Joanne Carlson Brown and Carole R. Bohn (New York: Pilgrim, 1989), 1–30.

35. Delaney, *Abraham on Trial*, 5.

36. Delaney, *Abraham on Trial*, 6.

37. Delaney, *Abraham on Trial*, 22.

38. Delaney, *Abraham on Trial*, 11.

39. Delaney, *Abraham on Trial*, 5, 11.

40. Delaney, *Abraham on Trial*, 18–19.

41. Delaney, *Abraham on Trial*, 7.

42. Delaney, *Abraham on Trial*, 22.

43. Interestingly, a strand of interpretation in rabbinic tradition emphasizes Isaac's willingness as victim. See Delaney, *Abraham on Trial*, 123–25; and Jan Willem Van Henten and Friedrich Avemarie, *Martyrdom and Noble Death: Selected Texts from Graeco-Roman, Jewish, and Christian Antiquity* (New York: Routledge, 2002), 141–42.

44. Delaney, *Abraham on Trial*, 22.

45. Delaney, *Abraham on Trial*, 116.

46. See Barbara Miller, *Tell It on the Mountain: The Daughter of Jephthah in Judges 11* (Collegeville, Minn.: Liturgical Press, 2005); Phyllis Trible,

Texts of Terror: Literary-Feminist Readings of Biblical Narratives (Philadelphia: Fortress Press, 1984), 92–116; "A Meditation in Mourning. The Sacrifice of the Daughter of Jephthah," *USQR* 36 (1981): 59–73.

47. Miller, *Tell It on the Mountain*, 18.

48. Miller, *Tell It on the Mountain*, 62–63.

49. Don C. Benjamin, *The Old Testament Story* (Minneapolis: Fortress Press, 2004), 65–69.

50. Benjamin, *The Old Testament Story*, 69.

51. See Colleen Carpenter Cullinan, *Redeeming the Story: Women, Suffering, and Christ* (New York: Continuum, 2004), 18–19; and Gloria Inés Loya, "Considering the Sources/Fuentes for a Hispanic Feminist Theology," *Theology Today* 54 (1998): 491–98, for remarks about how history has blamed Malintzín (the indigenous woman who was taken to serve as Cortez's interpreter) for the Conquest in the same way that some have blamed Eve for the so-called "Fall."

52. Similarly, see Ephesians 5:22-24; 1 Peter 3:1-2.

53. Phyllis Trible, *God and the Rhetoric of Sexuality* (Philadelphia: Fortress Press, 1978), 72–143. For other feminist treatments of Genesis 3, see Phyllis Bird, *Missing Persons and Mistaken Identities: Women and Gender in Ancient Israel* (Minneapolis: Fortress Press, 1997), 155–93; Athalya Brenner, ed., *A Feminist Companion to Genesis* (Sheffield: Sheffield Academic Press, 1997); Esther Fuchs, *Sexual Politics in the Biblical Narrative: Reading the Hebrew Bible as a Woman* (Sheffield: Sheffield Academic Press, 2000); Ivone Gebara, *Teología a Ritmo de Mujer* (Mexico, D. F.: Dabar, 1995), 47–63; Judith Plaskow, *Sex, Sin and Grace* (Washington, D.C.: University Press of America, 1980); and Gale Yee, *Poor Banished Children of Eve: Woman as Evil in the Hebrew Bible* (Minneapolis: Fortress Press, 2003).

54. Alternatively, Adrien Bledstein, "Was Eve Cursed? (Or Did a Woman Write Genesis?)," *Bible Review* 9 no. 1 (1993): 42–45, reads Genesis 3:16 as a warning that woman is attractive to man but will be in danger because he can rule over her. For a survey of a number of feminist analyses of Genesis 3, see Alice Ogden Bellis, *Helpmates, Harlots, and Heroes: Women's Stories in the Hebrew Bible* (Louisville: Westminster John Knox, 1994), 45–66.

55. Carol Meyers, "Gender Roles and Genesis 3:16 Revisited," in *A Feminist Companion to Genesis*, ed. Athalya Brenner (Sheffield: Sheffield Academic Press, 1997), 118–41; Meyers, *Discovering Eve: Ancient Israelite Women in Context* (New York: Oxford University Press, 1988).

56. Meyers, "Gender Roles," 130.

57. See further David L. Balch, *Let Wives Be Submissive: The Domestic Code in 1 Peter* (Chico, Calif.: Scholars, 1981); Sharyn Dowd, "1 Peter" in *Women's Bible Commentary*, 462–64; E. Elizabeth Johnson, "Colossians," in *Women's Bible Commentary*, 437–39; Johnson, "Ephesians," *Women's Bible Commentary*, 428–32; Osiek, "Women in House Churches," in *Common Life in the Early Church*, 300–15; Osiek and Balch, *Families in the New Testament World: Households and House Churches*, 118–23; Carolyn Osiek and Margaret Y. MacDonald, eds., with Janet H. Tulloch, *A Woman's Place: House Churches in Earliest Christianity* (Minneapolis: Fortress Press, 2006); and Schüssler Fiorenza, *In Memory of Her*, 251–84.

58. See Eldon J. Epp, *Junia: The First Woman Apostle* (Minneapolis: Fortress Press, 2005).

59. Osiek and MacDonald, "Ephesians 5 and the Politics of Marriage," in *A Woman's Place*, 19, 131.

60. Osiek and MacDonald, "Ephesians 5 and the Politics of Marriage," 141–42.

61. See David M. Scholer, "The Evangelical Debate over Biblical 'Headship,'" in *Women, Abuse, and the Bible: How the Bible Can Be Used to Hurt or Heal*, ed. Catherine Clark Kroeger and James R. Beck (Grand Rapids, Mich.: Baker, 1996), 28–56, who argues that "the Bible does not institute, undergird, or teach male headship and female submission, in either the traditionalist or complementarian forms of evangelical thought, which exclude women from equal participation in authority with men within the body of Christ, whether in ministry or marriage or any other dimension of life. Rather, the Bible affirms, supports, and teaches by precept and example a mutuality or equality in Christ for women and men, both in ministry and in marriage" (51).

62. Recounted by Carolyn Holderread Heggen, "Religious Beliefs and Abuse," in *Women, Abuse, and the Bible*, 19. See also Marie Evans Bouclin, *Seeking Wholeness: Women Dealing with Abuse of Power in the Catholic Church* (Collegeville, Minn.: Liturgical Press, 2006), 45–49, who discusses how the mechanism of women being socialized to defer to men's authority operates in situations of abuse of religious authority.

63. Gilbert Bilezikian, *Beyond Sex Roles: What the Bible Says about a Woman's Place in Church and Family*, 2nd ed. (Grand Rapids, Mich.: Baker, 1990), 211.

64. Elisabeth Schüssler Fiorenza was the first to propose such an interpretation in "A Feminist Critical Interpretation for Liberation: Martha and Mary: Lk. 10:38-42," *Rel & Int Life* 3 (1986): 21–36. The substance of this essay is also found in Schüssler Fiorenza's book, *But She Said: Feminist Practices of Biblical Interpretation* (Boston: Beacon, 1992), 57–76.

65. The verb *hypodexato*, "welcomed," in Luke 10:38 is a compound form of *dechomai*, "to receive," which refers in the Gospel of Luke not only to welcoming a person (so also 19:6) but also to receiving, hearing, or understanding the word (Luke 8:13; Acts 8:14; 11:1; 17:11).

66. For a detailed treatment of this text, see Barbara E. Reid, "The Power of Widows and How to Suppress It (Acts 6:1-7)," in *A Feminist Companion to the Acts of the Apostles*, ed. Amy-Jill Levine (New York: T & T Clark International, 2004), 71–88.

67. The noun *hyparchontōn* signifies monetary goods, and the possessive pronoun *autais*, "their," indicates that the money belonged to the women, not that they were holding the common purse and controlling the expenditures (as Judas is said to do in John 12:6).

68. See further Warren Carter, "Getting Martha Out of the Kitchen: Luke 10:38-42 Again," *CBQ* 52, no. 8 (1996): 264–80.

69. BDAG, 804.

70. See E. E. Ellis, "Paul and His Co-Workers," *NTS* 17 (1970/71): 437–52, especially 446–47, who shows that *adelphē*, "sister," carries ministerial connotations, for example, in Romans 16:1; Philemon 1:2. Mary Rose D'Angelo,

"Women Partners in the New Testament," *JFSR* 6 (1990): 65–86, also sees *adelphē* as a missionary title and views Mary and Martha as a missionary pair.

71. For further treatment on Luke's mixed message for women, see Barbara E. Reid, *Choosing the Better Part? Women in the Gospel of Luke* (Collegeville, Minn.: Liturgical Press, 1996); Turid Karlsen Seim, *The Double Message: Patterns of Gender in Luke-Acts* (Nashville: Abingdon, 1994); "The Gospel of Luke," in *Searching the Scriptures*, 2.728–62; and Jane Schaberg, "Luke," in *Women's Bible Commentary*, 363–80.

72. For epigraphical evidence of women's leadership in ministry in the early church, see Ute Eisen, *Women Officeholders in Early Christianity: Epigraphical and Literary Studies* (Collegeville, Minn.: Liturgical Press, 2000); and Carolyn Osiek and Kevin Madigan, *Ordained Women in the Early Church: A Documentary History* (Baltimore: Johns Hopkins University Press, 2005).

73. Similarly, Meister Eckhart (c. 1260–1327), Dominican monk and mystic, preached that Martha was the one who had already achieved the stage of integrating contemplation and action. He saw Mary as the novice in the contemplative life, and Martha's concern was that her sister not get stuck there, indifferent to the needs around her. See Eckhart, *Deutsche Predigten und Traktate* (Munich: C. Hanser, 1955), 286, with English translation in Matthew Fox, *Breakthrough: Meister Eckhart's Creation Spirituality in New Translation* (New York: Doubleday, 1991), 479–80; and Elisabeth Moltmann Wendel, *The Women around Jesus* (New York: Crossroad, 1993), 28–29. See also Loveday Alexander, "Sisters in Adversity: Retelling Martha's Story," in *A Feminist Companion to Luke*, ed. Amy-Jill Levine with Marianne Blickenstaff (Sheffield, U.K.: Sheffield University Press, 2002), 197–213; Pamela Thimmes, "The Language of Community: A Cautionary Tale (Luke 10.38-42)," in *A Feminist Companion to Luke*, 232–45; and Dorothee Soelle, "Mary and Martha: The Unity of Action and Dreams," in *The Window of Vulnerability: A Political Spirituality*, trans. Linda M. Maloney (Minneapolis: Fortress Press, 1990), 93–96.

74. See further Schneiders, *Written That You May Believe*, 171–83.

75. Mark 8:29; Matthew 16:16; Luke 9:20.

76. See Adeline Fehribach, *The Women in the Life of the Bridegroom: A Feminist Historical-Literary Analysis of the Female Characters in the Fourth Gospel* (Collegeville, Minn.: Liturgical Press, 1998) 83–113, who analyzes the function of Mary and Martha in John 11–12 in terms of the portrayal of Jesus as the messianic bridegroom who has come to enable those who believe in him to become children of God. See also Satoko Yamaguchi, *Mary & Martha: Women in the World of Jesus* (Maryknoll, N.Y.: Orbis, 2002), who presents a Japanese feminist interpretation of John 11:1–12:8.

77. For more detail on the Lucan portraits of Mary and Elizabeth, see Reid, *Choosing the Better Part?*, 55–85.

78. While Luke does not elaborate on this, Matthew recounts Joseph's struggle over how to act righteously once such shame has come upon them (Matt 1:18-25). In Matthew's Gospel, the focus is on Joseph and his obedient response to God.

79. The name given the child, *Iēsous* (Luke 1:31), is understood in popular etymology to derive from the Hebrew verb *yš`* ("save," see Matt 1:21). For more detail on the etymology, see Fitzmyer, *Luke*, 1.347.

80. In the two episodes in which she appears in the Gospel of John (2:1-12; 19:25-27), she is not named.

81. Since there is no punctuation in the Greek text, it is not clear how many figures there are in 19:25. See Raymond E. Brown, *The Death of the Messiah. From Gethsemane to the Grave: A Commentary on the Passion Narratives in the Four Gospels*, 2 vols. (New York: Doubleday, 1994), 2.1013-19. Sandra Schneiders, *Written That You May Believe: Encountering Jesus in the Fourth Gospel*, rev. ed. (New York: Crossroad, 2003), 233–54, shows that the Beloved Disciple in 19:26 is not another male figure that inexplicably appears, but is a symbol for the community of those who believe in Jesus, "made up of both Jesus' natural family (represented by his mother's sister) and his disciples (represented by Mary Magdalene), composing together the family of faith" (242).

82. Michael Gilgallon, "We Can, Must Learn from Our Errors" *NCR Online* 3, no. 5 (June 29, 2005), http://www.nationalcatholicreporter.org/globalpers/gp062905.htm (accessed September 25, 2005). Gilgallon, a priest of the diocese of Kansas City-St. Joseph, Missouri, has served in Bolivia since 1974. This quote is from an open letter to Pope Benedict XVI, pleading for attention to the forgotten Catholic brothers and sisters of Latin America.

83. Rarely in the Bible is the adjective *dikaios*, "righteous," applied to a woman. In the LXX, it is frequently attributed to God (for example, Deut 32:4; Pss 7:12; 118:137; Prov 21:12). The few individuals that are said to be "righteous" include Noah (Gen 6:9); Job (Job 1:1); Daniel (4 Macc 16:21); Ishbaal, the son of Saul (2 Sam 4:11); and the Servant of God (Isa 53:11). Tamar (Gen 38:26) is the only woman said to be "righteous," and it is her deception of Judah that earns her the title. In the Gospel of John, Jesus addresses God as *pater dikaie*, "righteous Father" (John 17:25). Righteous individuals in the New Testament include Joseph (Matt 1:19), John the Baptist (Mark 6:20), Simeon (Luke 2:25), Joseph of Arimathea (Luke 23:50), Cornelius (Acts 10:22), Abel (Heb 11:4; 1 John 3:12), and Lot (2 Pet 2:7). Elizabeth is the only woman to whom the term is applied. It is particularly significant that Luke uses *dikaios* of Elizabeth in light of the importance he gives this term in reference to Jesus. Luke has changed Mark's climactic declaration of the centurion at the death of Jesus from, "Truly this man was the Son of God!" (Mark 15:39), to, "Certainly this man was innocent (*dikaios*)" (Luke 23:47). And in his second volume, "the Righteous One" (*ho dikaios*) becomes a title of Jesus in three key speeches (Acts 3:14; 7:52; 22:14).

84. The theme of God bringing forth from the womb of a barren woman a key figure for Israel's salvation is an oft-repeated one. In this, Elizabeth is like Sarah (Gen 16:1), Rebecca (Gen 25:21), Rachel (Gen 30:1), the mother of Samson (Judg 13:2), and Hannah (1 Samuel 1–2).

85. See Genesis 4:26; 5:3, 28-29; 16:15; 17:19; Exodus 2:22; Judges 8:31. In the patriarchal narratives, however, there are instances in which the mother names the child: Genesis 4:1, 25; 16:11; 19:37-38; 29:32-35; 30:6, 8; 35:18; 38:4-5; Judges 13:24; 1 Samuel 1:20.

86. See further Jacqueline E. Lapsley, *Whispering the Word: Hearing Women's Stories in the Old Testament* (Louisville: Westminster John Knox, 2005), 69–75.

87. Anthony J. Tambasco, *A Theology of Atonement and Paul's Vision of Christianity* (Collegeville, Minn.: Liturgical Press, 1991), 71.

88. Anne E. Carr, *Transforming Grace: Christian Tradition and Women's Experience* (New York: Harper & Row, 1988), 188.

89. Mark W. Thomsen, *Christ Crucified: A 21st-Century Missiology of the Cross* (Minneapolis: Lutheran University Press, 2004), 26.

90. CODIMUJ, Con Mirada, *Mente y Corazón de Mujer*, 96, 138.

91. Mary Horn, "The Dark Night of Creation," in *Land and Place: He Whenua, He Wāhi. Spiritualities from Aotearoa New Zealand*, ed. Helen Bergin and Susan Smith (Auckland: Accent, 2004), 230.

Chapter 3 Notes

1. Amatenango del Valle is located 37 kilometers southeast of San Cristóbal de las Casas and has about seven thousand inhabitants. It is renowned for its clay figurines made by women artisans.

2. I am grateful to Rev. Delle McCormick, who introduced me to the community of women at Amatenango del Valle on November 13, 2002. These quotes are a compilation of the women's reflections translated from Tzeltal into Spanish for me by catechist Angelina Gómez. Similar remarks by other women are also found in CODIMUJ, *Con Mirada, Mente y Corazón de Mujer*, (Mexico, D. F.: Author, 1999), 19–23. See also an account by Paul Jeffrey, a United Methodist missionary in Central America, "The Quiet Revolution: Indigenous Women Struggle for Dignity" at www.gbm-umc.org/Response/articles/indigenous.html (accessed October 13, 2005).

3. See pp. 9–11, for a description of how Ruiz's vision enabled the formation of CODIMUJ and the grassroots Bible study groups for women. See also CODIMUJ, *Con Mirada, Mente, y Corazón de Mujer*, 29–35.

4. In the Gospel of Matthew, Jesus is explicitly called a prophet in 14:5; 21:11, 46. In the First Gospel, however, the theme is played out more strongly as prophecy fulfilled; the Matthean image of Jesus is more that of teacher whose words and deeds fulfill those of the prophets who came before, particularly Isaiah. See Matthew 1:22; 2:5, 15, 17, 23; 4:14; 5:17; 8:17; 12:17; 13:35; 21:4; 24:15; 26:56; 27:9. The theme is not prominent in the Gospel of Mark. Jesus speaks of prophets not being accepted by their own (6:4), and he is said to be like Elijah or one of the prophets of old (6:15; 8:28). John the Baptist is said to be "truly a prophet" (11:32), and Jesus warns his disciples against false prophets (13:22). For a reading of the Marcan scene of the Transfiguration as one that aims to situate Jesus within Israel's prophetic tradition and to invite disciples to live in the company of prophets and even to take on one's own shoulders the prophetic mantle, see William Reiser, *Jesus in Solidarity with His People: A Theologian Looks at Mark* (Collegeville, Minn.: Liturgical Press, 2000), 159–72. In the Gospel of John, Jesus is called a prophet in 4:19, 29; 6:14-15; 7:40-41; 9:17, and the "one about whom . . . the prophets wrote" (1:45). The Pharisees derisively insist that "no prophet is to arise from Galilee" (John 7:52). And in John 12:38, the unbelief of the people despite the signs that Jesus performs is explained as fulfilling the words of the prophet Isaiah (53:1).

5. Mary Rose D'Angelo, "Women in Luke-Acts: A Redactional View," *JBL* 109, no. 3 (1990): 441–61, advances that the public character of the work ("this was not done in a corner," Acts 26:26) causes the author to choose the category of prophet and prophecy to explain Jesus and the early communities, as this was a category accessible to the Greco-Roman world. Also, in using this familiar category from the Hebrew scriptures, "Luke defends the community against the horrid charge of religious innovation and shows the coherence of God's will and work" (451). The most extensive treatment of the theme of persecuted prophet in Luke and Acts is by Scott Smith Cunningham, *"Through Many Tribulations": The Theology of Persecution in Luke-Acts* (Sheffield, U.K.: Sheffield Academic Press, 1997). See also John T. Carroll, "Luke's Crucifixion Scene," in *Reimaging the Death of the Lukan Jesus*, ed. Dennis D. Sylva (Frankfurt A.M.: Anton Hain, 1990), 108–203; Severino Croatto, "Jesus, Prophet Like Elijah, and Prophet-Teacher Like Moses in Luke-Acts," *JBL* 124, no. 3 (2005): 451–65; Joseph A. Fitzmyer, *The Gospel According to Luke* (Garden City, New York: Doubleday, 1985), 1.22–23, 213–15; Robert J. Karris, *Luke: Artist and Theologian. Luke's Passion Account as Literature* (New York: Paulist, 1985); Donald Senior, *The Passion of Jesus in the Gospel of Luke* (Wilmington, Del.: Glazier, 1989), 28–31; and Joseph B. Tyson, *The Death of Jesus in Luke-Acts* (Columbia: University of South Carolina Press, 1986), 29–47.

6. Parallel accounts are found in Mark 6:30-44; Matthew 14:13-21; and John 6:1-14. Two other accounts of Jesus feeding a crowd of four thousand are found in Mark 8:1-10 and Matthew 15:32-39.

7. See Dale C. Allison, "Rejecting Violent Judgment: Luke 9:52-56 and its Relatives," *JBL* 121, no. 3 (2002): 459–78.

8. Similarly see Matthew 13:57; Mark 6:4; and John 4:44.

9. In his second volume, Luke further solidifies this identification with allusions to Deuteronomy 18:15 in Peter's speech in the temple (Acts 3:22-23) and in Stephen's speech in Acts 7:37. See Robert O'Toole, "The Parallels between Jesus and Moses," *BTB* 20 (1990): 22–29. For a fuller treatment of Luke's Transfiguration account, see Barbara E. Reid, *The Transfiguration: A Source- and Redaction-Critical Study of Luke 9:28-36* (Paris: Gabalda, 1993).

10. See the parallel in Matthew 11:10. See also Luke 3:4 and the parallels in Mark 1:2-3, and Matthew 3:3. On Luke's theme of both Jesus and John as Elijah, see Fitzmyer, *Luke*, 1.213-15; Raymond E. Brown, "Jesus and Elisha," *Perspective* 12 (1971): 84–104. The theme of John the Baptist as prophet is also found in Luke 1:76; 20:6; Matthew 21:26; John 1:21, 23, 25. See further Thomas L. Brodie, *The Crucial Bridge: The Elijah-Elisha Narrative as an Interpretive Synthesis of Genesis–Kings and a Literary Model of the Gospels* (Collegeville, Minn.: Liturgical Press, 2000).

11. Simeon's prophecy (Luke 2:34-35) first introduces this theme of the dual response to Jesus. Even in the first success stories of Jesus' mission in 5:17–6:11, the opposition by the Pharisees is juxtaposed with the amazement by others.

12. See also the parallel in Matthew 11:2-19. See further Barbara E. Reid, "Wisdom's Children Justified (Matt 11.16-19; Luke 7.31-35)" in *The Lost Coin: Parables of Women, Work, and Wisdom*, ed. Mary Ann Beavis (Sheffield: Sheffield Academic Press, 2002), 287–305.

13. See further Barbara E. Reid, "'Do You See This Woman?'—Luke 7:36-50 as a Paradigm for Feminist Hermeneutics," *BR* 40 (1995): 37–49; and Reid, *Choosing the Better Part? Women in the Gospel of Luke*, (Collegeville, Minn.: Liturgical Press, 1996), 107–23. See chapter 1 (pp. 50–51) of this book for an exploration of how she models self-giving love.

14. See also Mark 6:14-16; Matthew 14:1-2.

15. He speaks of his own death in explicit and parabolic ways in 9:22, 44; 12:50; 13:31-35; 17:26; 18:31-34 ; 20:9-18; 22:19-22.

16. Also found in Matthew 12:38-42.

17. Elisabeth Schüssler Fiorenza, *In Memory of Her: A Feminist Theological Reconstruction of Christian Origins* (New York: Crossroad, 1984), 135. Martin Hengel, *The Atonement: The Origins of the Doctrine in the New Testament*, trans. John Bowden (Philadelphia: Fortress Press, 1981), 41, raises the objection, however, that the category of prophet–martyr is inadequate for understanding the passion of Jesus, in that it neglects the uniqueness of Jesus' Messianic character.

18. In what follows, I rely on Kenneth E. Untener, *The Practical Prophet: Pastoral Writings* (New York: Paulist, 2007), 192–204.

19. Untener, *The Practical Prophet*, 198.

20. Luke's account (9:38-36) is unique. He does not say that Jesus was transfigured (compare Mark 9:2; Matt 17:2), but rather that the appearance of his face changed (Luke 9:29).

21. BDAG, 350.

22. See Beverly Wildung Harrison, "The Power of Anger in the Work of Love," *USQR* 36 (1981) 41–57.

23. Joyce E. Salisbury, *The Blood of the Martyrs: Unintended Consequences of Ancient Violence* (New York: Routledge, 2004), 148, explains that when Palestinian suicide bombers, for example, call themselves "self-martyrs" and are hailed as martyrs who go directly to heaven, "they are not martyrs in the oldest sense of the word because they are not bearing witness to their faith"; rather, they are sacrificing themselves for a cause, in a way that "retains the old idea of blood sacrifice in which the sacrifice of that which is most precious—life—is given away in trade for some benefit for one's land or people" (148). On the topic of martyrdom, see further G. W. Bowersock, *Martyrdom and Rome* (Cambridge: Cambridge University Press, 1995); Daniel Boyarin, *Dying for God: Martyrdom and the Making of Christianity and Judaism* (Stanford: Stanford University Press, 1999); and W. H. C. Frend, *Martyrdom and Persecution in the Early Church: A Study of a Conflict from the Maccabees to Donatus* (Oxford: Blackwell, 1965). On women in martyrdom, see Anne Jensen, *God's Self-Confident Daughters: Early Christianity and the Liberation of Women*, trans. O. C. Dean Jr. (Louisville: Westminster John Knox, 1996), 81–124. See also Elizabeth A. Castelli, *Martyrdom and Memory: Early Christian Culture Making* (New York: Columbia University Press, 2004). On the influence of the noble death tradition on the depiction of the Lucan Jesus, see Gregory E. Sterling, "*Mors philosophi*: The Death of Jesus in Luke," *HTR* 94, no. 4 (2001): 383–402. See also Robert Doran, "Narratives of Noble Death," in *The Historical Jesus in Context*, ed. Amy-Jill Levine, Dale C. Allison Jr., and John Dominic Crossan (Princeton, N.J.: Princeton University Press, 2006),

385–99; Jan Willem Van Henten and Friedrich Avemarie, *Martyrdom and Noble Death: Selected Texts from Graeco-Roman, Jewish, and Christian Antiquity* (New York: Routledge, 2002); Stephen J. Patterson, *Beyond the Passion: Rethinking the Death and Life of Jesus* (Minneapolis: Fortress Press, 2004), 39–68; Robin Darling Young, "The 'Woman with the Soul of Abraham': Traditions about the Mother of the Maccabean Martyrs," in *"Women Like This": New Perspectives on Jewish Women in the Greco-Roman World*, ed. Amy-Jill Levine (Atlanta: Scholars Press, 1991), 67–81. Charles Talbert, "Martyrdom in Luke–Acts and the Lukan Social Ethic," in *Reading Luke–Acts in its Mediterranean Milieu* (Leiden, Netherlands: Brill, 2003), 105–19, argues that the deaths of Jesus and Stephen in Luke–Acts are not depicted as the result of their political agitation or resistance to Rome, but rather as the outcome of a struggle within the people of God, with a positive influence on those within the people of God. See also Paul Debesse, *Viacrucis de América Latina: Mártires de Hoy*, 2a. ed. (Santa Fe de Bogotá, Colombia: Paulinas, 1991), who relates the stations of the cross to fourteen contemporary Latin American martyrs.

24. Salisbury, *The Blood of Martyrs*, 203.

25. Rita Nakashima Brock and Rebecca Ann Parker, *Proverbs of Ashes: Violence, Redemptive Suffering and the Search for What Saves Us* (Boston: Beacon, 2001), 40.

26. Nakashima Brock and Parker, *Proverbs of Ashes*, 40.

27. Jon Sobrino, "Ignacio Ellacuría, the Human Being and the Christian: 'Taking the Crucified People Down from the Cross,'" in *Love that Produces Hope: The Thought of Ignacion Ellacuría*, ed. Kevin F. Burke and Robert Lasalle-Klein (Collegeville, Minn.: Liturgical Press, 2006), 50–51.

28. Dorothee Sölle, *Theology for Skeptics: Reflections on God* (Philadelphia: Fortress Press, 1995), 99–108.

29. See further Jon Sobrino, *Christ the Liberator: A View from the Victims* (Maryknoll, N.Y.: Orbis, 2001); and Leonardo Boff, *Passion of Christ, Passion of the World*, trans. Robert R. Barr (Maryknoll, N.Y.: Orbis, 1987).

30. Sobrino, "Ignacio Ellacuría," observes, "When the prophet Rutilio Grande was murdered, the prophet Archbishop Romero emerged. When he was killed, the prophet Ignacio Ellacuría arose, though he had emerged earlier" (53).

31. See Cunningham, *"Through Many Tribulations."*

32. Similarly, see Matthew 5:10-12.

33. See also Mark 4:16-20; Matthew 13:20-23.

34. Similarly, see Mark 6:11; Matthew 10:14.

35. Similary, see Mark 8:34-35; Matthew 10:38-39; 16:24-25.

36. See Cunningham, *"Through Many Tribulations,"* 86; Fitzmyer, *Luke*, 1.787-88. Compare Paul's exclamation, "And why are we putting ourselves in danger every hour? I die every day!" (1 Cor 15:30-31). Simon of Cyrene (22:26) literally fulfills this instruction.

37. Warren Carter, *Matthew on the Margins: A Sociopolitical and Religious Reading* (Maryknoll, N.Y.: Orbis, 2000), 245–46.

38. An example of a host being held responsible for his guest is found in Acts 17:1-9, where Jason was attacked after Paul stirred up trouble in Corinth.

39. Similarly, see Mark 13:9-13; Matthew 10:26-31; 24:9-14.

40. See Cunningham, "Through Many Tribulations," 186–294, who shows how these promises of Jesus are played out in the lives of the first Christians as depicted in the Acts of the Apostles.

41. There is also the episode in Acts 16:16-19 in which a slave girl with a "spirit of divination" (16:16) rightly prophesies of Paul and Silas: "These men are slaves of the Most High God who proclaim to you a way of salvation" (16:17). Annoyed with her, Paul casts out the spirit, and her owners, now deprived of their income from her, have him and Silas thrown into prison. This is not an exorcism. The girl does not have an evil spirit; what she prophesies is true. As Ivoni Richter Reimer, Women in the Acts of the Apostles: A Feminist Liberation Perspective (Minneapolis: Fortress Press, 1995), 151–94, points out, this is a liberation for her only if we imagine her being taken into the Christian community and finding new life there.

42. Amazement is also the reaction to the message of the shepherds (2:18), to the naming of John by Elizabeth and Zechariah (1:63), and to Jesus' words (4:22; 20:26) and deeds (8:25; 9:43; 11:14, 38; 24:12, 41).

43. Luke 3:16; 4:1, 14, 18; 10:21. See further Odette Mainville, L'esprit dans l'oeuvre de luc (Quebec: Fides, 1991); and Max B. Turner, "Jesus and the Spirit in Lucan Perspective," TynB 32 (1981): 3–42. Similarly, in the Gospels of Matthew and Mark, all references to the Spirit are in relation to Jesus (Matt 1:18, 20; 3:11, 16; 4:1; 12:18, 28; 27:50; Mark 1:8, 10, 12), with the exception of Matthew 10:20, Jesus' assurance to the disciples that when they are handed over, the Spirit will speak through them (// Luke 12:12); Matthew 22:43, a reference to David speaking in the Spirit (// Mark 12:36; the Lucan parallel at 12:41-44 omits mention of the Spirit, but see Acts 4:25); and the final commission in Matthew 28:19, where disciples are sent to teach and baptize in the name of the Father, Son, and Spirit.

44. See further Mary Rose D'Angelo, "Women in Luke–Acts; D'Angelo, "Re-membering Jesus: Women, Prophecy, and Resistance in the Memory of the Early Churches," Horizons 19, no. 2 (1992): 199–218; Reid, Choosing the Better Part?, 30–34, 49–52.

45. See Reid, Choosing the Better Part?, 144–62; Elisabeth Schüssler Fiorenza, "A Feminist Critical Interpretation for Liberation: Martha and Mary: Lk. 10:38-42," Rel & Int Life 3 (1986): 21–36; Adele Reinhartz, "From Narrative to History: The Resurrection of Mary and Martha," in "Women Like This," 161–84; and Warren Carter, "Getting Martha Out of the Kitchen," CBQ 58 (1996): 264–80.

46. Fitzmyer, Luke, 1.927, remarks that Jesus' beatitude does not negate that of the woman, but rather formulates what Jesus considers of prime importance and merely corrects the inadequacy of the first.

47. The issue in 1 Corinthians 11:2-16 seems to involve head coverings, but it is unclear whether it concerns veils or hairstyles, and what it is Paul wants them to do remains uncertain. Some scholars have suggested that 1 Corinthians 14:34b-36 is a secondary gloss, since it appears to conflict with Paul's approval of women's prophecy in 1 Corinthians 11:2-16, but the evidence for this is weak. Others have proposed that Paul is dealing with a different kind of speaking, a different setting, or different women. Others

see Paul as refuting the attempts of the Corinthian men to keep women from speaking in the assembly, as noted in N. Flangan and E. Snyder, "Did Paul Put Down Women in 1 Cor 14:34-36?" *BTB* 11 (1981): 10–12; and D. Odell-Scott, "Let the Women Speak in Church. An Egalitarian Interpretation of 1 Cor 14:34-16," *BTB* 13 (1983): 90–93). Either way, the text reflects conflict over women's speaking. See further Antoinette Clark Wire, *The Corinthian Women Prophets: A Reconstruction through Paul's Rhetoric* (Minneapolis: Fortress Press, 1999); Wire, "1 Corinthians," in *Searching the Scriptures,* 2.176-79, 185-89; Jouette M. Bassler, "1 Corinthians," in *Women's Bible Commentary,* 416–19; Margaret M. MacDonald, "Reading Real Women through the Undisputed Letters of Paul," in *Women and Christian Origins,* ed. Ross Shepard Kraemer and Mary Rose D'Angelo (New York: Oxford University Press, 1999): 215–17; Jerome Murphy-O'Connor, "Sex and Logic in 1 Cor 11:2-16," *CBQ* 42 (1980): 482–500; Murphy-O'Connor, "1 Corinthians 11:2-16 Once Again," *CBQ* 50 (1988): 265–74; John P. Meier, "On the Veiling of Hermeneutics (1 Cor 11:2-16)," *CBQ* 40 (1978): 212–26; G. W. Trompf, "On Attitudes toward Women in Paul and Paulinist Literature," *CBQ* 42 (1980): 196–215; W. O. Walker, "1 Corinthians and Paul's Views Regarding Women," *JBL* 94 (1975): 94–110; and Elisabeth Schüssler Fiorenza, *In Memory of Her,* 226–33.

48. See further Karen Jo Torjeson, "Wisdom, Christology, and Women Prophets," in *Jesus Then and Now: Images of Jesus in History and Christology,* ed. Marvin Meyer and Charles Hayes (Harrisburg, Pa.: Trinity, 2001), 186–200; and Mary Rose D'Angelo, "Re-membering Jesus," 202. See also Schüssler Fiorenza, *In Memory of Her,* 130–40; and Schüssler Fiorenza, *Jesus: Miriam's Child, Sophia's Prophet. Critical Issues in Feminist Christology* (New York: Continuum, 1994).

49. Luke 2:18, 33; 4:22; 5:26; 7:16; 8:25, 37; 9:34, 43; 11:14; 20:26; 24:41.

50. Luke 4:14, 37; 5:15; 7:17; 8:34, 39; 23:5.

51. There are many features in Luke 1:26-38 that match the form of a call story. Xavier Léon-Dufour, "L'annonce à Joseph," in *Etudes d'Evangile* (Paris: Seuil, 1965), 65–81, has observed the similarities between annunciation of birth stories and call stories such as that of Moses (Exod 3:2-12) and Gideon (Judg 6:12-22, 33); similarly, see Klemens Stock, "Die Berufung Marias (Luke 1,26-38)," *Bib* 61 (1980): 457–91. See Raymond E. Brown, *The Birth of the Messiah: A Commentary on the Infancy Narratives in the Gospels of Matthew and Luke* (Garden City, N.Y.: Doubleday, 1993), 156, for an outline of the elements of annunciation of birth stories as seen in the birth of Ishmael (Gen 16:7-13), Isaac (Gen 17:1-20; 18:1-2, 10-15), Samson (Judg 13:3-23), John the Baptist (Luke 1:11-20), and Jesus (Matt 1:20-21; Luke 1:26-38). Portions of this section on Mary rely on my previous work in *Choosing the Better Part?,* 55–85.

52. It is probable that originally the entire Exodus hymn was led by Miriam, and not simply verse 21, which mirrors verse 1. That it was the women who would lead victory songs and dancing is reflected in 1 Samuel 18:7. See further George J. Brooke, "A Long-Lost Song of Miriam," *BAR* 20 (1994): 62–65. Brooke posits that a separate Song of Miriam, partially suppressed in the book of Exodus, has survived in part in a Qumran text, 4Q365. Further, he shows that Mary's Magnificat, the Song of Hannah (1 Sam 2:1-10), the victory hymn of Judith (Jdt 16:6,7,13), and two sections of the Qumran War Scroll (1QM 11,14) all sing of how the powerful are brought low by God's action

through those who are lowly. That this theme survives in songs associated with women reflects an effort on the part of the then current power structure to marginalize the threat of these poems. See also Rita J. Burns, *Has the Lord Indeed Spoken Only through Moses? A Study of the Biblical Portrait of Miriam* (Atlanta: Scholars Press, 1987); Phyllis Trible, "Bringing Miriam out of the Shadows," *BRev* 5 (1989): 14–25; and J. Gerald Janzen, "Song of Moses, Song of Miriam: Who Is Seconding Whom?" *CBQ* 54 (1992): 211–20.

53. The Greek word *eleos* used in Luke 1:50 is the word that often translates *ḥesed*, the Hebrew word used in Exodus 15:13.

54. See Drorah O'Donnel Setel, "Exodus," in *Women's Bible Commentary*, 36, who observes that Miriam's actions and lineage are priestly and proposes that her designation as prophet may be due to male transmitters of the tradition who found this title less objectionable than "priest."

55. Irene Nowell, *Women in the Old Testament* (Collegeville, Minn.: Liturgical Press, 1997). 52. See also Carmiña Navia Velasco, "El Dios que nos revelan las mujeres," 2–4, http://www.sjsocial.org/crt/dios.html (accessed December 13, 2001).

56. Rav Shlomo Aviner, *Women in the Bible*, trans. Lazar Sarna (Montreal: Jewel, 2004), 93, makes these observations concerning *Tosaphot Nidda* 50a at *HaKol*.

57. As Lisa Wilson Davison, *Preaching the Women of the Bible* (St. Louis: Chalice, 2006), 91, points out, our usual placid image of Mary has taken the edge off these words. "They have lost their power to stun and offend." Davison, citing Kathleen Norris, *Amazing Grace: A Vocabulary of Faith* (New York: Riverhead Books, 1998), 117, recalls one contemporary example of the danger of these words when, in the 1980s, the Guatemalan government banned the public recitation of the Magnificat. Elizabeth A. Johnson, "Mary, Mary, Quite Contrary," *U.S. Catholic* (December 2003): 15, quotes the same.

58. Nowell, *Women in the Old Testament*, 53.

59. Nowell, *Women in the Old Testament*, 54-55.

60. Because there is no punctuation in the original Greek, it is not clear whether there are two, three, or four women at the foot of the cross in John 19:25. See further Brown, *Death of the Messiah*, 1013–19, who opts for four. Sandra Schneiders, *Written That You May Believe: Encountering Jesus in the Fourth Gospel*, rev. ed. (New York: Crossroad, 2003), 233-54, decides on three. Mark 15:40 names Mary Magdalene, Mary the mother of James the younger and of Joses, and Salome as the women who were "looking on from a distance." Similarly, Matthew says that there were many women from Galilee, among whom were Mary Magdalene, Mary the mother of James and Joseph, and the mother of the sons of Zebedee (Matt 27:55-56).

61. In the Gospel of Matthew, among the women at the foot of the cross are Mary Magdalene, Mary the mother of James and Joseph, and the mother of the sons of Zebedee (Matt 27:55-56). It may be that Mary the mother of James and Joseph is meant to be understood as Jesus' mother, since at 13:55 two of Jesus' brothers' names are given as James and Joseph. Similarly, in Mark 15:40, the women viewing the crucifixion are Mary Magdalene, Mary the mother of James the younger and of Joses, and Salome (15:40). In Mark 6:3, James and Joses are named among Jesus' siblings.

62. Scholars debate the meaning of "sword" in 2:35. For some, for example, Frederick W. Danker, *Jesus and the New Age, According to St. Luke: A Commentary on the Third Gospel* (St. Louis: Clayton, 1972), 69; and I. Howard Marshall, *Commentary on Luke* (Grand Rapids, Mich.: Eerdmans, 1978), 123, it refers to Mary's anguish over her son's rejection and death. Others, such as Fitzmyer, *Luke*, 1.429-30; Brown, *The Birth of the Messiah*, 464; and Cunningham, "Through Many Tribulations," 49, understand it in relation to Ezekiel 14:17. I see no reason to dichotomize these two meanings; both can be within Luke's purview.

63. See further Elizabeth Johnson's final chapter, "Mary, Friend of God and Prophet," in her groundbreaking book, *Truly Our Sister: A Theology of Mary in the Communion of Saints* (New York: Continuum, 2003).

64. William E. Phipps, *Assertive Biblical Women* (Westport, Conn.: Greenwood Press, 1992), 86. Aviner, *Women in the Bible*, 160, lists other explanations given by the rabbis for the choice of Huldah over Jeremiah: Jeremiah was away traveling, or Huldah was chosen because as a woman she was more compassionate (*Mesillat Yesharim* §4).

65. Phipps, *Assertive Biblical Women*, 86.

66. Claudia V. Camp, "1 and 2 Kings," in *Women's Bible Commentary*, 115.

67. Camp, "1 and 2 Kings," 115.

68. The *Mishnah* is the body of authoritative explanations of the scriptures (oral teaching, or "repetition") by rabbis who lived between 50 B.C.E. and 200 C.E.

69. For preaching insights on Huldah in 2 Chronicles 34:19-28, see Davison, *Preaching the Women of the Bible*, 63–73.

70. Tamara Cohn Eskenazi, "Ezra-Nehemiah," in *Women's Bible Commentary*, 128-29. On Old Testament women prophets, see Tereza Cavalcanti, "The Prophetic Ministry of Women in the Hebrew Bible," in *Through Her Eyes: Women's Theology from Latin America*, ed. Elsa Támez (Maryknoll, N.Y.: Orbis, 1989), 118–39.

71. Material on Anna relies on my previous work, *Choosing the Better Part?*, 86–95.

72. This is a particularly Lucan theme: 3:21; 9:18, 28, 29; 11:1; 22:32, 41-45.

73. Luke 24:53; Acts 1:14; 2:42, 46; 3:1; 4:31; 6:4, 6; 7:59; 8:15; 9:11, 40; 10:2, 9; 11:15; 12:5,12; 13:2-3; 14:23; 16:25; 20:36; 21:5; 22:17; 26:29; 27:29; 28:8.

74. The Greek *heōs etōn ogdoēkonta tessarōn*, "until" or "up to eighty-four years" in 2:37, can mean either her present age is eighty-four or she has been a widow for eighty-four years.

75. J. K. Elliott, "Anna's Age (Luke 2:36-37)," *NovT* 30 (1988): 100–02.

76. The high number of references to widows in Luke and Acts (Luke 4:25-26; 7:11-17; 18:1-8; 20:47; 21:1-4; Acts 6:1-6; 9:36-43) likely reflects their growing influence and importance in ministry, as consecrated widows moved toward becoming a clerical order. See further Bonnie Bowman Thurston, *The Widows: A Women's Ministry in the Early Church* (Minneapolis: Fortress Press, 1989).

77. See in this book pp. 50–51. See also Matthew 26:1-16; John 12:1-11.

78. There are clearly two strands of tradition. Whether they represent two separate incidents in the life of Jesus or only one that has been preserved in slightly different variations is impossible to determine. The two strands have many points of similarity, and it is likely that details from the one passed over to the other in the oral retelling. See A. Legault, "An Application of the Form-Critique Method to the Anointings in Galilee (Luke 7.37-50) and Bethany (Matt 26.6-13; Mark. 4.3-9; John 12.1-8)," *CBQ* 16 (1954): 131–45.

79. See Holly Hearon, "The Story of 'The Woman Who Anointed Jesus' as Social Memory: A Methodological Proposal for the Study of Tradition as Memory," in *Memory, Tradition, and Text: Uses of the Past in Early Christianity,* ed. Alan Kirk and Tom Thatcher (Atlanta: SBL, 2005), 99–118, who analyzes the stable and unstable elements of the story in its different versions, finding three different emergent Christologies with differing implications in terms of identity formation and social interaction.

80. In the Gospel of John (12:1-11), the woman who anoints Jesus is Mary, the sister of Martha and Lazarus. In the other three accounts, she is nameless.

81. See James B. Pritchard, ed., *ANEP* (Princeton: Princeton University Press, 1969), 209. For the custom among Jews, see H. Strack and P. Billerbeck, *Kommentar zum Neuen Testament,* 6 vols. (Munich: Beck, 1922–1961) 427, 428.

82. Susan Miller, *Women in Mark's Gospel* (New York: T & T Clark, 2004), 132.

83. Miller, *Women in Mark's Gospel,* 133.

84. Miller, *Women in Mark's Gospel,* 142.

85. Miller, *Women in Mark's Gospel,* 138.

86. Schüssler Fiorenza, *In Memory of Her,* xiii.

87. See also Joanna Dewey, "The Gospel of Mark," in *Searching the Scriptures,* vol. 2, *A Feminist Commentary,* ed. Elisabeth Schüssler Fiorenza (New York: Crossroad, 1994), 501–02; Elisabeth Moltmann Wendel, *The Women around Jesus* (New York: Crossroad, 1993), 92–104; Donald Senior, *The Passion of Jesus in the Gospel of Mark* (Wilmington, Del.: Glazier, 1984), 42–48; and Mary Ann Tolbert, "Mark," in *Women's Bible Commentary,* 357–58.

88. See chapter 5 (pp. 159–60) for a fuller discussion of this text.

89. The interpretation presented here relies heavily on Schneiders, *Written That You May Believe,* 126–48. For another approach, see Luise Schottroff, "The Samaritan Woman and the Notion of Sexuality in the Fourth Gospel," in *What Is John?* 2 vols., ed. Fernando F. Segovia (Atlanta: SBL, 1998), 2.157-81, who sees the woman as one who is in a situation of extreme exploitation. She is a woman who has had to marry five times to survive, and now the man with whom she lives does not even offer her the security of a marriage contract. Her encounter with Jesus gave her the courage to put an end to the degrading situation and to find a new household in the community of believers in which she can survive and thrive. Jerome Neyrey examines the text from a social science perspective in "What's Wrong with This Picture? John 4, Cultural Stereotypes of Women, and Public and Private Space," *BTB* 24 (1994): 77–91.

90. See Raymond F. Collins, "The Representative Figures in the Fourth Gospel," *DRev* 94 (1976): 26–46, 118–32; Craig R. Koester, *Symbolism in the Fourth Gospel: Meaning, Mystery, Community*, 2d ed. (Minneapolis: Fortress Press, 2003), 33–77.

91. That Jesus and the woman meet at a well also serves the marital symbolism, as a number of famous couples in the Old Testament met at wells: Rebekah and Isaac (Gen 24:10-61), Jacob and Rachel (Gen 29:1-20), Moses and Zipporah (Exod 2:16-22). The theme of the bridegroom has also been established with the wedding feast at Cana (2:1-11) and John the Baptist's declaration that he is not the bridegroom but his friend (3:27-30).

92. Schneiders, *Written That You May Believe*, 140.

93. The translation of *mēti houtos estin ho christos* as a question and its interpretation as an invitation is advanced by Mary Coloe, *God Dwells with Us: Temple Symbolism in the Fourth Gospel* (Collegeville, Minn.: Liturgical Press, 2001): 106.

94. See Dorothy Lee, "Abiding in the Fourth Gospel: A Case Study in Feminist Biblical Theology," in *A Feminist Companion to John*, 2 vols., ed. Amy-Jill Levine with Marianne Blickenstaff (Sheffield, U.K.: Sheffield Academic Press, 2003), 2.64-78.

95. The remark of the people, "It is no longer because of what you said that we believe, for we have heard for ourselves" (v. 42) should not be understood as denigrating the woman's witness, but rather as part of the repeated pattern where one who comes to belief in Jesus brings others to him, and they encounter him directly for themselves.

96. Nicodemus does appear twice more in the narrative, in an increasingly positive light. He questions his fellow Pharisees about the legality of judging people without giving them a hearing when they are discussing arresting Jesus (7:50), and he accompanies Joseph of Arimathea in burying Jesus' body, bringing one hundred pounds of spices (19:39-40).

97. There is no warrant in the text for interpretations that see the woman coming to the well at noon rather than early morning, as was customary, because she was an outcast due to her sinfulness and she wished to avoid other people. There is nothing in the text that indicates that she should be seen as a sinner. Jesus never says to her, as he does to the man at the pool of Bethsaida, "Do not sin anymore" (5:14), or to woman caught in adultery, "Go your way and from now on do not sin again" (8:11). Moreover, one wonders, if she was such a pariah, how did the townspeople so readily accept her testimony when she told them about Jesus?

98. There are only four references to the twelve in the Fourth Gospel. Jesus asks the twelve, "Do you also wish to go away?" (6:67) after the bread-of-life discourse, which some find too hard to take. Then Jesus remarks, "Did I not choose you, the twelve? Yet one of you is the devil" (6:70), although there is no narration of the choice of the twelve. Judas is identified as one of the twelve (6:71), as is Thomas (20:24).

99. See Adeline Fehribach, *The Women in the Life of the Bridegroom: A Feminist Historical-Literary Analysis of the Female Characters in the Fourth Gospel* (Collegeville, Minn.: Liturgical Press, 1998), 45–81, who finds the Samaritan woman's role diminished in the gospel by other women who also play the

role of the betrothed of the messianic bridegroom. Mary L. Coloe, *God Dwells with Us: Temple Symbolism in the Fourth Gospel* (Collegeville, Minn.: Liturgical Press, 2001), 85–113, concentrates on the question of the place and nature of true worship in her analysis of the scene.

100. Because there is no punctuation in the Greek text, it is not possible to tell whether the evangelist intends two, three, or four women. See Brown, *The Death of the Messiah*, 2.1014-19.

101. See Maria-Luisa Rigato, "'Remember . . . Then They Remembered': Luke 24.6-8," in *A Feminist Companion to Luke*, ed. Amy-Jill Levine with Marianne Blickenstaff (Sheffield, U.K.: Sheffield University Press, 2002), 269–80.

102. See further Barbara E. Reid, *Choosing the Better Part?*, especially 198–204, on the Galilean women as disbelieved witnesses. On the muting of women's voices in Luke, see Mary Rose D'Angelo, "Women in Luke–Acts: A Redactional View," 441–61.

103. Luke 16:16 gives the clue that the Third Evangelist thinks of salvation history in terms of two distinct moments: the time of the Law and the prophets, and the new age of the renewed people of God who follow the Way of Jesus. John the Baptist is a hinge figure that bridges the two.

104. See chapter 2 (pp. 76–79), on Luke's depiction of Martha and Mary and the struggle it reflects in the Lucan community. See Elisabeth Moltmann-Wendel, "Motherhood or Friendship," in *The Power of Naming: A Concilium Reader in Feminist Liberation Theology*, ed. Elisabeth Schüssler Fiorenza (Maryknoll, N.Y.: Orbis, 1996), 292–306; and Moltmann-Wendel, *Rediscovering Friendship*, 66–81, who shows how the church's tradition has put Mary, the mother of Jesus, in the foreground, while pushing Mary Magdalene, the first proclaimer of the resurrection, to the back of the stage.

105. The designation of Mary Magdalene as "apostle to the apostles" dates at least to the third century, to Hippolytus of Rome's commentary on the Song of Songs. In what follows, I rely substantially on Sandra Schneiders, *Written That You May Believe*, 202–23.

106. See note 87 for references on analyses of representative characters in the Fourth Gospel.

107. There are strong overtones of the lover who seeks for the one whom her heart desires in Song of Songs 3:1-5.

108. See Schneiders, *Written That You May Believe*, 219–23, for more detailed analysis of this difficult verse. The imperative is in the present tense, which indicates that the command is to stop doing something, that is, that Mary not continue to cling to her previous way of knowing Jesus. The NAB translation, "Stop holding on to me," captures this better than the translations "Do not hold on to me" (NRSV and NIV) or "Do not cling to me" (NJB). In addition, the verb *haptomai* does not connote "cling" or "hold"; the verb *krateō* would convey this notion. *Haptomai*, as Schneiders observes, "often means not simply, or even primarily, the physical gesture of laying one's hands on a person, but rather interpersonal relating such as being deeply touched by a person's kindness or touched by the Evil One, as in 1 John 5:18, which is the only other place the word occurs in the Johannine corpus" (219–20). Further, she reads Jesus' words about ascending as a question: "Am I as yet (or still)

not ascended?" The implied answer is, "No, you are indeed ascended, that is, glorified." Jesus is not suspended between resurrection and glorification; in John's Gospel, passion, death, resurrection, ascension, and glorification, are all one moment. "Jesus' ascension to the Father, that is, his glorification, is precisely the reason Mary will now encounter him in the community of the church rather than in his physical or earthly body" (220). For further exploration of the significance of the bodily resurrection in John 20, see Sandra Schneiders, "The Resurrection (of the Body) in the Fourth Gospel: A Key to Johannine Spirituality," in *Life in Abundance: Studies of John's Gospel in Tribute to Raymond E. Brown*, ed. John R. Donahue (Collegeville, Minn.: Liturgical Press, 2005), 168–98, and the response to Schneiders by Donald Senior, *Life in Abundance*, 199-203. For a comprehensive survey of interpretations of John 20:17, see Harry Attridge, "'Don't Be Touching Me': Recent Feminist Scholarship on Mary Magdalene," in *A Feminist Companion to John*, 2.140-66.

109. There is an enormous body of contemporary literature on Mary Magdalene. Important sources include Ann Graham Brock, *Mary Magdalene, the First Apostle: The Struggle for Authority* (Cambridge, Mass.: Harvard University Press, 2003); Esther DeBoer, *Mary Magdalene: Beyond the Myth* (Harrisburg, Pa.: Trinity, 1997); Dierdre Good, ed., *Mariam, the Magdalen, and the Mother* (Bloomington: Indiana University Press, 2005); Holly E. Hearon, *The Mary Magdalene Tradition: Witness and Counter-Witness in Early Christian Communities* (Collegeville, Minn.: Liturgical Press, 2004); Karen King, "Prophetic Power and Women's Authority: The Case of the Gospel of Mary Magdalene," in *Women Prophets and Preachers through Two Millennia of Christianity*, ed. Beverly M. Kienzle and Pamela J. Walker (Berkeley: University of California Press, 1998), 21–41; Katherine Ludwig Jansen, *The Making of the Magdalen: Preaching and Popular Devotion in the Later Middle Ages* (Princeton, N.J.: Princeton University Press, 2000); Ingrid Maisch, *Mary Magdalene: The Image of a Woman through the Centuries* (Collegeville, Minn.: Liturgical Press, 1998); Carla Ricci, *Mary Magdalene and Many Others: Women Who Followed Jesus* (Minneapolis: Fortress Press, 1994); Jane Schaberg, *The Resurrection of Mary Magdalene: Legends, Apocrypha, and the Christian Tradition* (New York: Continuum, 2002); "Thinking Back through Mary Magdalene," in *A Feminist Companion to John*, 2.167-89; Mary R. Thompson, *Mary of Magdala: What the DaVinci Code Misses* (New York: Paulist, 2006); and Carmiña Navia Velasco, "Violencia Histórica Contra María de Magdala," *RIBLA* 41 (2002): 107–16. For an analysis of the androcentric and patriarchal overtones in the characterization of Mary Magdalene, see Fehribach, *The Women in the Life of the Bridegroom*, 143–67.

110. For more detailed analysis of why these verses are considered redactional, see Reid, *Choosing the Better Part?*, 192–93.

111. Don C. Benjamin, "The Persistent Widow," *TBT* 28 (1990): 212–19.

112. The verbs *ērcheto*, "kept coming" (v. 3), and *ouk ēthelen*, "refused" (v. 4), are in the imperfect tense, which indicates repeated or sustained action in the past.

113. The verb *hypōpiazō* is a boxing term that means literally "to strike under the eye" (BDAG, 1040). See also Paul's use of it in 1 Corinthians 9:26-27. Some take it to have a metaphorical meaning, such as, "bothering" (NAB), "pestering" (NJB), or "wear out" (NRSV). But this ill fits the story line, where the judge is already worn down, and it misses the impact of the ludicrous scenario of a seemingly powerful judge being cowed by a supposedly helpless widow.

114. Ivoni Richter, "El poder de una protagonista. La oración de las personas exluidas (Luke 18,1-8)," *RIBLA* 25 (1997): 59–68. See also Barbara E. Reid, "La Viuda y el Juez (Lc 18, 1-8) Desde la Perspectiva de una Hermeneútica Feminista," *QOL. Revista Bíblica Mexicana* 37 (2005): 69–82.

115. Hebe Bonafini, president of the "Mothers of the Plaza de Mayo," quoted in *Cadernos do 3o Mundo* 80 (June 1985): 48, cited by Tereza Cavalcanti in "The Prophetic Ministry of Women in the Hebrew Bible," in *Through Her Eyes: Women's Theology from Latin America*, ed. Elsa Támez; (Maryknoll, N.Y.: Orbis, 1989), 137–38. For other feminist perspectives on this parable, see Mary W. Matthews, Carter Shelley, and Barbara Scheele, "Proclaiming the Parable of the Persistent Widow (Luke 18.2-5)," in *The Lost Coin: Parables of Women, Work, and Wisdom*, ed. Mary Ann Beavis (Sheffield: Sheffield Academic Press, 2002), 46–70; and Luise Schottroff, *The Parables of Jesus*, trans. Linda M. Maloney (Minneapolis: Fortress Press, 2006), 188–94.

116. Cynthia Crysdale, *Embracing Travail: Retrieving the Cross Today* (New York: Continuum, 1999), 57.

117. Pedro Casaldáliga, "Mystik der Befreiung," in *Mystik de Befreiung: Ein Portrait des Bischofs Pedro Casaldáliga n Brasilien*, by Teófilo Cabastrero (Wuppertal, Ger.: Jugenddienst, 1981), 13, cited in Dorothee Soelle, *The Silent Cry: Mysticism and Resistance*, trans. Barbara and Martin Rumscheidt (Minneapolis: Fortress Press, 2001), 288.

118. Soelle, *The Silent Cry*, 230.

119. See CODIMUJ, *Con Mirada, Mente y Corazón de Mujer*, 47–54.

120. CODIMUJ, *Con Mirada, Mente y Corazón de Mujer*, 130.

121. CODIMUJ, *Con Mirada, Mente y Corazón de Mujer*, 134.

122. CODIMUJ, *Con Mirada, Mente y Corazón de Mujer*, 139.

123. The following comments were made by the *asesoras* of CODIMUJ at a meeting in San Cristóbal de las Casas, on November 11, 2002.

124. CODIMUJ, *Con Mirada, Mente y Corazón de Mujer*, 141–42.

125. The following incident took place at a three-day gathering of deacons, deacon candidates, and catechists in January 2005, at which I was privileged to share reflections about women in the New Testament. See also the account by Richard Galliardetz, "Accountability in the Church: Report from Chiapas," *New Theology Review* 19 (2006): 33–45.

126. CODIMUJ, *Con Mirada, Mente y Corazón de Mujer*, 152.

127. Casaldáliga, "Mystik der Befreiung," 87, cited in Soelle, *The Silent Cry*, 288–89.

Chapter 4 Notes

1. Margaret M. Leddy, *Domestic Violence: A Pastoral Response Guide* (M.A.P.S. thesis submitted at Catholic Theological Union, Chicago, 2004), 10.

2. The author of Hebrews, using similar imagery and language of cultic sacrifice, asserts, "Without the shedding of blood there is no forgiveness of sins" (Heb 9:22). Actually, there were other means, for example, contrition of heart (Ps 51:19), fasting (Joel 2:12), and almsgiving (Sir 3:29). See Joachim Jeremias, *The Eucharistic Words of Jesus* (Philadelphia: Fortress Press, 1966). 229–31, on various means of atonement in Judaism). The author of Hebrews then says that there is no more need for offerings because sins are forgiven through Jesus' sacrifice: "Where there is forgiveness . . . there is no longer any offering for sin" (Heb 10:18).

3. Robert J. Schreiter, *In Water and in Blood: A Spirituality of Solidarity and Hope* (New York: Crossroad, 1988), 53–62.

4. In the scriptures, "cup" frequently refers to the suffering of Israel (Isa 51:17; Jer 25:15, 49:12, 51:7; Lam 4:21; see also *Mart. Isa. 5:13*). In its two other instances in Matthew, it refers to that borne by Jesus. When the mother of the sons of Zebedee request privileged places for them, Jesus asks if they can "drink the cup" that he is about to drink (Matt 20:22-23). In Gethsemane, he implores the Father to let "this cup" pass from him (26:39).

5. Moses typology in the First Gospel is strong. The threats to the infant Jesus' life (2:16-18) mirror those toward Moses (Exod 1:15-22). Matthew depicts Jesus as authoritative teacher of the Law, often instructing from a mountaintop (5:1; 15:29; 17:1; 28:16). Many see the evangelist's arrangement of five major blocks of teaching as a deliberate parallel to the five books of the Law of Moses. Explicit references to Moses occur at 8:4; 17:3-4; 19:7-8; 22:24; 23:2.

6. As in Matthew 20:28 *pollōn*, "many" has a comprehensive sense, reflecting a Semitic expression where "many" is the opposite of "one," thus the equivalent of "all." See W. D. Davies and Dale C. Allison, *The Gospel According to St. Matthew*, 3 vols. (Edinburgh: T & T Clark, 1988, 1991, 1997), 3.474. An echo of Isaiah 53:12 may be heard in this phrase. The preposition *peri* carries the connotation usually conveyed by *hyper*, "on account of, for." It also has a sense of encircling, encompassing, "around" (BDAG, 798; Maximilian Zerwick, *Biblical Greek* (Rome, 1963), §96.

7. In the phrase "for the forgiveness of sins" (*eis aphesin hamartiōn*), the preposition *eis* indicates not only the end in view (Zerwick, *Biblical Greek*, §87) but also signifies motion into a thing (BDAG, 288), in this case, movement into a way of forgiveness.

8. All of the following references to blood and bloodshed are unique to Matthew except for the word over the cup at the Last Supper (compare Matt 26:28; Mark 14:24; Luke 22:20). In the Lucan parallel to Matthew 23:30 (Luke 11:47, 49), Jesus speaks of killing prophets but does not speak of blood or bloodshed.

9. It is deplorable to use this verse to place blame on Jews of all times for the death of Jesus.

10. Here it is *pas ho laos*, "the people as a whole," not *ho ochlos*, "the crowd."

11. See Joseph A. Fitzmyer, "Anti-Semitism and the Cry of 'All the People' (Matt 27:25)," *TS* 26 (1965): 189–214, who also understands this verse to be explanatory, not condemnatory. He sees 27:25 as the climax of a theme whereby Matthew aims to explain to Jewish Christians why it is that "the nations" have accepted the gospel more readily than have the Jews.

12. Similarly, Robert H. Smith, "Matthew 27:25: The Hardest Verse in Matthew's Gospel," *CurrTM* 17, no. 6 (1990): 421–28, argues that Matthew intends the reader to see the irony in this verse and to weep with him for the crowd that does not comprehend that the blood of Jesus was on them for their blessing.

13. Scholars debate whether Judas sincerely repents or is simply regretful. J. Ramsey Michaels, for example, "The Parable of the Regretful Son," *HTR* 61 (1968): 15–26, argues that *metameletheis* in 27:3, as well as in 21:29, 32 (the parable of the two sons), signifies futile regret, not repentance, which would be indicated with *metanoeo*, as in Matthew 3:2; 4:17; 11:20-21; 12:41. However, there does not appear to be as significant a difference in the meaning of the two verbs as Michaels would advocate. See BDAG, 639–40. Moreover, in 21:32, *metamelomai* is connected with the change of mind that leads to faith, for which John the Baptist calls. See further the discussion in Davies and Allison, *The Gospel According to St. Matthew*, 560–63.

14. See also John 7:53–8:11. Here, neither the noun *aphesis*, "forgiveness," nor the verb *aphiemi*, "to forgive," occurs. Rather, the discussion concerns Jesus' refusal "to condemn," *katakrino*, a woman caught in adultery.

15. Other places in the New Testament where faith is linked with forgiveness include Luke 7:50; Acts 10:43; 13:38-39; 26:17-18.

16. Similarly, see Mark 11:25. There is no parallel for Matthew 6:14-15 in Luke's version of the Our Father (11:1-4). Luke's wording is slightly different: "forgive us our sins (*hamartias*), for we ourselves forgive (*aphiomen*) everyone indebted (*opheilonti*) to us" (Luke 11:4). Where Matthew (6:12) uses *opheilemata*, "debts," Luke (11:4) has *hamartias*, "sins." Matthew's term reminds disciples that offenses against others include monetary inequities from systemic injustices. See Deuteronomy 15 for prescriptions for relaxation of debts in the sabbatical year. Luke also captures this nuance by using the verb form *opheilonti*, "owing a debt," in the second clause of 11:4. Another difference is that Luke has "forgive" in the present tense, *aphiomen*, whereas Matthew uses the perfect tense, *aphekamen*, "we have forgiven." The perfect tense connotes a past action of which the effect endures into the present. Luke's version can be understood as saying that reception of divine forgiveness and offer of human forgiveness are concurrent, whereas Matthew makes reception of divine forgiveness contingent on willingness to forgive others.

17. Luke's version of the saying (17:3-4) is far more brief. The parable is unique to Matthew.

18. It is probable that this concluding verse was added to the parable by the evangelist. See Jan Lambrecht, *Out of the Treasure: The Parables in the Gospel of Matthew*. Louvain Theological and Pastoral Monographs

10; (Louvain: Peeters Press; and Grand Rapids: Eerdmans) 1991, 53–68. For a more detailed analysis of the tradition history of the parable. For a more detailed analysis of the whole parable, see Barbara Reid, *Parables for Preachers: Year A* (Collegeville, Minn.: Liturgical Press, 2001), 131–42.

19. Marta, in Ate, a neighborhood of Lima, Peru, at a meeting to prepare for a workshop entitled "Nonviolence in the Household," April 16, 2003.

20. Margaret M. Leddy, *Domestic Violence: A Pastoral Response Guide* (M.A.P.S. thesis submitted at Catholic Theological Union, Chicago, 2004), 22.

21. On the relationship between Jesus and John the Baptist, see John P. Meier, *A Marginal Jew: Rethinking the Historical Jesus*, 3 vols. (New York: Doubleday, 1994), *Mentor, Message, and Miracles* 2.116-30; and Jerome Murphy-O'Connor, "John the Baptist and Jesus: History and Hypotheses," *NTS* 36 (1990): 359–74.

22. On the dynamics and strategies of reconciliation, see Robert J. Schreiter, *Reconciliation: Mission & Ministry in a Changing Social Order* (Maryknoll, N.Y.: Orbis, 1992); and Schreiter, *The Ministry of Reconciliation: Spirituality & Strategies* (Maryknoll, N.Y.: Orbis, 1998).

23. It is only in the Pauline letters that the noun *katallagē*, "reconciliation," and the related verbs *katallassō* and *apokatallassō*, "to reconcile," are found.

24. BDAG, *katallagē*, 521.

25. BDAG, *katallassō*, 521.

26. We will examine *sōzō*, "to save," shortly.

27. This is the same assertion Paul makes with regard to justification in Romans 3:21-26.

28. In Paul, the word *kosmos* does not have the pejorative connotation that it does in the Gospel of John.

29. This is the only instance in which the verb *eirēnopoieō*, "peacemaking," occurs in the New Testament. The noun *eirēnopoioi*, "peacemakers," appears in the Sermon on the Mount, where they are pronounced "blessed" (Matt 5:9).

30. New Testament scholars are split on whether the letter to the Colossians was written by Paul or by a follower who took on the mantle of the apostle.

31. Almost all New Testament scholars are agreed that Ephesians was not written by Paul.

32. The only other instance of the verb *katallassō* in the New Testament is 1 Corinthians 7:11, where Paul speaks of the reconciliation of a wife to her husband. There is a single instance of the verb *diallassomai*, "be reconciled," in the Gospel of Matthew, where Jesus advises, "When you are offering your gift at the altar, if you remember that your brother or sister has something against you, leave your gift there before the altar and go; first be reconciled (*diallagēthi*) to your brother or sister, and then come and offer your gift" (Matt 5:23-24).

33. Joseph Fitzmyer, *The Gospel According to Luke* (Garden City, N.Y.: Doubleday, 1985), 1.222.

34. From an inscription from Ephesus, dating to A.D. 48. See Fitzmyer, *Luke*, 1.204. See further W. Foerster and G. Fohrer, "*sōzō*," *TDNT* 7 (1971): 965–1024.

35. Hebrew *môšîa'* literally means "anointed," usually rendered in Greek as *christos*, "Christ."

36. See, for example, 1 Samuel 10:19; Isaiah 45:15, 21; Wisdom 16:7; 1 Maccabees 4:30; Sirach 51:1.

37. The evangelists use *sōtēr* only in Luke 1:47; 2:11; John 4:42; and Acts 5:31; 13:23; and *sōtēria* occurs only in Luke 1:69, 71, 77; 19:9; John 4:22; Acts 4:12; 7:25; 13:26, 47; 16:17; 27:34.

38. The verb *sōzō* occurs fourteen times in Matthew, thirteen times in Mark, eighteen times in Luke, six times in John, and thirteen times in Acts of the Apostles.

39. Fitzmyer, *Luke*, 1.222. The title *sōtēr* occurs mainly in the later New Testament letters. In most instances, it is a title for Jesus: Ephesians 5:23; 1 Timothy 1:1; 2 Timothy 1:10; Titus 1:4; 3:6; 2 Peter 1:1; 2:20; 3:2, 18; 1 John 4:14. Some references are to God as Savior: Luke 1:47; 1 Timothy 2:3; 4:10; Titus 1:3; 2:10; 3:4; Jude 25. In two instances can be found the phrase "our God and Savior Jesus Christ": Titus 1:13; 2 Peter 1:1. The universality of salvation comes to the fore in the Johannine writings, where Jesus is said to be "Savior of the world" (John 4:42; 1 John 4:14). Similarly, 1 Timothy 2:4 says that he "desires everyone to be saved." By contrast, the author of Ephesians speaks of him as Savior of the church (Eph 5:23).

40. For the use of *sōzō* in connection with deliverance from sickness, disability, or demons, see Matthew 9:21, 22; Mark 5:23, 28, 34; 6:56; 10:52; Luke 6:9; 8:36, 48, 50; 17:19; 18:42. In Matthew 8:25; 14:30, it refers to rescue from the sea.

41. See Matthew 9:22; Mark 5:34; 10:52; Luke 7:50; 8:12, 48, 50; 17:19; John 4:42; Romans 1.16; Ephesians 1.13; 2 Thessalonians 2:13; 2 Timothy 3:15; 1 Peter 1:5.

42. This is the NAB translation. The NRSV translates, "Your faith has made you well." The verb *sōzō* means both "heal" and "save."

43. Fitzmyer, *Luke*, 1.223, observes that in the Gospel of Luke, "while the verb *sōzō* often depicts Jesus' effect on individuals during his ministry, the title *sōtēr* is never given to him during that ministry. It is a title born of the totality of his work, esp. as that was understood after the resurrection."

44. These, along with John 3:16, are the few times that the Fourth Evangelist uses *kosmos* in a positive sense. Most often, it refers to the realm opposed to Jesus.

45. Fitzmyer, *Luke*, 1.204-05.

46. The author of Colossians equates redemption with forgiveness, using the verb *hruomai*, "to draw out of danger, rescue, save" (BDAG, 907). He says that the Father "has rescued us from the power of darkness and transferred us into the kingdom of his beloved Son, in whom we have redemption (*errysato*), the forgiveness of sins" (Col 1:13-14).

47. For other feminist reflections on salvation, see L. Susan Bond, *Trouble with Jesus: Women, Christology, and Preaching* (St. Louis: Chalice, 1999), 120–26, who explores the metaphor "salvage" in place of "salvation." Ivone Gebara, *Teología a ritmo de mujer* (Mexico, D.F.: Ediciones Dabar, 1995), 67–89, explores the human search for saviors, examining the figures of both Jesus and his mother.

48. Walter Wink, *Engaging the Powers: Discernment and Resistance in a World of Domination* (Minneapolis: Fortress Press, 1992), 175–86.

49. BDAG, 80.

50. A similar formulation is found in 1 Peter 2:23: "When he was abused he did not return abuse; when he suffered he did not threaten; but he entrusted himself to the one who judges justly." When this image of Jesus as a passive victim is taken by an abused person as the model to emulate, the effect is deadly.

51. For example, see Romans 12:9; 1 Thessalonians 5:22; 1 Corinthians 5:13; Ephesians 6:13.

52. See further Hans Dieter Betz, *The Sermon on the Mount: A Commentary on the Sermon on the Mount, Including the Sermon on the Plain (Matthew 5:3–7:27 and Luke 6:20-49)*, ed. Adela Yarbro Collins (Minneapolis: Fortress Press, 1995), 280–81. Walter Wink, *Engaging the Powers*, 184–86, shows that, in the majority of instances of *antistēnai* in the LXX, Philo, and Josephus, the connotation is "resist violently," or use "armed resistance in military encounters." See also Ephesians 6:13, where it is employed with military imagery.

53. See www.cverdad.org.pe/ingles/pagina01.php (accessed February 23, 2007).

54. See http://www.cverdad.org.pe/ingles/apublicas/p-fotografico/e_yuyanapacha.php (accessed February 23, 2007).

55. The commission gave their final report on August 28, 2003, after two years of investigation, collecting the testimony of some 69,280 persons. See further http://www.cverdad.org.pe/ingles/pagina01.php (accessed February 23, 2007).

56. *Boletín de la Comisión de la Verdad y Reconciliación*, no. 7 (March 2003): 4.

57. *Boletín de la Comisión*, 4–5.

58. "Myths and Facts," in *Rainbow House Domestic Violence Training Manual* (Chicago: 2004), 7, cited in Leddy, *Domestic Violence*, 23.

59. For example, see Matthew 5:28, 26; 6:2, 5, 16; 8:10; 10:15, 23, 42; 11:11; 13:17; 14:33; 16:28; 17:20; 18:3, 13, 18, 19; 19:23, 28; 21:21, 31; 23:36; 24:2, 34, 47; 25:12, 40, 45; 26:13, 21, 34; John 1:51; 5:19, 24, 25; 6:26, 32, 47, 53; 8:34, 51, 48; 10:1, 7; 12:24; 13:16, 20, 21; 14:12; 16:20, 23.

60. R. Scott Appleby comments on this in *The Ambivalence of the Sacred: Religion, Violence, and Reconciliation* (New York: Rowman & Littlefield, 2000), 203. Appleby's book is one of a burgeoning body of writings that attests to the workability of processes of forgiveness and reconciliation in contemporary situations of conflict transformation. See also William Bole, Drew Christiansen, and Robert T. Hennemeyer, eds. *Forgiveness in International Politics: An Alternative Road to Peace* (Washington, D.C.: United States Conference of Catholic Bishops, 2004); Marc Golpin, *Holy War, Holy Peace: How Religion Can Bring Peace to the Middle East* (Oxford, U.K.: Oxford University Press, 2002); *Between Eden & Armageddon: The Future of World Religions, Violence, and Peacemaking* (Oxford: Oxford University Press, 2000); Joseph F. Kelly, *Responding to Evil* (Collegeville, Minn.: Liturgical Press, 2003); Edward Leroy, *Facing Terrorism: Responding as Christians* (Louisville: Westminster John Knox, 2004); Schreiter, *Reconciliation*; Schreiter, *The Ministry of Reconciliation*; James C. Scott, *Weapons of the Weak: Everyday*

Forms of Peasant Resistance (New Haven, Conn.: Yale University Press, 1985); Glen Stassen, ed., *Just Peacemaking: Ten Practices for Abolishing War*, 2nd ed. (Cleveland: Pilgrim, 2004); Desmond Tutu, *No Future without Forgiveness* (New York: Doubleday, 1999); and Miroslav Volf, *Exclusion & Embrace: A Theological Exploration of Identity, Otherness, and Reconciliation* (Nashville: Abingdon, 1996). Relating social peacemaking to New Testament interpretation are Gil Bailie, *Violence Unveiled: Humanity at the Crossroads* (New York: Crossroad, 1999); and Willard M. Swartley, *Covenant of Peace: The Missing Peace in New Testament Theology and Ethics* (Grand Rapids, Mich.: Eerdmans, 2006).

61. Tutu, *No Future without Forgiveness*, 23.

62. Appleby, *Ambivalence of the Sacred*, 44.

63. See further Donald W. Shriver Jr., *An Ethic for Enemies: Forgiveness in Politics* (New York: Oxford University Press, 1995); and William Bole, Drew Christiansen, and Robert T. Hennemeyer, *Forgiveness in International Politics . . . an Alternative Road to Peace* (Washington, D.C.: United States Conference of Catholic Bishops, 2004).

64. Bole, et al., *Forgiveness in International Politics*, 51–53.

65. Remarks from his homily delivered on October 29, 2006, at Catholic Theological Union, Chicago, on the occasion of the dedication of the new academic center. A transcription can be found at www.suntimes.com/lifestyles/religion/117886,CST-NWS-cardtranscript3.article (accessed November 1, 2006).

66. Matthew 11:15; 13:3, 9, 43; 15:10; 21:33.

67. Matthew 9:10-13; 11:19; 22:1-14; Luke 5:27-32; 7:34; 15:1-2; 19:1-10.

68. Jesus is shown healing and exorcising in Matthew 4:23-25; 8:1-4, 5-13; 14-17; 8:28–9:1; 9:2-8, 18-26; 11:5; 12:9-14, 22; 14:14; 17:14-21, 18; 20:29-34; Mark 1:21-28, 29-34, 39, 40-45; 2:1-12; 3:1-6; 5:1-20, 21-43; 8:22-26; 9:14-27; 10:46-52; Luke 4:31-37, 38-41; 5:12-14, 17-26; 6:6-11, 18-19; 7:1-10, 21; 8:2, 40-56; 9:11, 37-43; 11:14; 13:10-17; 14:1-6; 17:11-17; 18:35-43; 22:51; Acts 10:38; John 4:46-54; 6:2; 5:1-18; 7:53-8:11; 9:1-41; 11:1-46. See further Elaine M. Wainwright, "'Your Faith Has Made You Well': Jesus, Women, and Healing in the Gospel of Matthew," in *Transformative Encounters: Jesus and Women Re-Viewed*, ed. Ingrid Rosa Kitzberger (Leiden, Netherlands: Brill, 2000), 224–44; and Wainwright, *Women Healing/Healing Women: The Genderisation of Healing in Early Christianity* (London: Equinox, 2006).

69. See previous discussion, pp. 77–78, for the range of meanings of *diakonein*.

70. See Ligia Valdivieso Eguiguren, "Género y Medicina Natural y Andina," *Alpanchis* 57 (2001): 235–39.

71. See the article written November 22, 2006, by Greg Moses, "Dissident Women of Chiapas and Oaxaca: MonkeyWrench Event," austin.indymedia.org/newswire/display/34913/index.php (accessed February 21, 2007), in which he tells of the efforts of Zapatista women in Chiapas to work collectively to recover their knowledge of indigenous herbs and to reclaim their role and art as healers, which they have exercised in their communities for tens of thousands of years.

72. Matthew 8:14-15 // Mark 1:29-34 // Luke 4:38-41.

73. As Bruce Malina and Richard Rohrbaugh, *Social Science Commentary on the Synoptic Gospels* (Minneapolis: Fortress Press, 1992), 181, observe, "Since marriages in first-century Palestine were patrilocal, the fact that Peter's mother-in-law was in his house may mean that she was a widow with no living family members to care for her."

74. Wainwright, *Towards a Feminist Critical Reading*, 177–91.

75. The verbs *egeirō* (Mark 1:31; Matt 8:15) and *anistēmi* (Luke 4:39) are the same verbs that are used of Jesus' resurrection, for example, Acts 2:24, 30; 3:15, 26; 5:30; 10:40; 13:33, 37; 17:31; 1 Thessalonians 4:16; 1 Corinthians 6:14; 15:15, 51.

76. For analyses of the Marcan version of the story, see Susan Miller, *Women in Mark's Gospel* (New York: T & T Clark, 2004), 17–30; and Deborah Krause, "Simon Peter's Mother-in-Law—Disciple or Domestic Servant? Feminist Biblical Hermeneutics and the Interpretation of Mark 1.29-31," in *A Feminist Companion to Mark,* ed. Amy-Jill Levine with Marianne Blickenstaff (Sheffield: Sheffield Academic Press, 2001), 37–53. Krause warns against idealizing Simon's mother-in-law's service and recognizes the text as a site of competing and conflicting power relations.

77. For more on Joanna, see Elisabeth Moltmann Wendel, *The Women around Jesus* (New York: Crossroad, 1993), 131–44. For a reconstruction of how Joanna and Mary may have come to know Jesus and how they collaborated as his patrons, see Marianne Sawicki, "Magdalenes and Tiberiennes: City Women in the Entourage of Jesus," in *Transformative Encounters*, 181–202; and Sawicki, *Crossing Galilee: Architecture of Contact in the Occupied Land of Jesus* (Harrisburg, Pa.: Trinity, 2000).

78. Jane Schaberg, "Luke," in *Women's Bible Commentary*, 287, notes the smallness of the geographic area and argues for day trips. She further observes that if this kind of practice were scandalous, it is curious that there is no mention or explicit defense of it in the traditions. Malina and Rohrbaugh, *Social Science Commentary*, 334, think that there is no scandal if the women are widows who are understood to serve the surrogate family of Jesus' disciples in place of their biological family. Similarly, see Kathleen Corley, *Private Women, Public Meals* (Peabody, Mass.: Hendrickson, 1993), 118–19.

79. For example, see Ben Witherington III, "On the Road with Mary Magdalene, Joanna, Susanna, and Other Disciples—Luke 8:1-3," *ZNW* 70 (1979): 243–48; and Witherington III, *Women in the Ministry of Jesus* (Cambridge: Cambridge University Press, 1984), 116–18.

80. Luke 11:21; 12:15, 33, 44; 14:33; 16:1; 19:8; Acts 4:32.

81. Corley, *Private Women*, 111. See also Richard Pervo, *Profit with Delight: The Literary Genre of the Acts of the Apostles* (Philadelphia: Fortress Press, 1987); Shelly Matthews, *First Converts: Rich Pagan Women and the Rhetoric of Mission in Early Judaism and Christianity* (Stanford: Stanford University Press, 2001); and Matthews, "Elite Women, Public Religion, and Christian Propaganda in Acts 16," in *A Feminist Companion to Acts of the Apostles,* ed. Amy-Jill Levine with Marianne Blickenstaff (Sheffield: Sheffield Academic Press, 2004), 111–33, on Luke's interest in portraying the Christian movement as a legitimate one, with adherents of high status. See also James A. Arlandson, "Lifestyles of the Rich and Christian: Women, Wealth, and

Social Freedom," in *A Feminist Companion to Acts of the Apostles*, 155–70; and Arlandson, *Women, Class, and Society in Early Christianity: Models from Luke-Acts* (Peabody, Mass.: Hendrickson, 1996).

82. See further Carmen Bernabé Ubieta, "Mary Magdalene and the Seven Demons in Social Science Perspective," in Kitzberger, *Transformative Encounters*, 203–23.

83. Jane Schaberg, *The Resurrection of Mary Magdalene: Legends, Apocrypha, and the Christian Testament* (New York: Crossroad, 2002), 77–80, 199, 232; and Robert Price, "Mary Magdalene, Gnostic Apostle?" *Grail* 6 (1990): 73–74.

84. The account of Mary of Egypt is recorded in a seventh-century Greek text attributed to Sophronius (c. 560–638), in which Mary relates her story to the monk Zosimus, who found her in the desert toward the end of her life.

85. For detailed analysis of the story of Tabitha, see Ivoni Richter Reimer, *Women in the Acts of the Apostles: A Feminist Liberation Perspective*, trans. Linda M. Maloney (Minneapolis: Fortress Press, 1995), 31–69. See also Janice Capel Anderson, "Reading Tabitha: A Feminist Reception History," in *A Feminist Companion to the Acts of the Apostles*, 22–48; Mary Ann Getty-Sullivan, *Women in the New Testament* (Collegeville, Minn.: Liturgical Press, 2001), 235–40; Clarice J. Martin, "The Acts of the Apostles," in *Searching the Scriptures. Vol. 2: A Feminist Commentary*, ed. Elisabeth Schüssler Fiorenza (New York: Crossroad, 1994), 781–82; Gail R. O'Day, "Acts," in *Women's Bible Commentary*, 309–10; and Bonnie Thurston, *Women in the New Testament: Questions and Commentary* (New York: Crossroad, 1998), 120–22.

86. BDAG, 609.

87. Thurston, *Women in the New Testament*, 120.

88. 1 Timothy 5:16 gives regulations for the emerging order of widows, which became prominent from the late first through the third centuries. See further Thurston, *Women in the New Testament*, 121–22; and Thurston, *The Widows* (Philadelphia: Fortress Press, 1989).

89. F. Scott Spencer, "Women of 'the Cloth' in Acts: Sewing the Word," in *A Feminist Companion to Acts of the Apostles*, 134–54, sees an echo of the ideal woman of Proverbs 31:19, who diligently works at home to manufacture clothing for the family.

90. Other women named in the New Testament who were heads of house churches include Nympha (Col 4:14), Phoebe (Rom 16:1), Prisca (1 Cor 16:19; Rom 16:5), Lydia (Acts 16:40), Mary (Acts 12:12), and possibly Chloe (1 Cor 1:11).

91. Getty-Sullivan, *Women in the New Testament*, 239.

92. "Good works" (*erga agatha*) occurs in Romans 2:7; 13:3; 2 Corinthians 9:8; Ephesians 2:10; Phillipians 1:6; Colossians 1:10; 1 Timothy 2:10; 5:10; 2 Timothy 2:21; 3:17; Titus 1:16; 3:1. "Doing good" (*agathon poiēsai*) occurs in Mark 3:4; 6:9; John 5:29; Romans 2:10.

93. Richter Reimer, *Women in the Acts of the Apostles*, 36.

94. There is a play on words in Spanish: *la reina* is "the queen," and God's reign is *el reino de Dios*.

95. See further Marco Tavanti, *Las Abejas: Passivist Resistance and Syncretic Identities in a Globalizing Chiapas* (New York: Routledge, 2003); and Teresa

Ortiz, *Never Again a World without Us: Voices of Mayan Women in Chiapas, Mexico* (Washington, D.C.: EPICA, 2001), 167–95.

96. From a personal interview in Mexico City, January 9, 2005. See also Samuel Ruiz con la colaboración de Carles Torner, *Cómo me Convirtieron los Indígenas* (Santander, Spain: Sal Terrae, 2002).

97. *Boletín de la Comisión de la Verdad y Reconciliación*, no. 7 (March 2003): 6–7.

Chapter 5 Notes

1. Marcia Good shared this experience at a workshop at Dominican Center/Marywood, Grand Rapids Michigan, January 26, 2005.

2. See Dorothy Lee, *Flesh and Glory: Symbolism, Gender and Theology in the Gospel of John* (New York: Crossroad, 2002), 135–65, on the symbols of motherhood in the whole of the gospel. See also Barbara E. Reid, "The Cross and Cycles of Violence," *Interpretation* 58, no. 4 (2004): 376–85.

3. The Greek word in John 1:13 is *andros*, which refers specifically to males, unlike *anthrōpos*, which connotes both women and men.

4. See also Luke 1:13, 57; 23:29. See BDAG, "*gennaō*," 193.

5. This is especially evident in John 3:4, where Nicodemus asks Jesus, "Can one enter a second time into the mother's womb and be born [*gennēthēnai*]?" The verb *gennaō* occurs also in John 3:3, 4, 5, 6, 7, 8; 8:41; 9:2, 19, 20, 32, 34; 16:21; 18:37.

6. Kathleen P. Rushton, "The (Pro)creative Parables of Labour and Childbirth (John 3:1-10 and 16:21-22)," in *The Lost Coin: Parables of Women, Work, and Wisdom*, ed. Mary Ann Beavis (Sheffield: Sheffield Academic Press, 2002), 212–13. See especially John 1:13; 3:3, 5, 6, 8.

7. See Josephine Massyngbaerde Ford, *Redeemer, Friend, and Mother: Salvation in Antiquity and in the Gospel of John* (Minneapolis: Fortress Press, 1997), 193, for references. Another interpretation is that blood and water symbolize true humanity, so John 19:34 can be understood as having an antidocetic thrust. See Ford, *Redeemer, Friend, and Mother*, 194, for references from patristic writings.

8. Raymond E. Brown, *The Gospel According to John i-xii* (Garden City, N.Y.: Doubleday, 1966), 12.

9. Lyn Bechtel, "A Symbolic Level of Meaning: John 2.1-11 (The Marriage in Cana)," in *A Feminist Companion to the Hebrew Bible in the New Testament*, ed. Athalya Brenner (Sheffield: Sheffield Academic Press, 1996), 248, notes that "[i]n the Hebrew Bible culture and religion are often referred to as the people's 'mother,'" and suggests that "John does not refer to 'the mother of Jesus' as Mary because he is not talking about Jesus' biological mother Mary. He is referring to Judaism, Jesus' matrix." She reads Jesus' reply to his mother in verse 4 as distancing himself from his matrix, Judaism. However, see Judith Lieu, "The Mother of the Son in the Fourth Gospel," *JBL* 117, no. 1 (1998), 71, for arguments against such a reading.

10. This is also the way he addresses the Samaritan woman at the well (John 4:21), the woman whom others wanted to stone (8:10), and Mary Magdalene at the empty tomb (20:15). See also Matthew 15:28; Luke 13:12.

As Brown, *John*, 1.99, observes, "It was Jesus' normal, polite way of addressing women," and is not disrespectful. Nor is Jesus' response, *ti emoi kai soi*, "What to me and to you?" (2:4). As in 2 Kings 3:13; and Hosea 14:8, this expression signals disengagement from a situation when someone is asked to get involved in a matter which he feels is not his business (see Brown, *John*, 1.99). As Lieu, "Mother of the Son," 67, observes, this question should not be read as Jesus disengaging from his mother's parental authority, as in Luke 2:41-52, nor should we envision the kind of tension between Jesus' blood kin and his new family of disciples, as the Synoptic evangelists portray (Mark 3:31-35 // Matt 12:46-50 // Luke 8:19-21).

11. On the symbol of water in the Fourth Gospel, see Larry Paul Jones, *The Symbol of Water in the Gospel of John* (Sheffield: Sheffield Academic Press, 1997); Craig R. Koester, *Symbolism in the Fourth Gospel: Meaning, Mystery, Community*, 2nd ed. (Minneapolis: Fortress Press, 2003), 175–206; and Dorothy Lee, *Flesh and Glory: Symbolism, Gender, and Theology in the Gospel of John* (New York: Crossroad, 2002), 65–87.

12. See Lieu, "Mother of the Son," 65–69, for a detailed analysis of the links between John 2:1-11 and 19:25-27 as the resolution of the enigma.

13. See Schneiders, *Written That You May Believe*, 233–54, on the Beloved Disciple as a representative character in this scene. On this and other representative figures in the Fourth Gospel, see Raymond F. Collins, "The Representative Figures in the Fourth Gospel," *DRev* 94 (1976): 26–46, 118–32; and Koester, *Symbolism*, 33–77.

14. Sandra Schneiders, *Written That You May Believe*, 241. Ingrid Rosa Kitzberger, "Transcending Gender Boundaries in John," in *A Feminist Companion to John. Vol. 1*, ed. Amy-Jill Levine with Marianne Blickenstaff (New York: Sheffield Academic Press, 2003), 206, says of Jesus' mother in John 19:25-27, "As she loses her son Jesus, another son is 'born' to her when Jesus entrusts her and the Beloved Disciple to each other." Lieu, "Mother of the Son," 69, cautions that we should treat with extreme skepticism interpretations that see 19:25-27 as establishing a new relationship between Jesus and his mother, by which she would have ongoing intercession with Jesus.

15. Schneiders, *Written That You May Believe*, 241–42, notes that, when speaking to his mother, Jesus does not address the Beloved Disciple as "son" and that the expression *eis ta idia*, usually translated "into his own home," is a neuter expression (literally, "to one's own") in which there is no masculine possessive pronoun "his." Thus, there is no indication of the gender of the one receiving the mother of Jesus. She proposes that the most logical reading is that in this scene, the Beloved Disciple is symbolized by the women standing with the mother of Jesus at the cross: Mary of Clopas and Mary Magdalene. The family of faith is comprised of Jesus' natural family, his mother and her sister; and his disciples, represented by Mary Magdalene.

16. Mark 8:31; 9:31; 10:34; Matthew 16:21; 17:23; 20:19; Luke 9:22; 18:33; 24:7, 21, 46. See also Acts 10:40.

17. Some, such as Theodore of Mopsuestia (*In Joanne* [Syr.]—CSCO 116:39), understand it as a reference to the third day after the baptismal scene of John 1:29-34. Others count from the day of Philip's and Nathanael's call. See Brown, *John*, 1.97. Lyn M. Bechtel, "A Symbolic Level of Meaning:

John 2.1-11 (The Marriage in Cana)," in *A Feminist Companion to the Hebrew Bible*, 246, asserts that "on the third day" ties the Cana story to Jesus' resurrection because narratively, this is the third day after the baptismal scene (John 1:29-34), and in Romans 6:3-4, Paul connects baptism with the death of Jesus.

18. Schneiders, *Written That You May Believe*, 121, notes that juxtaposing water and spirit should have alerted Nicodemus to the true meaning of spiritual birth, because the two are found in the promise of renewal in Ezekiel 36:25-27, "I will sprinkle clean water upon you . . . and a new spirit I will put within you."

19. Schneiders, *Written That You May Believe*, 120, links verse 5 with verse 6, "what is born of the flesh is flesh, and what is born of the Spirit is spirit," and sees birth from water (v. 5) in synonymous parallelism with birth from flesh (v. 6). Thus, she understands Jesus to be speaking of "two births, one of water and another of spirit. The first is human birth of flesh from flesh; the second is spiritual birth of spirit from spirit." Judith Lieu, "Scripture and the Feminine in John," in *A Feminist Companion to the Hebrew Bible*, 238, cautions, "We should not think of a dualism in which that birth again/from above is alien to and contrasted with the birth from a mother; for John earthly experience is a 'sign' which points to and enfleshes divine truth." Accordingly, I propose that "birth in water and Spirit" can also be taken to refer to one birth that is spiritual. Throughout the Fourth Gospel, water has a spiritual significance, as in the "living water" Jesus offers the Samaritan woman in 4:10.

20. John 19:30 is a proleptic giving of the Spirit to the disciples, which is completed in 20:22 when the risen Christ breathes on the disciples, saying, "Receive the Holy Spirit."

21. The image is explained more fully in John 12:32-33: "'and I, when I am lifted up from the earth, I will draw all people to myself.' He said this to indicate the kind of death he was to die."

22. Robert Kysar, "The Making of Metaphor: Another Reading of John 3:1-15," in *"What Is John?" Readers and Readings of the Fourth Gospel*, ed. Fernando F. Segovia (Atlanta: Scholars Press, 1996), 39–40.

23. Lieu, "Scripture and the Feminine," 231.

24. Schneiders, *Written That You May Believe*, 120. See further Ben Witherington III, "The Waters of Birth: John 3.5 and 1 John 5.6-8," *NTS 35* (1989): 155–60; Robert Fowler, "Born of Water and the Spirit (Jn 3:5)," *ExpTim* 82 (1971): 159; Margaret Pamment, "John 3:5: 'Unless One Is Born of Water and the Spirit, He Cannot Enter the Kingdom of God,'" *NovT* 25 (1983): 190; and D. Spriggs, "Meaning of 'Water' in John 3:5," *ExpTim* 85 (1974): 149–50.

25. John 6 also provides a rich array of maternal metaphors, with the images of Jesus feeding and giving nourishment with his body and blood. See Massyngbaerde Ford, *Redeemer*, 124–34; María Clara Bingemer, "Women in the Future of the Theology of Liberation," in *The Future of Liberation Theology: Essays in Honor of Gustavo Gutiérrez*, ed. Marc H. Ellis and Otto Maduro (Maryknoll, N.Y.: Orbis, 1989), 486; and Sallie McFague, "Mother God," in *Motherhood: Experience, Institution, Theology*, ed. Anne Carr and Elisabeth Schüssler Fiorenza. Concilium, *Religion in the Eighties* 206.

(Edinburgh: T & T Clark, 1989), 141, on how a woman's feeding others with her own body through the process of gestation, birth, and nursing embody Eucharist.

26. See Brown, *John*, 326–27 for a description of the ceremonial processions to the spring of Gihon and the pouring of the water from golden pitchers into funnels at the altar of the Temple, which was done each of the seven days of the Feast of Dedication.

27. See also Luke 1:41, 44; 2:21; 11:27; 23:29; John 3:4. It can also mean "belly, stomach," as in Matthew 15:17; Mark 7:19; Luke 15:16; 1 Corinthians 6:13; Revelation 10:9. *Koilia* can also be understood as the seat of inward life, of feelings and desires. The functional equivalent of this in English is "heart." See BDAG, *"koilia,"* 550.

28. For a fuller discussion of the interpretive possibilities, see Brown, *John*, 1.320-24.

29. Stephen D. Moore, "Are There Impurities in the Living Water that the Johannine Jesus Dispenses?" in *A Feminist Companion to John*, 1.87.

30. María Clara Bingemer, "Women in the Future of the Theology of Liberation," in The Future of Liberation Theology: Essays in Honor of Gustavo Gutiérrez, eds. Marc H. Ellis and Otto Maduro (Maryknoll, N.Y.: Orbis, 1989), 475.

31. Lieu, "Mother of the Son," 73–74, cautions against interpretations in which the pain of the mother is transferred to the child to refer to the birth of the Messiah or the messianic age. Rushton, "Parables of Labour and Childbirth," 212, also notes how often in commentaries a transfer takes place to emphasize the "birth of a child" with no mention of a woman at all.

32. Rushton, "Parables of Labour and Childbirth," 216–220. See p. 217 for parallels between Daughter of Zion and the Servant. See Kathleen P. Rushton, "The Woman in Childbirth of John 16:21: A Feminist Reading in (Pro)creative Boundary Crossing," in *Wholly Woman, Holy Blood: A Feminist Critique of Purity and Impurity*, ed. Kristin DeTroyer, Judith A. Herbert, Judith Ann Johnson, and Anne-Marie Korte (Harrisburg, Pa.: Trinity Press International, 2003), 83–85, for an analysis of how the Isaian Daughter of Zion relates to the biblical barren women traditions.

33. Rushton, "Woman in Childbirth," 91. In addition, the word *thlipsis*, "anguish," found in John 16:21, was widely used in Christian writings to speak about the labor pains of the end time: Mark 13:19, 24; Matthew 24:9, 21, 29; Acts 14:22; 1 Corinthians 7:26; 10:11; 2 Corinthians 4:17; Revelation 2:10; 7:14.

34. Rushton, "Parables of Labour and Childbirth," 220–21. Other references to the coming hour are found in John 5:25, 28; 7:30; 8:20; 12:23; 16:2, 4, 25, 32; 17:1.

35. Rushton, "Parables of Labour and Childbirth," 221, points out that this is said only by Jesus or the one who is understood to be the Messiah: John 1:9; 3:19; 6:14; 9:39; 11:27; 12:46; 16:28; 18:37.

36. Virginia Ramey Mollenkott, *The Divine Feminine: The Biblical Imagery of God as Female* (New York: Crossroad, 1983), remarks on the placement of the beginning of Psalm 22 on the lips of the crucified Jesus in the synoptic tradition ("My God, my God, why have you forsaken me?" Psalm 22:1; Mark

15:34; Matt 27:45). She observes that the psalm "contains many harrowing details that well describe crucifixion" juxtaposed with the midwife image. She proposes, "We may imagine that in the hour of his own anguished 'birth contractions' on the cross, Jesus tried to comfort himself by remembering that God had been the midwife drawing him out of the womb of his own mother. Since God had been with him 'from my mother's womb,' Jesus, like the Psalmist, may have felt justified in hoping that God would not 'stand aside' now, when 'I have no one to help me'" (33).

37. Massyngbaerde Ford, *Redeemer, Friend, and Mother*, 165. Ford quotes the text from William Hugh Brownlee, "Messianic Motifs of Qumran and the New Testament," *NTS* 3 (1956–57): 23–24. See also Judith Lieu's ("Mother of the Son," 73–74), comments on this text, who notes that "waves of death" (1QH 3:8-9) may be a play on "mouth of the womb." She comments, "The womb can sometimes be viewed as a grave, and the woman as the mediator of birth through death, birth and death, provides the proper context for the Johannine passage" (74).

38. Massyngbaerde Ford, *Redeemer*, 43.

39. María del Rosario, at a gathering of *asesoras* of the women's Bible study groups in the diocese of San Cristóbal de las Casas, Chiapas, Mexico, November 12, 2002. As the women become more and more empowered, their pain gives way to joy at the dignity, self-esteem, solidarity, and competence in biblical theological reflection that is born in them.

40. It is not until Genesis 3:20 that the first woman is named "Eve."

41. Lieu, "Mother of the Son," 74, notes that it does not, for example, occur in Isaiah 26:17-19 or 66:14.

42. See also Luke 22:45, where in Gethsemane, Jesus finds his disciples asleep "because of grief," *apo tēs lypēs*. The verb *lypeō* is used in the same way as the noun *lypē*, as in Matthew's Gethsemane scene, where Jesus begins to "be grieved," *lypeisthai* (Matt 26:37). For other instances of the verb *lypeō* in the Gospels, see Matthew 14:9; 17:23; 18:31; 19:22; 26:22; Mark 10:22; 14:19; John 21:17.

43. Lieu, "Mother of the Son," 74–75, notes the predilection of the Fourth Evangelist for motifs from the opening chapter of Genesis: the prologue (1:1-18) echoes Genesis 1; John 20:22 evokes Gen 2:7; John 8:44 alludes to the Cain narratives of Genesis 4; and the motif of the garden in Genesis 2–3 is reprised in John 18:1, 26; 19:41; 20:15.

44. See previous, chapter 2 (pp. 73–74), for other interpretations of Genesis 3:16. See also Rushton, "Parables of Labour and Childbirth," 214–15; Bechtel, "Rethinking the Interpretation of Genesis," 77–117; and Carol L. Meyers, "Gender Roles and Genesis 3.16 Revisited," in *A Feminist Companion to the Hebrew Bible*, 118–41.

45. Rushton, "Parables of Labour and Childbirth," 215.

46. Meyers, "Gender Roles," 138–39.

47. Bechtel, "Rethinking the Interpretation of Genesis," 112.

48. "'Theology from the Perspective of Women,' Final Statement: Latin American Conference, Buenos Aires, Argentina, Oct. 30—Nov. 3, 1985," in *Through Her Eyes: Women's Theology from Latin America*, ed. Elsa Támez (Maryknoll, N.Y.: Orbis, 1989), 152.

49. For a discussion and further references on those who attempt to explain this phenomenon historically and medically rather than symbolically, see Brown, *John*, 2.946-48; Brown, *The Death of the Messiah. From Gethsemane to the Grave: A Commentary on the Passion Narratives in the Four Gospels*, 2 vols. (New York: Doubleday, 1994), 2.1088-92; and W. D. Edwards, W. J. Gabel, and F. E. Hosmer, "On the Physical Death of Jesus Christ," *Journal of the American Medical Association* 255 (1986): 1455-63. For a sampling of the enormous body of literature on the spiritual meaning of the pierced side of Jesus, see Brown, *Death of the Messiah*, 2. 1178-79, n. 95.

50. Massyngbaerde Ford, *Redeemer, Friend, and Mother*, 195. The author of Hebrews uses a similar image: ". . . we have courage to enter the sanctuary by the blood of Jesus, by the new and living way that he opened for us through the curtain (that is, through his flesh)" (Heb 10:19-20).

51. Kitzberger, "Transcending Gender Boundaries," 204.

52. See Brown, *John*, 2.950, for comments on 1 John 5:6-8, which has the same confluence of water, blood, spirit, and testimony as John 19:34-35.

53. Massyngbaerde Ford, *Redeemer, Friend, and Mother*, 196. This meaning is more obvious in the Marcan crucifixion scene, where "Jesus cried out (*eboēsen*) with a loud voice" (Mark 15:34), forming an inclusion with John the Baptist crying out (*boōntos*) in the desert to herald the Messiah (Mark 1:3).

54. The following references and quotations are taken from Massyngbaerde Ford, *Redeemer, Friend, and Mother*, 196-97.

55. See Caroline Walker Bynum, *Jesus as Mother: Studies in the Spirituality of the High Middle Ages* (Berkeley: University of California Press, 1982).

56. Quoted in Bynum, *Jesus as Mother*, 153. Another image associated with the pierced side of Jesus is that of an "open door," by which a believer "may enter whole," into the heart of Jesus, "the sure seat" of his mercy (William of St. Thierry, quoted in Bynum, *Jesus as Mother*, 120). In addition to speaking of "the holes in the wall of his [Jesus'] body, in which, like a dove, you may hide," Aelred of Rievaulx (d. 1167), among others, thinks of the blood and water from the side of Christ as offering nourishment: "Then one of the soldiers opened his side with a lance and there came forth blood and water. Hasten, linger not, eat the honeycomb with your honey, drink your wine with your milk. The blood is changed into wine to gladden you, the water into milk to nourish you" (from *De institutione*, chap. 31, *Opera omnia* 1:671, quoted in Bynum, *Jesus as Mother*, 123).

57. Julian of Norwich, *Showings* (New York: Paulist, 1978), 292.

58. Julian of Norwich, *Showings*, 296-97. For a different interpretation of the Johannine crucifixion scene, see Adeline Fehribach, *The Women in the Life of the Bridegroom: A Feminist Historical-Literary Analysis of the Female Characters in the Fourth Gospel* (Collegeville, Minn.: Liturgical Press, 1998), 115-42. Fehribach sees the death of Jesus as a blood sacrifice that establishes a patrilineal kinship group. With Jesus portrayed as giving birth to the children of God, women's roles and powers are co-opted and the birthing role of his mother obliterated.

59. Massyngbaerde Ford, *Redeemer, Friend, and Mother*, 200.

60. Kitzberger, "Transcending Gender Boundaries," 193; and María Clara Bingemer, "Mujer y Cristología: Jesucristo: y la salvación de la mujer," in

Aportes para una Teología desde la Mujer, ed. María Pilar Aquino (Madrid: Editorial Biblia y Fe, 1988), 89–90. See also Elizabeth A. Johnson, "The Maleness of Christ," in *The Power of Naming: A Concilium Reader in Feminist Liberation Theology,* ed. Elisabeth Schüssler Fiorenza (Maryknoll, N.Y.: Orbis, 1996), 307–15.

61. Aquino, *Our Cry for Life,* 145–47; Massyngbaerde Ford, *Redeemer, Friend, and Mother,* 198; Rushton, "Woman in Childbirth," 96; and McFague, "Mother God," 142. See further Sallie McFague, *Body of God: An Ecological Theology* (Minneapolis: Fortress Press, 1993), for a more extensive exploration of the image of all creation coming from the womb of God.

62. See Aquino, "The God of Life and the *Rachamim* of the Trinity," and "Speaking of God in the Feminine," in *Our Cry for Life,* 130–38; María Clara Bingemer, "Reflections on the Trinity," in *Through Her Eyes,* 56–80.

63. See Barbara E. Reid, *Parables for Preachers. Year C* (Collegeville, Minn.: Liturgical Press, 2000), 177–91, 227–36, 293–307; Reid, *Choosing the Better Part?,* 169–94.

64. María Clara Bingemer, "Women in the Future of the Theology of Liberation," 485.

65. Shirley Gillett, "No Church to Call Home," in *Women, Abuse, and the Bible: How Scripture Can Be Used to Hurt or to Heal,* ed. Catherine Clark Kroeger and James R. Beck (Grand Rapids, Mich.: Baker, 1996), 108–09.

66. Julia Esquivel, "Conquered and Violated Women," in *The Power of Naming,* 113.

67. Esquivel, "Conquered and Violated Women," 113-14.

68. Traditions in both rabbinic Judaism and Christianity interpret birth pangs, based on Genesis 3:16, as punishment for sin. Thus, Josephus writes that Yochebed gave birth to Moses without birth pangs, which Moses' parents interpreted as a sign of God's favor (*A.J.* 2.218). Likewise, Mary, according to *Proto-evanglium Jacobi* (19), gave birth to Jesus without any birth pangs. See Tal Ilan, *Jewish Women in Greco-Roman Palestine* (Peabody, Mass.: Hendrickson, 1996), 116.

69. Nonetheless, the notion of Jesus' death as sacrificial and as atoning for sins is so prevalent that some scholars read this into the Johannine version. Raymond Brown, for example, in his comment on 19:34 remarks that John seems to think of Jesus "as going to his death as a sacrificial victim" (*John,* 2.951) and notes that "one of the strict requirements of Jewish sacrificial law was that the blood of the victim should not be congealed but should flow forth at the moment of death." See also Koester, *Symbolism,* 244–45.

70. The foregoing analysis is from Sandra Schneiders, "The Resurrection (of the Body) in the Fourth Gospel: A Key to Johannine Spirituality," in *Life in Abundance: Studies of John's Gospel in Tribute to Raymond E. Brown, S.S.,* ed. John R. Donahue, S.J. (Collegeville, Minn.: Liturgical Press, 2005), 168–98, esp. 186–87.

71. Massyngbaerde Ford, *Redeemer, Friend, and Mother,* 200–201, calls attention to this allusion and notes that the connection between Ezekiel 34 and John 20:23 has been made since at least since the fourth century, when it is found in *Apostolic Constitutions* II, 20.4.

72. Massyngbaerde Ford, *Redeemer, Friend, and Mother,* 201.

73. Elizabeth A. Johnson, *She Who Is: The Mystery of God in Feminist Theological Discourse* (New York, N.Y.: Crossroad, 1992), 177–78. See Bynum, *Jesus as Mother*, 133, for remarks on the how the sentimentalizing of maternal images by medieval monks and mystics functioned. She notes, "It was peculiarly appropriate to a theological emphasis on an accessible and tender God, a God who bleeds and suffers less as a sacrifice or restoration of cosmic order than as a stimulus to human love." McFague, "Mother God," 139, observes that we should "not suppose that mothers are 'naturally' loving, comforting, or self-sacrificing. Our society has a stake in making women think that they are biologically programmed to be these things, when, in fact, a good case can be made that the so-called qualities or stereotypes of mothers are social constructions—women are not born, but become, mothers through education and imitation."

74. In the United States, it is estimated that one woman is beaten every fifteen seconds, one woman is raped every three to six minutes. In Torreón, Mexico, the director of *Centro ¡Sí Mujer!* estimates that domestic abuse occurs in 70 percent of the homes; in rural Chiapas, it is closer to 90 percent. For U.S. statistics, see Family Violence Prevention Fund, "Domestic Violence is a Serious, Widespread Social Problem in America: The Facts," www.endabuse.org/resources/facts/ (accessed March 3, 2007). See also AARDVARC, "Domestic Violence Statistics, www.aardvarc.org/dv/statistics.shtml (accessed March 3, 2007). For recent figures in México, see Adrián Reyes, "Gender Violence Continues to Claim its Victims," InterPress Service News Agency, ipsnews.net/news.asp?idnews=34338 (accessed March 3, 2007). For global information see the UNICEF report "Domestic Violence against Women and Girls," *Innocenti Digest* 6 (June 2000), www.unicef-icdc .org/publications/pdf/digest6e.pdf (accessed March 3, 2007).

75. Rushton, "Parables of Labour and Birth," 208.

76. Rushton, "Parables of Labour and Birth," 223.

77. Massyngbaerde Ford, *Redeemer, Friend, and Mother*, 38, does not provide the evidence on which she bases this assertion. Carolyn Osiek and Margaret Y. MacDonald, *A Woman's Place: House Churches in Earliest Christianity* (Minneapolis: Fortress Press, 2006), 20, note that "in antiquity giving birth was by far the greatest threat to a young woman's life." See also their discussion of "Giving Birth, Labor, Nursing, and the Care of Infants in House-Church Communities," in *A Woman's Place*, 50–67. Tal Ilan, *Jewish Women*, 116–19, examines literary and inscriptional evidence. She contests the estimate of G. Mayer, *Die jüdische Frau in der hellenistisch-römischen Antike* (Stuttgart, Ger.: 1987), 93, that about 50 percent of women died in childbirth and advances that the figure was closer to 5 percent, based on the number of ossuaries of women buried with their children.

78. United Nations State of the World Population Report, 2000.

79. United Nations State of the World Population Report 2005. The maternal mortality figure is from 2000. The statistics measuring infant mortality are from 1993–2003, www.un.org/esa/population/publications/worldmortality/WMR2005.pdf (accessed January 10, 2007). By contrast, in the United States, the maternal mortality rate is only 17 per 1,000; only 7 children per 1,000 die as infants; and 8 children per 1,000 die before their fifth birthday.

80. McFague, "Mother God," 139, remarks on how dangerous and oppressive maternal language can be when it suggests that women who are not mothers are not true or fulfilled women and when it gives power to an image that has been used to oppress women over the centuries. She cautions that we must be careful to see the maternal model of God as only *one* model; we must also speak of God as sister, midwife, and in other female terms. See also her chapter, "God as Mother," in *Models of God*, 97–123; and Johnson, *She Who Is*, 177–78.

81. McFague, "Mother God," 139.

82. See further Kitzberger, "Transcending Gender Boundaries," 173–207.

83. See Karen Mary Dávalos, "'The Real Way of Praying,' The Via Crucis, *Méxicano* Sacred Space, and the Architecture of Domination," in *Horizons of the Sacred: Mexican Traditions in U.S. Catholicism*, ed. Timothy Matovina and Gary Riebe-Estrella (Ithaca, N.Y. and London: Cornell University Press, 2002), 41–68, who describes how women who have lost sons to gang violence in the Pilsen neighborhood of Chicago connect their sufferings with that of Mary and of the lamenting women of Jerusalem (Luke 23:27-31).

84. Jeannette Rodríguez, *Our Lady of Guadalupe: Faith and Empowerment among Mexican-American Women* (Austin: University of Texas Press, 1994), 121.

85. Davalos, "The Real Way of Praying," 51.

86. Davalos, "The Real Way of Praying," 51.

87. Davalos, "The Real Way of Praying," 60.

88. Davalos, "The Real Way of Praying," 61, recounts that some residents see the *Via Crucis* as having an impact on reducing the amount of gang violence and number of bars, and on preserving and increasing home ownership in the neighborhood.

89. Davalos, "The Real Way of Praying," 67.

90. Bingemer, "Women in the Future of the Theology of Liberation," 482.

91. The Third Evangelist portrays the giving of the Spirit in a different manner from the Gospel of John. In Luke's narrative, there is a forty-day period of appearances of the risen Christ, after which he ascends. He instructs his disciples to remain in Jerusalem until they receive the promised Spirit (Acts 1:4-5). Mary is named as present with the eleven, the other women, and with Jesus' siblings when the empowering Spirit descends on them at Pentecost (Acts 1:14). Unfortunately, the gospels tell nothing more of Mary's ministry with the community. Ancient legends say that she traveled to Ephesus in the companionship of the Beloved Disciple, where she died.

92. As my colleague Carmen Nanko-Fernández observed, there can also be a positive aspect to machismo in that men take responsibility for their wives and families, being very protective of them, rather than abusive. It is also important to note the effects of colonization on men in Latin America, who replicate in their homes the violence that has been directed at them. This is not to excuse domestic violence, but it is a factor that must be taken into account. For an analysis from the perspective of men who are perpetrators of domestic violence and a program outlining a pastoral respone to them, see Álvaro Amaniel Dávila Salazar, *El Acompañamiento Pastoral del Hombre Latino Abusivo* (M.A.P.S. thesis, Catholic Theological Union, Chicago, 2004).

93. Rodríguez, *Our Lady of Guadalupe*, 71.

94. Rosa María Gil and Carmen Inoa Vázquez, *The María Paradox: How Latinas Can Merge Old World Traditions with New World Self-Esteem* (New York: G. P. Putnam's Sons, 1996), 7, quoted by Nora O. Lozano-Díaz, "Ignored Virgin or Unaware Women: A Mexican-American Protestant Reflection on the Virgin of Guadalupe," in *A Reader in Latina Feminist Theology*, ed. María Pilar Aquino, Daisy L. Machado, and Jeanette Rodríguez (Austin: University of Texas, 2002), 204–16. Lozano-Díaz also details the difficulties posed for Protestant Mexican-American women, many of whom prefer to ignore Mary because she is so intimately tied with Catholic faith. But since Guadalupe is not only a religious symbol but a cultural one as well, Lozano-Díaz proposes a retrieval of Guadalupe's liberative value through cultural and feminist perspectives. She notes that the Bible is a powerful resource to challenge traditional images of Guadalupe, finding an active and assertive Mary in the annunciation scene and the Magnificat (Luke 1:26-38; 46-55) and Mary portrayed as a committed and active disciple, not just a mother in Acts 1:14, where she is named among the disciples who receive the empowering Holy Spirit at Pentecost. See also Aquino, *Our Cry for Life*, 171–77, on restrictive and liberative images of Mary.

95. Quoted in Lozano-Díaz, "Ignored Virgin," 210.

96. Rodríguez, *Guadalupe*, 130.

97. Rodríguez, *Guadalupe*, 129.

98. Rodríguez, *Guadalupe*, 130–31.

99. See Margaret Randall, "Guadalupe, Subversive Virgin," in *Goddess of the Americas: La Diosa de las Américas. Writings on the Virigin of Guadalupe*, ed. Ana Castillo (New York: Riverhead, 1996), 113–23.

100. María Victoria González, *Mujer Marginada* (Bolivia: CISEP, 1988), 27, cited in Vicenta Mamani Bernabé, *Identidad y Espiritualidad de la Mujer Aymara* (LaPaz, Bolivia: Misión de Basilea-Suiza, 2000), 88.

101. Rodríguez, *Guadalupe*, 139.

102. Rodríguez, *Guadalupe*, 150–153. In this, Rodríguez is influenced by Elizabeth A. Johnson, "Mary and the Female Face of God," *TS* 50, no. 3 (1989): 501–26.

103. Rodríguez, *Guadalupe*, 151.

104. Rodríguez, *Guadalupe*, 145.

105. Rodríguez, *Guadalupe*, 151.

106. Rodríguez, *Guadalupe*, 128.

107. My translation from the Spanish of Ivone Gebara, *Teología a ritmo de mujer*, trans. from Portuguese original by José Ma. Hernández (Mexico, D.F.: Ediciones Dabar, 1995), 136–37.

108. Ivone Gebara, "The Mother Superior and Spiritual Motherhood: From Intuition to Institution," in *Motherhood: Experience, Institution, Theology*, 48.

109. Cynthia Crysdale, *Embracing Travail: Retrieving the Cross Today* (New York: Continuum, 1999), 27. For an exploration of the Gospel of Luke through the lens of women's pregnant bodies and Earth, which shares this mode of being, see Ann F. Elvey, *An Ecological Feminist Reading of the Gospel of Luke: A Gestational Paradigm* (Lewiston, N.Y.: Edwin Mellen, 2005).

Conclusion Note

1. Julia Esquivel, "I Am Not Afraid of Death," in *Threatened with Resurrection: Prayers and Poems from an Exiled Guatemalan* (Elgin: Brethren Press, 1982), 65.

Select Bibliography

Adams, Carol J. and Marie Fortune, eds. *Violence Against Women and Children. A Christian Theological Sourcebook.* New York: Continuum, 1995.

Andraos, Michel. *Praxis of Peace. The Pastoral Work and Theology of Bishop Samuel Ruiz and the Diocese of San Cristobal de las Casas, Chiapas, Mexico.* Ph.D. diss., Toronto School of Theology, 2000.

Aquino, María Pilar, ed. *Aportes para una Teología desde la Mujer.* Nuevo Exodo 5. Madrid: Editorial Biblia y Fe, 1988.

_____. *Our Cry for Life. Feminist Theology from Latin America.* Maryknoll: Orbis, 1993.

Aquino, María Pilar and Elisabeth Schüssler Fiorenza, eds. *In the Power of Wisdom. Feminist Spiritualities of Struggle.* Concilium 2000/5. London: SCM, 2000.

Aquino, María Pilar, Daisy L. Machado, and Jeanette Rodríguez, eds. *A Reader in Latina Feminist Theology.* Religion and Justice. Austin: University of Texas, 2002.

Bracamontes, Maricarmen. *Jesús de Nazaret y las Mujeres de su Tiempo.* 3ra ed. Mexico, D.F.: Schola, 2005.

Brock, Rita Nakashima and Rebecca Ann Parker. *Proverbs of Ashes. Violence, Redemptive Suffering, and the Search for What Saves Us.* Boston: Beacon, 2001.

Brown, Raymond E. *The Death of the Messiah. From Gethsemane to the Grave. A Commentary on the Passion Narratives in the Four Gospels.* 2 vols. ABRL. Garden City: Doubleday, 1994.

Bustamante, Mercedes Olivera, ed. *De Sumisiones, Cambios y Rebeldías. Mujeres Indígenas de Chiapas.* Vol. 1. Tuxtla Gutiérrez: Universidad de Ciencias y Artes de Chiapas, 2004.

Carroll, John T. and Joel B. Green, eds. *The Death of Jesus in Early Christianity.* Peabody, Mass.: Hendrickson, 1995.

CODIMUJ, *Con Mirada, Mente y Corazón de Mujer.* México, D.F., 1999.

Cullinan, Colleen Carpenter. *Redeeming the Story. Women, Suffering, and Christ.* New York: Continuum, 2004.

Dreyer, Elizabeth A., ed. *The Cross in Christian Tradition. From Paul to Bonaventure.* New York: Paulist, 2000.

Finlan, Stephen. *Problems With Atonement: The Origins of, and Controversy About, the Atonement Doctrine.* Collegeville: Liturgical Press, 2005.

Ford, Patricia Henry and Maricarmen Bracamontes. *Mujeres y Derechos Humanos. Perspectivas y Alternativas. Aportes Sociales y Eclesiales.* 3d rev. ed. Mexico, D.F.: Ediciones Schola, CEDIMSE, 2001.

Gebara, Ivone. *Out of the Depths. Women's Experience of Evil and Salvation.* Translated by Ann Patrick Ware. Minneapolis: Fortress Press, 2002.

_____. *Teología a ritmo de mujer.* México, D.F.: Ediciones Dabar, 1995. Translated by José Ma. Hernández. Original: *Teologia em ritmo de mulher* (São Paulo: Ediciones Paulinas, 1992).

Grey, Mary. *Feminism, Redemption and the Christian Tradition.* Mystic, CT: Twenty-Third Publications, 1990.

Heim, S. Mark. *Saved from Sacrifice. A Theology of the Cross.* Grand Rapids: Eerdmans, 2006.

Hengel, Martin. *The Atonement: The Origins of the Doctrine in the New Testament.* Philadelphia: Fortress Press, 1981.

Isasi-Díaz, Ada María. *En La Lucha. A Hispanic Women's Liberation Theology.* Minneapolis: Fortress Press, 1993.

_____. *La Lucha Continues. Mujerista Theology.* Maryknoll: Orbis, 2004.

_____. *Mujerista Theology. A Theology for the Twenty-first Century.* Maryknoll: Orbis, 1996.

Johnson, Elizabeth A. *She Who Is. The Mystery of God in Feminist Theological Discourse.* New York: Crossroad, 1992.

Kroeger, Catherine Clark and James R. Beck, eds. *Women, Abuse, and the Bible. How the Bible Can be Used to Hurt or Heal.* Grand Rapids: Baker, 1996.

Levine, Amy-Jill with Marianne Blickenstaff, ed. *A Feminist Companion to Mark.* FCNT 2. Sheffield: Sheffield Academic Press, 2001.

Levoratti, Armando J., ed. *Comentario Bíblico Latinoamericano. Nuevo Testamento.* Estella, Navarra: Editorial Verbo Divino, 2003.

Mamani Bernabé, Vicenta. *Identidad y Espiritualidad de la Mujer Aymara.* LaPaz: Misión de Basilea-Suiza, 2000.

Massyngbaerde Ford, Josephine. *Redeemer. Friend and Mother. Salvation in Antiquity and in the Gospel of John.* Minneapolis: Fortress Press, 1997.

Moltmann-Wendel, Elisabeth. *Rediscovering Friendship. Awakening to the Promise and Power of Women's Friendships.* Minneapolis: Fortress Press, 2000.

Newsom, Carol and Sharon Ringe, eds. *Women's Bible Commentary. Expanded Edition with Aprocrypha.* Louisville: Westminster/John Knox, 1998.

Ortiz, Teresa. *Never Again A World Without Us. Voices of Mayan Women in Chiapas, Mexico.* Washington, D.C.: EPICA, 2001.

Patterson, Stephen J. *Beyond the Passion. Rethinking the Death and Life of Jesus.* Minneapolis: Fortress Press, 2004.

Rankka, Kristine M. *Women and the Value of Suffering. An Aw(e)ful Rowing Toward God.* Collegeville: The Liturgical Press, 1998.

Reid, Barbara E. *Choosing the Better Part? Women in the Gospel of Luke.* Collegeville: Liturgical Press, 1996.

_____. "The Cross and Cycles of Violence." *Int* 58/4 (2004): 376-89.

_____. "Telling Mark's Story of the Cross." *CurTM* 32/6 (Dec. 2005): 426-33.

Richter Reimer, Ivoni, *Women in the Acts of the Apostles. A Feminist Liberation Perspective* Minneapolis: Fortress Press, 1995.

Rodríguez, Jeannette. *Our Lady of Guadalupe. Faith and Empowerment among Mexican-American Women.* Austin: University of Texas Press, 1994.

Ress, Mary Judith. *Ecofeminism in Latin America.* Maryknoll: Orbis, 2006.

Rovira, Guiomar. *Mujeres de Maíz. La voz de las indígenas de Chiapas y la rebelión Zapatista.* México, D.F.: Ediciones Era, 1997.

Ruether, Rosemary Radford. *Women and Redemption: A Theological History.* Minneapolis: Fortress Press, 1998.

Ruiz, Samuel, in conversation with Jorge Santiago, *Seeking Freedom. On Time and History, Prophecy, Faith and Politics, and Peace.* Translated by Michel Andraos. Toronto: Toronto Council of the Canadian Catholic Organization for Development and Peace, 1999.

Ruiz, Samuel con la colaboración de Carles Torner. *Cómo me Convirtieron los Indígenas.* Servidores y Testigos 92. Santander: Sal Terrae, 2002.

Salisbury, Joyce E. *The Blood of Martyrs. Unintended Consequences of Ancient Violence.* New York: Routledge, 2004.

Schneiders, Sandra M. *Written That You May Believe. Encountering Jesus in the Fourth Gospel.* Rev. ed. New York: Crossroad, 2003.

Schreiter, Robert J. *The Ministry of Reconciliation. Spirituality & Strategies.* Maryknoll: Orbis, 1998.

_____. *Reconciliation. Mission & Ministry in A Changing Social Order.* The Boston Theological Institute Series 3. Maryknoll: Orbis, 1992.

Schüssler Fiorenza, Elisabeth. *Jesus. Miriam's Child, Sophia's Prophet.* New York: Continuum, 1994.

_____. *Wisdom Ways. Introducing Feminist Biblical Interpretation.* Maryknoll: Orbis, 2001.

Sobrino, Jon. *The Principle of Mercy: Taking the Crucified People from the Cross.* Maryknoll, New York: Orbis, 1994.

Sölle, Dorothee. *The Silent Cry. Mysticism and Resistance.* Translated by Barbara and Martin Rumscheidt. Minneapolis: Fortress Press, 2001.

_____. *Stations of the Cross. A Latin American Pilgrimage.* Translated by Joyce Irwin Minneapolis: Fortress Press, 1993.

Sotelo, Nicole. *Women Healing From Abuse. Meditations for Finding Peace.* New York: Paulist, 2006.

Támez, Elsa. ed. *Through Her Eyes. Women's Theology from Latin America.* Maryknoll: Orbis, 1989.

Tavanti, Marco. *Las Abejas: Passivist Resistance and Syncretic Identities in a Globalizing Chiapas*. Religion in History, Society, and Culture 1. New York: Routledge, 2003.

Thomsen, Mark W. *Christ Crucified. A 21ˢᵗ-Century Missiology of the Cross*. Minneapolis: Lutheran University Press, 2004.

Trelstad, Marit, ed. *Cross Examinations. Readings on the Meaning of the Cross Today*. Minneapolis: Augsburg Fortress Press, 2006.

Williams, Rowan. *Christ on Trial. How the Gospel Unsettles Our Judgement*. Grand Rapids: Eerdmans, 2000.

Indexes

NAMES AND SUBJECTS

mercy seat, 20, 30
metaphors, 1–3, 29. *See also* specific
  metaphors
Meyers, Carol L., 74
Miller, Susan, 109
mimetic desire, 33
Miriam (prophet), 103, 104–5
Moltmann-Wendel, Elisabeth, 38
Moses (prophet), 90–91, 93
mother images, 162–63
Mother of Jesus, 174–79. *See also*
  Mary (mother of Jesus)
Moyano, María Elena, 54
mujerista theology, 8, 187 n.24

Nanko-Fernández, Cármen, 4
Noadiah (prophet), 107
nonviolence, 142, 152

obedience
  of biblical women, 76–83
  as deadly, 67–76
  to God, 57–86
  by Jesus, 58, 61–66, 84
  and listening, 63–64
  myth and disobedience, 73–74
  parable, 59–61
  questioning, 67–69
  by women, 57–58
Oingt, Marguerite, 166
Osborne, Kenan B., 185 n.4
Our Lady of Guadalupe, 176–79

Parker, Rebecca Ann, 96
Paul (apostle)
  birthing imagery of, 173
  on death of Jesus, 19–20, 26–27,
    131–32, 192 n.8
  on God's love, 29–30
  on heroic death, 28
  on obedience, 63
  ransom metaphor, 23–24
  on salvation, 134, 137
  scapegoat metaphor, 25

Pilate, Pontius, 23, 92, 109, 126, 185
  n.4
popular religiosity, 8
prayer
  and forgiveness, 127
  and Jesus, 63–64
prophetic martyrs, 87–121
  costs of, 104–6
  defined, 95
  disciples of, 96–99
  false prophets, 94–95
  followers of, 117–19
  Jesus as, 89–93
  and resurrection, 96
  rewards, 97
  risk-taking by, 117–18
  true prophets, 93–94, 95
  women as, 99–121
Puah (biblical figure), 83

ransom metaphor, 2, 23–25, 30
reconciliation, 124–25, 128, 131–33,
  137–39, 143, 151–53
redemption metaphor, 23–25
religiosity. *See* popular religiosity
remembering
  and healing, 139–42
  hermeneutics of, 6
repentance, 130–31
resurrection
  and abuse, 14
  of Jesus, 112–15
  of prophets, 96
  of Tabitha, 149–50
Romero, Oscar, 96
Rosado Nuñes, María José F., 13
Ruiz, Samuel, Don, 9, 89, 152

sacrifice
  and atonement, 17–20, 26, 193
    n.12
  cultic, 20–21, 30, 39
  definitions, 36–38
  Jesus on, 38–39

BIBLICAL PASSAGES

Old Testament

New Testament

Apocrypha